Routledge Revivals

The Process of Literature

Originally published in 1929, *The Process of Literature* is a study of the art of letters considered from a new point of view, as a process of human activity rather than as a series of objects produced by that activity. It examines in detail "the process of literature" from the stimulus of the writer by their experience of life to the reader's reaction to what has been created as a result of that stimulus and describes just how a book comes into being. It was intended for the writer, critic, and teacher, as well as the professional psychologist.

Today it can be read in its historical context.

The Process of Literature
An Essay Towards Some Reconsiderations

Agnes Mure Mackenzie

First published in 1929
by George Allen & Unwin Ltd

This edition first published in 2025 by Routledge
4 Park Square, Milton Park, Abingdon, Oxon, OX14 4RN

and by Routledge
605 Third Avenue, New York, NY 10017

Routledge is an imprint of the Taylor & Francis Group, an informa business

© 1929 Agnes Mure Mackenzie

All rights reserved. No part of this book may be reprinted or reproduced or utilised in any form or by any electronic, mechanical, or other means, now known or hereafter invented, including photocopying and recording, or in any information storage or retrieval system, without permission in writing from the publishers.

Publisher's Note
The publisher has gone to great lengths to ensure the quality of this reprint but points out that some imperfections in the original copies may be apparent.

Disclaimer
The publisher has made every effort to trace copyright holders and welcomes correspondence from those they have been unable to contact.

A Library of Congress record exists under LCCN: 30004026

ISBN: 978-1-032-90433-7 (hbk)
ISBN: 978-1-003-55803-3 (ebk)
ISBN: 978-1-032-90437-5 (pbk)

Book DOI 10.4324/9781003558033

THE
PROCESS OF LITERATURE

AN ESSAY TOWARDS SOME
RECONSIDERATIONS

By

AGNES MURE MACKENZIE
M.A., D.LITT.

LONDON
GEORGE ALLEN & UNWIN LTD
MUSEUM STREET

FIRST PUBLISHED IN 1929

All rights reserved
PRINTED IN GREAT BRITAIN BY
UNWIN BROTHERS LTD., WOKING

FILIOLÆ OPUSCULUM (SED VERO SUUM)
ACCIPIAT MATER DILECTISSIMA
ABERDONENSIS UNIVERSITAS

" I think that the sickliest notion of physics, even if a student gets it, is that it is 'the science of molecules, atoms, and the ether'. And I think that the healthiest notion, even if a student does not wholly get it, is that physics is 'the science of taking hold of bodies and pushing them'."—W. S. FRANKLIN, quoted by W. James in *Pragmatism*

FOREWORD

ONLY a few weeks ago, an eminent physicist summed up the recent changes in our outlook on the material world by saying that the objects which we had been used to consider as *things*, now appear to us as series of *events*. This change in outlook is in fact one of the most important intellectual developments of our generation. It has already, in the last twenty years, affected the mental sciences no less than the physical: the modern psychologist thinks no longer in terms of states or conditions of the mind, but of processes. Such a fundamental change in point of view must necessarily be of far-reaching effect: it has, as indeed is very common knowledge, made it possible for psychology to throw a new and valuable light on the sciences of medicine and sociology, of anthropology and comparative religion. It may also, as this book attempts to show, bring new factors to the study of æsthetics.

The curious futility, for all practical purposes, of a mental science practised by fine minds, whose subject is so important as the range of activities we call the arts, is indeed remarkable. I venture to affirm that it has been due almost entirely to our habit of studying any art as a group of static *things* possessing certain properties. If, instead, we realise that an art is a sequence of dynamic *process*, and that its material productions (statues, pictures, books) are merely the outward expression of a stage—and not the final stage—in the process, a great many classical difficulties disappear: the relation of art to the whole process of human life—the meaning of art for mankind—becomes apparent, and a deal of cloudy metaphysic evaporates.

This point of view, the habit of regarding an art as a process of human activity rather than as a series of objects produced by that activity, has been foreshadowed here and there already, in the occasional statements of great artists with regard to their own practice of their art. But to the non-creative critic and the general public it is still new enough to be unfamiliar and even, perhaps, a little disconcerting. Yet the whole trend of our current thought makes towards its acceptance, and there is no doubt that the conception will soon be as familiar (for instance to the teacher of literature) as the conception of an earth revolving about the sun—an idea which would have startled Dante or Plato.

I have tried in this book to study a specific art, that we call literature, in these newer terms, and to describe the chains of process it involves, from the stimulus of the writer by his experience of life to the reader's reaction to what has been created as the result of that stimulus; and further, to relate this special sequence of processes to the general system that is human life at large. Such a study has a certain novelty, not alone from its point of view, but because it is only very recently that general psychology has provided the means for a survey of certain phases of these processes, and thrown light on the strange business of "creation".

Naturally, such a study, especially as pioneer work, must have its difficulties. I have tried to meet these honestly as they arose, describing and as far as possible explaining each phase of the process in its logical (and psychological) order, and shirking neither the unorthodox nor (what nowadays is more tempting) the strictly orthodox, if either of them seemed to fit the facts. If a consistent theory emerges, I can claim that at least it was not formed a priori. If my treatment appears in places egoistic, if I seem to illustrate too much from my own experience in two professions, I can only say that I know my own mind better than I do anyone else's, and have no reason to think it differs from the ordinary. I have endeavoured to be as untechnical as possible, for this book is intended for the writer, critic, and teacher, as well as the professional psychologist: but sometimes to let the careless reader think he understood me was to blunt the edge of my meaning for the careful one. I have tried, however, when technical terms were needful for exactness, to give such practical illustration of their meaning as would make it clear to any intelligent person who had not chanced to meet with them before.

Miss J. S. Templeton, M.A., of St. Hild's College, Durham, has been good enough to read this book in MS. and to give me some valuable criticism, and my sister, Miss J. M. Mackenzie, M.A., of the London Association for Mental Welfare, has by her continued interest in it been of the greatest possible assistance in its writing.

ST. JOHN'S WOOD
May 1929

CONTENTS

FOREWORD 9

CHAPTER
I. PROLEGOMENA: ART AS A FUNCTION OF HUMANITY 17
THE NATURE AND END OF ART: sensory perception common to man and beast: man's use of it as basis of science and art: distinction between these: the object-matter of art: the immediate purpose of art: the means of art: provisional definition
THE PROCESS OF ART: end and stimulus of art: art as extension of intense experience by its transference to further subjects: definition expanded

II. PROLEGOMENA: ART, THE ARTS, AND THE ARTIST 29
THE RELATION OF ÉLAN VITAL AND THE ART-IMPULSE: art a specialised form of the basic creative urge: some theories of their relation
THE ARTIST: causes of this specialised impulse in the individual: characteristics of the impulse: means of its exercise: definition of the artist

III. THE WRITER AT WORK: A CONCRETE EXAMPLE 42
Fiction as fullest example of the creative process: development of theme of *Othello*: choice of its subject: development of its characters from the subject: choice of form: lay-out

IV. THE WRITER AND HIS STIMULUS 59
THE NATURE OF THE STIMULUS AS PERCEIVED: must be the object of intense experience: its essential nature does not necessarily determine that of the experience: object must signify something important: need not be material: need not be present: may be complex
THE NATURE OF THE SUBJECT PERCEIVING: power of apperception: sensitiveness to quality of human experience as such: (place of emotion in such experience: recent changes of attitude:) vital impulse: scope and direction of personality: volition

14   THE PROCESS OF LITERATURE

CHAPTER   PAGE
V. THE NATURE OF THE PROBLEM OF CONVEYANCE   78

Artist's experience conveyed by material object: relations between artist, his initial stimulus, and conveying object: conveying object arouses experiend in another subject: it may be image of the stimulus-object: but experiend cannot always be conveyed by reproduction of original stimulus: need to create new image that will convey it

VI. THE WRITER AND THE APPREHENSION OF HIS THEME   84

THE NATURE OF SUCH APPREHENSION: (relation of required new image to stimulus-object:) necessity for apprehension of the latter's experiential value: apprehension both passive and active: involves more than schematisation by the reason: necessitates power of perceiving and apperceiving quality, as such, of experience: part of volition: large and small themes

THE RESULT OF SUCH APPREHENSION: apprehended experience crystallises in percept: rise of this to consciousness: nature of such percept: relation of conscious to subconscious elements: symbolic pre-image: effect of such apprehension and of lack of it

VII. THE WRITER AND THE DISCOVERY OF HIS SUBJECT   101

THE NATURE OF THE SUBJECT: cases in which experiend may be conveyed by reproduction of either stimulus or "symbolic pre-image": cases where this is inadequate: necessity for re-embodiment of experiend in fresh image of an imagined phase of experience: forms of this

THE PROCESS OF DISCOVERING THE SUBJECT: formation of new images: interaction of psychical dispositions: chains of subconscious process: effect of instinctive impulse upon these: relation of this to present problem: development of a system of images: effect of reason: expansion of system, voluntary and involuntary

CONTENTS

CHAPTER	PAGE
VIII. THE WRITER AND THE DEVELOPMENT OF HIS SUBJECT	124

THE NATURE OF SUCH DEVELOPMENT: writer has formed image of phase of experience which is capable of conveying the experiend: but image not yet fully adapted to this end: selection of elements: selection of means for their presentation

THE PROCESS OF THE DEVELOPMENT: analysis of images: nature and relation of components: process of analysis: conscious and subconscious imagination: the rational element: "inspiration": volition

IX. THE WRITER AND THE CONVEYANCE OF HIS SUBJECT   142

THE NATURE OF CONSTRUCTION: preparation of fully imagined subject to act on consciousness of reader: relation of this to its actual projection

THE METHOD OF CONSTRUCTION: the all-inclusive method: its possibilities: the selective method: its possibilities: the process of selection: the rational element: instinctive impulse: "inspiration": arrangement of selected images: effects of this

X. THE WRITER AND HIS WRITING   165

THE NATURE OF THE MEDIUM: associative interrelations of writing, speech, and thought: real medium of writer articulated sound: (effect of association of this with visual signs:) words, their significance: central meaning and associative overtones: latent and overt allusion: the grouping of words: its significance: the logical grouping: the rhythmical grouping: metre: psychological effect of all these in regard to conveyance of experiend: the ideal of writing

THE EMPLOYMENT OF THE MEDIUM: analysis of images and concepts: association of these with articulate sounds: apperception of verbal images: discrimination of words: discrimination of arrangements of words: the lack of these: use of verbal associations in practice

CHAPTER	PAGE
XI. THE READER	211

THE READER AS PASSIVE: completion of the literary process: effect on reader as writer envisages it: association of script, articulate sound, and idea: association of ideas in systems: reactions to ideas: modifications of this process in practice: "fallacies of reading"
THE READER AS ACTIVE: the reader an autonomous personality: his reactions as such: perception of the experiend: assimilation of it to the general content of his mind: evaluation: "fallacies of criticism": the reader as writer: art as an object of experience

XII. THE EFFECT OF THE PROCESS   250

The effect of literature on life: literature as a substitute for life: literature as an escape from life: literature as a discipline for life: nature of will as balance of perception and conation: art as discipline of perception: art as discipline of conation: effect of these on evolutionary process

APPENDIX A   273

APPENDIX B   279

INDEX   283

THE PROCESS OF LITERATURE

CHAPTER I

PROLEGOMENA: ART AS A FUNCTION OF HUMANITY

"No man has knowledge of another by means of his own actions and passions, as a brute beast; nor does it happen that one man can enter into another by spiritual insight, like an angel, since the human spirit is held back by the grossness and opacity of its mortal body. It was therefore necessary that the human race should have some sign, at once rational and to be perceived through the senses, for the inter-communication of its thoughts."

DANTE ALIGHIERI, *De Vulgari Eloquentia*

ADAM gave names to the beasts in Paradise: but not even his dog bestowed a name on Adam. Whether or not one believes man has "a soul", there is no denying that while his actual sensory experience is similar in its process, so far as we know, to that of any other of the mammals, he does something with it none of them show heed for: he fashions his knowledge into art and science. He is a spoonful of dust in a pail of water, but he measures the volume of the sun and stars, and can change a quarry of stone to Chartres Cathedral. That he should do so is not reasonable: he cannot eat the dimensions of the sun, and to build a cathedral, even with reliable labour, is much more likely to shorten his days than increase them: yet he will spend a passion of toil on either, and pay the briefness of life with its abundance.

Science and art have two qualities in common: they are functions of the same subject, *humanum genus*, and they deal with the same object, human experience. But between them comes this important difference. The basis of science is exact arithmetic: two and two of anything are always four, whether one thinks of cabbages or planets. But the synthesis of art differs in kind: the whole is greater than the sum of the parts—add two to four, and the answer is a million, and

> Out of three sounds (is framed)
> Not a fourth sound, but a star.

The major ground of the diversity is that while the scientist deals with things as he assumes they are in themselves, the artist is concerned with things as they are in his experience: the epistemologist may decide which ground is firmer, and we, meanwhile, concern ourselves with art.

Art, then, we consider as a function of humanity, whose object is not what stimulates man's experience, but rather the whole experience itself—its stimulus, certainly, but also, as importantly, its quality, what it feels like. It grasps these things and proceeds to record them in such fashion that the subjective experience is solidified, as it were, given an actual objective existence, independent of the mind which originally underwent it. Ronsard and the trees of his forest of Gastine have passed out of the world we know. Ronsard's experience of his forest has not. I can hold his thought in my hand by crossing the room, and re-experience it, bring it to life, by looking down at a few marks on paper.

It is necessary here to put in a caution. It is not true, as is often loosely said, that art is the *expression* of experience. That has been one of the most fashionable of fallacies, even with thinking people, and still is popular. Its results have made so much good mirth for gods and men that one cannot condemn it without tenderness: one would not dispense with Signor Marinetti. But for a serious investigation one must keep a little closer to the facts. If, in the manner of our forefathers, I raise my voice to a sudden anguished howl, it may be entirely adequate as the expression—that is, the discharge in action—of my emotions: the efferent nerves have reacted well and truly to the stimulus brought them by the afferents. But the world at large, though it may be acutely aware of the fact of my anguish, will not know whether I have lost my lover, upset the porridge-pot, or had a tooth out. Miss Gertrude Stein or Herr Arp may not agree, but one feels it would be a more subtle form of art, in the former situation (though doubtless more difficult), if I modulated my howl to something like the air of *Lord Gregory*, or in the latter two "swore tersely and with variety", after the manner of Fastidius Brisk.

"Expression", then, is inadequate as definition, because it leaves out so much of the facts. "Gahn, yeh bloody swine", or "Da-arling Googles" may *express* an emotion as fully as Dryden's vivisection of Buckingham or the various thing John Donne wrote for Anne More, and they involve considerably less trouble. But as art I think it may be said without exaggeration that they are a little less than adequate: they need, at least, the support of voice and gesture, to say nothing of an embrace or a half-brick. The Buckingham passage of *Absalom and Achitophel*, the *Valediction forbidding Mourning*, subsist by themselves. The content has been enclosed in an adequate form, that preserves it in an independent being, and makes it susceptible of a re-experience by a subject other than its original one. That is the test. Art is not only expression, but conveyance. Unless it is that, it is not art at all, but merely a reflex action of the nerves.

This definition is so unfashionable (though better folk than I have arrived at it) that I must give its test at the same time. Take any "expressionist" of the straiter creed, and promise him a maintenance for life, a perfectly unlimited supply of art-materials, and the most absolute liberty of expression, *on condition no one shall see his work but himself*. You will be safe enough, for he won't take it. Either he really does want to create an *objet d'art* or he wants to be talked about as being an artist: but in either case, he must have an audience. And why should he, unless he wants them to apprehend something—the nature of the universe, of a daisy, of a glass of beer, or the extreme importance of his remarkable self? The fact that every artist of any sense destroys a lot of his own work is not against this: I have already, in the first rough draft of this chapter, crossed out more pages than I have preserved: but if I knew the book would not be published, I would never go to the trouble of writing it. In the last resort, a man is his own audience. If nobody else reads his MS. he will . . . but even then, an ideal audience, in both senses of the word, reads over his shoulder. When Van Huysum copies in minutest detail the form and texture and colour of a tulip, he desires to convey to us his experience of the tulip: and part of that experience, by the way, was a forgetfulness of Van Huysum experiencing in his intense apprehension of the thing experienced. When Herr Arp represents *Paolo and Francesca* by screwing two fragments of an ordinary jigsaw on to a board, he may be *expressing* himself: but to express himself means, surely, to *convey* to someone else that he experiences profound and unusual emotion over the unfortunate lovers. If we compare his aim with that of Van Huysum, we shall find the basic point of difference is merely that his apprehension of the object of emotion, and even perhaps of the emotion itself, yields, shall we say, to his apprehension of that emotion's profundity and originality. One recalls, perhaps, those patrons of the B.B.C. who are more concerned with "getting Amster-

HUMANITY AND ART

dam" than with listening to what they have got when it arrives.

So far, we have concerned ourselves with Art. But, we must remember, there is no such thing, any more than one ever meets the Modern Woman. They are both conveniences of conversation. There are the arts, though happily for man. These do exist: and the Albert Memorial does not invalidate Salisbury Cathedral... though I have known a writer in the *London Mercury* talk as if Wren did! But now there emerges something rather queer. Art is a function of the human spirit. Its essence, whatever it is, is intangible. The Cnidian Demeter, for instance, is something more than an equal bulk of marble, and though a dead man is materially the same as a live one, he does not paint or sing or write a novel. Yet none the less, when we classify the arts, the basis of classification is dead matter, or at all events, some property of matter. Sculpture is human experience conveyed by means of three-dimensional space. Painting is human experience conveyed by ratios of light-vibration in spatial relations of two dimensions. Music conveys its content by the vibration of air in various temporal ratios, and literature by a medium more complex in itself than any of these, whose nature we shall investigate later on.

In the light of this odd circumstance we amend our definition. Art is the conveyance of human experience, *by means of certain properties of matter*.

Is this, then, adequate as definition? No: it is not. It is true as far as it goes, but it goes too far. If I say to the waiter, "I will have a grilled steak", I convey to him, by certain properties of matter (the vibrations set up in the air by my vocal organs), a portion of my experience—my desire, which may be a very intense experience, for that particular form of nourishment. Yet most people would not affirm that this "conveyance" was art. I dare not say all: but I should not affirm it myself, at any rate. The definition, therefore, must be narrowed. To use the words in their strict logician's meaning, it is too *general*: it defines by the genus only, as if I said "Ink is a fluid". We must make it more *specific*—add species to genus, as we might say, "Ink is a fluid used for writing". The species there is the teleological one—the thing is considered in terms of its aim or purpose, and that particular category will serve us here. Art, then, we take as "the conveyance of human experience by means of certain properties of matter, and *for a certain end*".

This leads the analysis a little farther. What is this end? To be more concrete, why does a man take the trouble to write a book? It is a tiresome business, even as mere manual labour: often, dismissing a hundred and fifty thousand words in typescript with a scathing six or so (as a publisher's reader), I have thought, as novelist, " 'Did these bones cost no more the breeding than to play at loggats with 'em?' " . . . and remembered, as critic, that to treat them otherwise was an injustice to the competent. Why should one risk writer's cramp, which is most unpleasant, to say nothing of other possibilities?

In point of fact, there are more reasons than one, and it behoves us to distinguish carefully, for not all books are art, any more than all art is books. Of the thirteen thousand eight hundred and ten published in Great Britain in 1927, a large part were written from the same motive that makes a man talk very loudly in a public place: another division were written purely for money; and the major part of those not avowedly fiction because in the academic profession (*cuius pars parva eram*) one is expected to publish something at frequent intervals.

HUMANITY AND ART

Let us avoid a smug superiority. If the great artist has the luck to survive the opening campaigns, it is seldom he does not make a decent fortune. I hardly think Shakespeare wrote *King Lear* for money, but he probably saw to it Burbage paid the royalties: he seems to have had an excellent business head. The academic motive, if rather more dubious than the financial, need not be fundamental either; and as for conceit, a gentleman named Milton confessed that he rather badly wanted fame. I am not throwing stones at anyone who sells his work for the best price in money, reputation, or dignities: I have got all the money I could for my own books, and only wish there had been more of it: I acquired a doctorate on the first one that looked appropriate for a thesis: and I relish praise as much as the next man. But these are by-products. Very useful by-products: they who serve the altar must live somehow to serve it, and if they can live by the altar, it saves vitality. At the same time, they have no business to be fundamental motives: the man who makes them so, cripples himself. If he follows the Muses for their loaves and fishes, they can effect no work of grace on him. "Genap under nihthealm, swa he no wære"—"fit retribution, empty as his deeds".

There is only one valid excuse for any man to attempt creative art, and that is that he simply cannot help it. Creating art is like creating life: a desire, however intense, will not achieve it. Yet once that the conception has taken place, and the first rudimentary spark of life is kindled, only a ruinous violence will prevent the thing conceived from coming to birth . . . whatever may be its state when it is born.

The artist, then, "conveys experience" because he must, because he cannot help it, except by doing violence to himself. But this will take us very little farther. Two men, at the same window, look out on a sunset. Neither regards it with indifference: but one goes to bed contentedly and leaves it at that. The other is driven to an agony of effort to reproduce it on a square of canvas. Why?

The answer is not very easy to put in words: but the basic factors of the artist's experience, as nearly as I can phrase them, would seem to be more or less these. Thanks to some "pre-established harmony" between himself and the object in question—perhaps the "more than ordinary organic sensibility"* to which Wordsworth refers—he has had a given experience so intense and vivid that its intensity gives it a peculiar value, as if his life, in undergoing it, had somehow transcended normal limitations. He has lived, for a moment, more largely, more abundantly. But life is lived in time, and not eternity. Of necessity, then, the moment must go past. Something within himself resolves against this, is too acutely aware of the moment's value to be satisfied with the mere extension of it that may be provided by his personal memory, which must perish with his frail life and even before that be confined within the limit of himself. He feels, as we say, that he "must get that down", and goes about as he may to make the experience endure, to give it some independent body of its own, so that, apart from him, it has means of existence and can live in the experience of others, though he himself has been dead a thousand years.

The latter point is of some importance to him. It is experience as such that he wishes to make permanent: and experience implies subject as well as object, the experiencing mind as well as the thing experienced. He, its first subject, must die: and the object itself, a celan-

---

* This phrase, an odd one in the mouth of a man whose outlook was far from materialist, suggests an interesting anticipation of the theory of emotion formulated later on by James and Lange, and more recently so brilliantly expanded by W. McDougall.

HUMANITY AND ART

dine or a sunset, the charge of a desperate army, someone's singing, may be a good deal more evanescent than he. He must create a new, perdurable object, that shall arouse his experience, as near as may be, in other subjects after he is dead. This object itself may be very unlike that other which gave rise initially to the experience: what likeness has a stream of sounds or a row of black marks on paper to a face

> Clad in the beauty of a thousand stars?

But they can make us know what it was like to have seen Helen pass by the Scæan Gate, when the old men turned and watched her because of her beauty . . . and Helen herself was not the initial object of Homer's experience, for he never saw her, nor Christopher Marlowe either. But Marlowe had seen the stars he uses for sign of her, and Homer had seen or dreamed what she was the sign of—a sign like the letters that set down his verse. The image and letters are a kind of sacrament: they convey to us more than they can be in themselves.

It may be objected, "This is very well: you can make it fit *Tamburlaine* or *Paradise Lost*, or even *Sir Patrick Spens* or *The Egoist*. But how does it cover *Patience* or *Duncan Gray*?" The full response must wait for the rest of this book: but here, at all events, I may observe that delight is an experience like another, and delight in a mirthful object may be fully as acute as another kind. As to the record of a triviality—a girl scrawling a name on the sand, for example . . . are you quite sure that that was the whole content of the experience Landor was transcribing? "What about *Bulldog Drummond*?" adds someone else. Well, I enjoyed that hero's adventures heartily. But in the first place, I rather imagine that Captain McNeile himself would hardly consider it as serious art, though it probably did more good to the community than a deal of art with a clear right to the word. Nevertheless, there is room for it in my definition. There *is* an intensity of experience—Captain McNeile's enjoyment in spinning a lively story, or keeping us running after his intrigue. I will grant that this is a good deal less intense (not to say profound) than that which underlies *Macbeth* or *Hamlet*. But the author's gusto over both this and the adventures themselves that one thing and another suggested to his lively imagination was quite intense enough to demand "getting down",* though the "extension to fresh subjects" which it demanded was conceived of, probably, as spatial rather than temporal.

This last distinction brings in the executant artist—the singer or instrumentalist, actor or dancer—as well as him who is usually thought of as the creator. Here again the extension is spatial rather than temporal, for the new, or conveying, object is impermanent—the art of Duse is gone with last year's snow.

But as a rule, when we consider the body of what we think of as "the arts", the newer object is meant to endure, either in itself or in some recording process, as when notes are printed in a musical score. The outlines are fixed in stuff that outlasts their maker, and art, causing to endure that consciousness which is life, becomes man's answer to mortality.

The process, considered objectively, may be summed up thus: A man comes in contact with a certain object which causes in him a state of consciousness whose quality as a means to life is to him so high that he is compelled

---

* This does the author rather less than justice: he had an obviously sincere enjoyment of seeing courage and resourcefulness in action and in the triumph of the decencies after a sporting conflict. (And that same delight was the seed of the *Odyssey*.) But in taking the first well-known "thick-ear yarn" that came to my mind, I purposely considered it on its lowest terms.

HUMANITY AND ART

to perpetuate it in itself, independently of himself its subject. To do this, he must find some second object—not necessarily that which has aroused it in himself—that will arouse it again in other subjects, and then convey to them a sense of this object such as to arouse an experience which is, so far as possible, his own. From the psychological point of view, therefore, a work of art is essentially a sign conveying a given experience to other minds than that of the original subject of the experience: and this is true whatever the scale of the conveying sign may be. There is no essential difference, for example, between a simple metaphor in two words and a complex piece of creative literature: the difference between *War and Peace* and the phrase "Roma Mater" is one of scale and complexity, not of kind. The sea cannot laugh: but the phrase "the laughter of the waves", though in fact it describes a thing that does not exist, creates in our minds the image of a real condition of the sea, not easily to be otherwise conveyed. So Mr. Pickwick's adventures never happened; but the description of them creates in our minds the image of an experience of peculiar quality, not easily to be otherwise conveyed.

It is the purpose of the remaining chapters of this book to study the manner in which a man's experience becomes objectified in such a sign, and that in which the sign itself fulfils the function for which he has created it. It will be considerably to our future convenience to find a set of brief and simple symbols to express the relationship between the artist, his experience, his work of art, and his audience, in the most general terms, and such that in dealing with any phase of the process we may keep in mind its relation to the whole. We may therefore express the point of view arrived at by means of a very simple little diagram: a certain given Object, O^1, causes a man to become the Subject of (that is, to undergo) a vivid experience. Thereupon the man who is the subject of this initial experience, and whom we will call S^1, creates another Object, O^2, the work-of-art, which can arouse this experience again in the consciousness of fresh Subjects, SS^2, who are, as we say, his "public", or his "audience". The relations between these various subjects and objects of experience —a relation whose growth and development is the process of art—may then be summed briefly thus: O^1 affects S^1, who creates O^2, which in turn affects S^2, or $O^1 \to S^1 \to O^2 \to S^2$.

CHAPTER II

PROLEGOMENA: ART, THE ARTS, AND THE ARTIST

"All the inventive arts maintain, as it were, a sympathetic connection between each other, being no more than various expressions of one internal power, modified by different circumstances, either of an individual or of society."

P. B. SHELLEY, *Essay on the Literature, Arts, and Manners of the Athenians*

THE formula arrived at in the preceding chapter may serve to clear the ground, at all events, and to indicate a line for the approach. But its air of compact finality is deceitful, for it begs no less than three important questions.

Take our formula again, for brevity: $O^1 \to S^1 \to O^2 \to SS^2$. . . . Here are the questions: (1) Why should S^1's experience of O^1 arouse in him the desire to make it permanent? (2) How does S^1 go about to discover O^2? (3) In what way does O^2 convey the *experiend* to SS^2 . . .? The discussion of these three questions will be the subject-matter of most of this book, though in considering Nos. 2 and 3 I shall perforce restrict myself to a handling of them in terms of a single art. No. 1 may be tackled in the present chapter.*

I have suggested a proximate answer, in fact, already: the experience has had an intensity which gave life a new fullness and keenness, "more abundance". We shall do well to consider this point a moment.

Now it is of the very essence of life itself that, wherever we find it, it has a powerful impulse to *continue*, to extend itself. This extension is normally twofold: the individual

---

* I am advised to warn the reader who is unaccustomed to the conceptions of general psychology that he may do better to omit the remainder of this chapter and pass on at once to Chapter III.

unit strives to extend itself in terms of itself—i.e., to go on living: and the individual unit strives to extend itself in terms of the race—i.e., to reproduce itself in some posterity. From the protozoa onward, all life, whether vegetable or animal, shares this impulse: man is subject to it, and the lettuces in his garden.

But as we pass from unconscious life to conscious, and thence to self-conscious, the primary urge undergoes some well-marked changes. It remains the same in essence: but its manifestations alter very markedly with the nature of the being in which it is manifested, and that being's place in the scale of evolution. Let us consider for a moment that function of it which is so fundamental in life that we must consider the impulse to it not so much a development as an actual part of the basic urge that is life itself in action: the impulse of the living creature to reproduce its kind. All normal living creatures have this impulse, which manifests itself to consciousness as a desire: but in normally developed human beings, and in some other species, especially certain birds, the desire is in practice more specific than that. It includes an idea that the reproduction shall involve the collaboration of a particular partner: if another be substituted, the desire is felt to be in some measure frustrated—in many cases, indeed, to be thwarted altogether. The precise nature of this modification to the blind basic urge to reproduce the kind varies from individual to individual. Even in the general average of humanity, it is the general instinct that awakens first, and the subject looks round, more or less consciously, for the first person who is likely to help him to satisfy it: * he is, as we say, "in love with love". But in the more fully developed human being, the spring that either awakens the instinct in the

---

* This is the course of events in the lower animals—who have no art.

first place, or enables it to crystallise from a blind urge to an enduring cognitive and conative disposition, is an acute awareness of some individual who is perceived, very intensely, to contain the possibilities of a considerable enhancement of life. The primal instinctive impulse, to create life as such, develops (phylogenetically or even ontogenetically) into a desire to enhance not mere quantity of life, but also, and very intensely, *quality*—the quality of the subject's own in the first place, but as the instinct develops into a sentiment in which it is reinforced by other instincts, there is also a desire to enhance the quality of life for the collaborating person, for their children, and even for the world at large: any porter or taximan knows well enough that a man in love is generally openhanded.*

The other instincts run this course as well as the sexual, because they have a common ground with it phylogenetically. At bottom they reduce themselves to the various means of satisfying the two fundamental needs, the desire of the individual to continue himself, and the desire to reproduce himself, in terms of his status in the scale of evolution. As he develops, he finds that in the case of each specific instinct which serves these ends, the desire is growing for *quality* as well as *quantity* of satisfactions. (Compare a dog with a bone and the point of view of Brillat-Savarin.) In every direction there is this growing desire for quality of life, and it comes to seek its end as such, and consciously.

But always at base of it there is the primary urge to *continue*—to continue both the self and the species to

---

* Cf. the code of *l'amour courtois*—see Part I of *The Romaunce of the Rose*:
        Resoun wol that a lover be
        In his yiftes more large and free
        Than cherles that been not of loving . . . etc.
               (Amor's charge to the lover.)

which it belongs. And this, collaborating with the desire for quality of life, fuses to a compound impulse—a new desire *to continue this "quality" as such*, in the life of the species, beyond that of the individual.

That is, I think, the main genetic outline. It is more complex, by a good deal, than the recently popular one of Herren Freud and Jung, which is based on the same facts, or at least on some of them. But when one is trying to explain a complex process, simplicity may not always be a virtue. It is simpler to say that the urge to create enhancements of life is a perversion of that urge to create life itself which they and M. Bergson have described variously* as the *libido* and *l'élan vital*, and which (in Jung's view of it at all events) seems to be simply life as such in native and undifferentiated action. This is a good deal easier to deal with, as a theory, than my hypothesis of a complex derived instinctive disposition—a horrifying term in itself, for which I apologise. It works, in fact, beautifully so long as you do not look closely at the facts.

I have no wish to belittle the achievements of Herr Freud or Herr Jung. They are great pioneers in the advance of mental science; they have put psychology in their debt for ever, and to its base. But in so doing they often committed outrages against logic from a fundamental inability to distinguish between an observed datum and an inferred conclusion, as between a valid and an invalid inference. To examine fully the fallacies of their assumptions on art would take up more space than a book of the scope of this one can afford, for this chapter is, after all, no more than a clearing of the ground for my real issues. But putting it as briefly as possible, to consider the creation of the Samothracian Victory, the Eroica Symphony, the Odyssey, or the windows of the Sainte Chapelle, as a sort of disease

* The terms chosen are not uncharacteristic of two national cultures.

or short-circuiting of the sexual instinct, is rather like saying, "I see with my foot", and to the answer, "Nonsense!" replying blandly, "But *my* definition of 'foot' includes organs of vision". To which there is certainly no more to be said!

The instinct to create life itself and the instinct to create that which will enhance it are related to each other rather as sight is related to hearing. Neither of these senses is a perversion or even modification (a much less question-begging word) of the other. They have, however, a common genetic basis, the sense of touch, as manifested by the lower forms of life. As this becomes more finely adjusted and specialised in the process of phylogenetic development, it breaks up into differentiated functions. In the same fashion the impulses of art and sex spring from a common basis, the need of life for extension of itself. Why that need should be, as why matter should move, may properly be called an Ultimate Question, and as such I leave it thankfully to ontologists. " 'It's gey and easy speirin',' said the beggar-wife to me."

There is one point in the relation of the two impulses that is worth a moment's further consideration. It has been observed, somewhat crookedly by Herr Freud and his school and more clearly by Plato, that the total of life-force, *élan vital*, or Professor Nunn's *hormé*,* in the individual, may be guided to some extent through either of these manifestations—i.e., into sex-activity or into the activity of any other form of creation, whether of a picture or a government. The Freudians of the strait sect of believers regard this process merely as a draining of an activity which is essentially sexual in itself into non-sexual channels, a process which they describe as its

* The term *libido* is a singularly unfortunate one: if it is not to have its full accepted Latin meaning, why use it?—and if it is, it is a spectacular case of the fallacy *species pro genere*.

sublimation—another word unhappily chosen, for if it is to mean anything, it is not only out of harmony with the conception of art as a perversion of the fundamental instinct, but is also a petitio principii. It is no doubt a greater thing to use one's *élan vital* to create *Hamlet* than to use it to create, say, Patrick Mahon—or even, to be less extreme, the writer of this book. But when Mary Arden used hers to create William Shakespeare, she surely did a rather larger thing than creating *Hamlet*: in effect, by that one exercise of *élan vital*, she created the possibility of the whole thirty-seven plays, with the sonnets thrown in. One takes one's chance, with either the book or the baby! But however unfortunate his terminology, Freud has come near the truth, though he has not reached it. Art and sex-activity are not two cases of the same impulse, in the one case thwarted, in the other free. But the fundamental urge from which both are derived may be drained to some extent from the one to the other. Any individual man has only a given quantity of *élan vital*, though Smith may have a much larger amount than Jones or than he had himself a year ago: and it stands to reason that if it is made to flow in the direction X there will be a less amount to flow towards Y and Z.

We assume, then, not that the art-impulse is derived from the sex-impulse, but that they are both the differentiated manifestations of a primitive urge*—a point borne out by the fact that if the art-impulse does not become manifest until high in the evolutionary scale, the sex-impulse also is not found until life has evolved some distance from the bottom of it.† Yet though they

* To give a concrete parallel, suppose I desire some active exercise. I may play tennis or have a bout with the foils. Both these activities would in that case derive from my desire for exercise, but neither is a modification of the other.

† Asexual reproduction is general among the protozoa, and is even found in some rather higher forms.

ART, THE ARTS, AND THE ARTIST

have the same root, their manifestations are not equally extensive. The one instinct is common to all normal human beings: it may in rare cases never be aroused, or in less rare, not find its exercise, but it is part of the very concept "man" or "woman". But the other is by no means universal, and though it is bad reasoning to consider it a disease of the sex-impulse, there is often enough good cause, if not good reason, to consider it a disease of personality. Indeed, it has always been felt as something rather abnormal—"fine frenzy", no doubt, but frenzy all the same, something foreign to the common mode of living.

Why should a man be endowed with this abnormal, or at all events extra-normal, addition to the ordinary range of instinctive propensities? The only possible answer is simply that, as the exercise of any developed instinctive ability presupposes a perception of (*a*) its object and (*b*) the means of dealing with the object, he is naturally endowed with the perception necessary in this particular case. Ask, "Why is he so endowed?" and the only answer possible is, "Because he happens to be made that way, as he is made tall or short, myopic or remarkably keen-sighted". It is some innate disposition in the individual . . . which is merely an impressive way of saying, "We don't know".

"Poets are born, not made", says the old proverb. But a man who knew what he was talking about* adds, "they are made as well". And both are right. A poet, a maker ($\pi o \iota \eta \tau \acute{\eta} s$, and the M.S. *makar*) is so called because he makes something to convey his experience of life— i.e., common speech describes him in terms of that stage of the art-process which can be directly perceived by those around him. His training to achieve that conveyance may sweat the soul out of him for half a lifetime.

* Ben Jonson, in his prefatory verses to the First Folio Shakespeare.

The content of the experience necessarily extends with the extension of his life.* But the faculty ("power", "ability", "means of doing", ex *facere*) of the primary perceptions is something in the nature of the man. If we knew all that exist of the data of psychology and biology, we might arrive at some notion of its causes, but they would not take us any nearer to its reason.

The only science that can help us here is that of speculative theology. And even that can go no farther than the possibility of an uncontradicted hypothesis—that as one aspect or *persona* of the Godhead is essentially creative, then the spark of divine in life, and the flame in man, partake in their degree of this property. As a Catholic Christian, I have no difficulty in believing this possible, even probable. But I am also aware that an hypothesis requires more than an absence of convincing contradiction before it can be considered fully proved.

In any case, we do not need to know. Men have discovered a great many valuable facts about electricity: it cooks my breakfast and drives my vacuum cleaner, irons out my washing, takes me to the British Museum, and lights my work for me when I have got there. Yet no one knows *what* it is, let alone *why*. We can take for granted the ultimate reason for our faculty,† and study, more profitably, the question of its nature and mode of function.

We have noticed already that any instinctive impulse connotes a power of perceiving both the object of its exercise and the means to that exercise, or as Professor McDougall has defined it rather more fully, "an instinct is an innate disposition which determines the organism

* "Imagination is useless without knowledge. Nature gives in vain the power of combination unless study and observation supply materials to be combined."—Samuel Johnson, *Life of Butler*.

† I hope psychologically trained readers will suspend their natural suspicions of this word.

ART, THE ARTS, AND THE ARTIST

to *perceive* (to pay attention to) any object of a certain class and to experience in its presence *a certain emotional excitement* and *an impulse to action* which finds expression in *a certain mode of behaviour with regard to that object*"*. Notice, the art-impulse implies all these things. A man has the "organic sensibility" to perceive a certain class of objects with unusual keenness, and the power of such a strong emotional reaction to it† that he feels the need to put his experience beyond reach of perishing. But he is not an artist unless he conceives (less clearly, perhaps, but with equal intensity) the particular "mode of behaviour" that this implies—is conscious not only of a desired activity with regard to the object perceived, but of the appropriate means to this activity—i.e., he not only wants to "get down" his experience, but has some sense of the means of doing so. "Mute Miltons" do not exist. If his MS. had perished (and paper is terribly perishable stuff) Milton might well have been inglorious. But if he had been mute he would no more have been Milton than a red ribbon would be a red ribbon if it were a blue one. The only artists who do not create are those who are killed before they have time to achieve the "getting down" process, as a mother may die before her child is born. And their claim, in any individual case, is somewhat more difficult to prove than hers.‡

---

* *An Outline of Psychology*. The italics are mine.
† Op. cit., "The emotional qualities have . . . a cognitive function; they signify to us primarily not the nature of things, but rather the nature of our impulsive reaction to things. . . . The function they primarily subserve is cognition not of the object but of the subject, of the state or activity of the organism."
‡ A few days before rereading this sentence, I chanced to wander into the Panthéon, and was confronted by a memorial tablet to writers who died in French service during the war—men of one art and country in a not very long war. There were five hundred and sixty of them. In a number like that, one can assume the presence of a good many men of considerable talent and some of genius.

The artist, then, along with this experience, which may have any conceivable kind of object and any emotional quality known to man, has not only the urge to make it permanent, but some inkling of a means of doing so. Now these means are considerably varied. A is a sculptor, B a dramatist. X, to express his sense of his lady's beauty, makes noises: Y lays oil-paint over canvas. Let us consider these differences a little.

While it is true, in a sense, as we have said in passing, that the artist perceives the object of his experience, the fundamental content of the perception is not a mere cognition of the object as such, but some emotional quality it reveals to him. Rembrandt was not painting a butcher's shop: he was painting the delight derived from its colour and light and shadow. And the fundamental quality that makes the artist is neither his perception of the material universe in action—a seagull or a film-camera has more of that than either Rembrandt or Shakespeare—nor his skill in the means to recreate its sensory image. He needs both of these, but they are not the main thing. The intensity of the experience, that makes him desire its perpetuation, is in the emotional quality of the objects perceived.* Unless he *feels* profoundly what he perceives—unless it is emotionally significant to him— it is of no use to him as a matter of art, nor can he make it significant to his audience, except in so far as they may be moved to a certain wonder at his technical skill, as they are at that of a very clever juggler.

None the less, although they are useless alone, he does

---

* Intensity of sensory perception and intense emotional quality of experience are not the same thing. Suppose I have my photograph taken by a magnesium flash. My sensory perception of the light is very intense: but (if I am expecting it) the experience has practically no emotional quality. On the other hand, a second's half-perception in a stranger, of a fleeting and shadowy likeness to someone who has meant very much to us, may move us deeply.

ART, THE ARTS, AND THE ARTIST 39

require a vivid sensory and intellectual perception of the objects themselves which carry this emotional quality. (A skeleton is not a man, nor even the most important thing about a man, but he finds one rather necessary, all the same.) This perception, in practice, may be limited to certain classes of such objects, and generally is, as in the extreme case of a blind musician. A painter may be acutely aware of the emotional significance of objects present to his sight, but have no sense whatever of that of objects present to his hearing.

What is true of the present image is true of the recollected one. Image and emotional quality being inseparably united, when the same emotion is roused by another image, it tends to bring up a memory of that with which it has been connected previously. The artist has not only an acute sensitiveness to those present, but a vivid and supple recollection of those past. This faculty, again, will probably be restricted in practice to certain *classes* of objects.

Precisely what these are—that is to say, precisely what class of sensory and intellectual percept and concept will affect a man most, be most valuable to him as the vehicles of emotional experience, depends very largely on his physical make-up. A normal man uses both hands: but he does not use them both indifferently. He may even, in fact, make equal use of them, but it will seldom be the same use. I know a man who writes with his right hand, shoots with his left, and draws with both: a fencer who uses the foil with one hand and the sabre with the other. But normally, a man is, as we say, right- or left-handed, and in the same way, though he may have a normal sensory equipment, his perceptions are *predominantly* visual, motor, or auditory. (It is logically possible that they might even be gustatory or olfactory, but I have not heard of a human case of either, though a dog notoriously "thinks through his nose".*) This fact applies to the artist as to everyone else. The images that matter most to him will be those that reach him through his favourite group of sense-perceptions. The artist whose main experience comes in terms of sound, or of sound and movement together, will be a musician. A visual or visual-motor type will paint, or if the motor element is very strong, become a sculptor. The writer would seem to be the type in which all three kinds of perception are most equally balanced. His technical equipment, at any rate, demands a sensitiveness to both motor and auditory qualities, but he would seem to possess, as a rule, a stronger visualising power than the musician.† This statement requires a certain supplement. When I say "writer", I am thinking of the writer quâ competent artist. The issue is somewhat fogged in his case by the fact that when we use the word colloquially we are apt to make it mean "anyone who writes stuff that gets printed", which is almost like calling a "monumental mason" a sculptor. The confusion is worse, of course, because though comparatively few people draw, model, or compose, everybody in a civilised country is capable of putting words on to paper, and the material part of a book will look the same whether it is written by Jane Austen or Gene Stratton Porter. However, since recent developments in the other arts have considerably simplified access to the titles of painter, sculptor, or musician, the writing profession may cease to be quite so crowded with people who write merely because there is nothing else they can do.

This classification of the arts by the psychological

* Miss J. S. Templeton informs me that she has come across a case of a boy of twelve, whose perceptions appeared to be predominantly olfactory. He was rather "backward" but not mentally defective.

† This point is more fully dealt with in Chapter X.

ART, THE ARTS, AND THE ARTIST 41

equipment of the artist is less familiar than that which divides them by their media. But the facts are the same, only seen from the genetic point of view. To say that music is an art which presents emotional experience by auditory images and to say that it is the art of a man who, receiving most of his emotional experience in auditory terms, uses these naturally to convey and perpetuate it, may sound like Tweedledum and Tweedledee. But as a matter of fact, the latter description of it, though it makes us look at the same facts as the former, makes us see them in a rather different light. Music becomes a process, not a product. And art that is experienced *as a product* is like an electric bulb with the light switched off.

So far, then, we have arrived at this. What makes a man an artist in the first place is the innate possession of a "complex derived instinctive disposition" (i.e., of a certain arrangement and balance of innate tendencies) which leads him to react strongly to the emotional significance of objects perceived, by means of a particular activity—the attempt to separate the idea of the emotionally charged experience from himself, and give it an existence of its own apart from his. The material medium through which this activity will work—i.e., the particular art that he will practise—is determined by the fact that his physical organism reacts more readily to one class of sensory stimuli than to another.

CHAPTER III

THE WRITER AT WORK: A CONCRETE EXAMPLE

"Behold with your eyes how that (he) laboured."
The Wisdom of Jesus the Son of Sirach

THE ground having been cleared to some extent by an examination, from the genetic and the teleological points of view, of the process of art in its most general terms, it is possible to proceed to the immediate purpose, and consider the process of a specific art, that of literature. Now, it has been stated already that the process of art is essentially one of *conveyance*: and conveyance implies, as Holofernes might have said, a person to convey, an object conveyed, a means of conveyance, a means of reception, and a person to receive. That is, the process requires for its completeness the collaboration of two persons at least: a book that has not been read does not exist: it is merely in a state of suspended being, with potential existence, but not actual. By "book", of course, I mean in this connection what we think of when we think of *Pride and Prejudice*—that is to say, what Jane Austen had in mind to tell us: the other sense of book— ink, paper, and binding-case—might, of course, exist independently of a reader—at least, if the compositor did not speak its language! But my copy of *Pride and Prejudice* is not the comedy of Elizabeth and Darcy, but merely the instrument that conveys it to me.

Since the two parts of the collaboration are not contemporary, but follow in a necessary sequence, it will be both logical and convenient to discuss them separately, taking the writer's part first. To it, then, I propose to devote the next eight chapters, discussing first those

A CONCRETE EXAMPLE 43

very important processes that take place before the pen goes into the ink. But since the great danger, in any general account of a psychological process, is a loss of touch with the concrete facts concerned, it will, perhaps, be as well if before we begin to study the process in general we examine its working in an individual case. The best illustration would be what we call "fiction"— literature that achieves its end by describing the actions and passions of people who are created in accordance with the author's purpose. Here the process of creation is more elaborate, because more completely depersonalised than in those types of literature where a man expresses his own (real or imagined) experience directly, as in lyrical verse, the essay, the travel book, the autobiography, or the various works which set forth observed fact or deduced opinion. But though the process is more involved, it is, as I hope to show, the same in essentials. The best illustration that I could find would be a novel, and the specimen I could handle most convincingly would naturally be one of my own, as there I *know* what the actual process was, instead of deducing it from a mingling of analysis and experience. This choice, however, has the disadvantage that the reader of the present book may quite possibly have read none of my others. And it would be better, for the present lecture-table demonstration, that I should put before him a book he knew.*

Accordingly, I will take a play of Shakespeare's, which will have the advantage of being a much more manageable size than any novel at all likely to be equally well known. I am aware, of course, that to consider a play as literature (though heaven knows there is precedent enough!) is a remarkably uncritical proceeding. The *Hamlet* in my bookcase is not a play at all, but merely, as one might say, the score for one. And it was plays, not scores for plays,

* See, however, Appendix A.

that Shakespeare set out to create, as Beethoven made symphonies, and not scores for symphonies. At the same time, the score may itself be literature: and further, before it reaches the dramatist's pen, the psychological processes of its creation do not differ materially from those of a novel, while the differences are easy to indicate.

The example I would like to take, as the play of simplest psychological texture (genetically considered) would be *Troilus and Cressida*, for there a simple and logically patterned theme is embodied in a subject* that holds it with scarcely any admixture. It is a beautiful illustration, but unfortunately the play is almost the least known of Shakespeare's works: and most readers' vision of it has apparently been thoroughly confused by critics who in defiance of plain English have determined that a play with such a title *must* be a romantic love-tale on the lines of Chaucer's *Troylus and Creseyde*† or Shakespeare's own *Romeo and Juliet*, and were consequently bewildered by what they got: if you stick to it that a man is talking French when he happens, in point of fact, to be talking English, your grasp of his meaning may not be very certain. Instead of *Troilus*, then, I will take *Othello*. Here the initial situation—the subject, if you like—is similar, and

---

* This distinction between "theme" and "subject" is a very important one, and unfortunately our terminology has worn loose through the carelessness of common usage. The grounds of the differentiation will appear hereafter. Here I will say that the "subject" of a book is what most people (including reviewers) will think of if you ask, "What is it about?" The subject of *Jane Eyre* is the adventures of a governess. The theme, on the other hand, is what a book says *by means of its subject*. The theme of *Jane Eyre* is what Charlotte Brontë conveys to us by recounting those particular adventures. The same theme may be expressed by means of several quite different subjects: and two books on similar subjects may have different themes.

† See end of preceding note. *Troylus and Creseyde* and *Troilus and Cressida* have identical subjects, but radically different themes. And in *The Winter's Tale* and *The Tempest*, though the subjects (and the handling) are quite different, the theme is exactly the same.

A CONCRETE EXAMPLE

again it has been laid out rather simply, while the structure built on it is richer in the incidental content that goes to make up the texture of the work. The theme of the play, however, is a compound one: at any rate, it derives from one used already—used first, in fact, in the play I have just rejected. It will be as well, therefore, to go back and examine first the growth of this theme.

The beginning, as usual, is an intense experience, highly charged with emotion. Shakespeare, we know from his own confession, had been betrayed by a woman he trusted.* (The æsthetic result, of course, might have been the same if he had had an acute realisation of someone else's betrayal: but we know that in his case the experience was direct, and that it was reinforced in intensity by a simultaneous betrayal by a friend he had deeply loved and trusted and by the apprehension of betrayal, in turn, in store for this friend himself.)† Now, this experience, of course, was a matter of intellect no less than emotion. His intellectual perception had grasped it also, played on it, and drawn various conclusions from it, and from the light which it gradually threw on life in general. These conclusions speedily gave him themes, or elements at least of a theme, for plays. In *Troilus and Cressida* you

* He had not only trusted her: his previous plays show a pretty high opinion of women in general—compare, even as late as *Twelfth Night*, the instructive difference between the conception of Olivia in that play and that of the equivalent figure in Riche's *Apolonius and Silla*, from which Shakespeare probably lifted the bones of his plot.

† The idea of a man losing his illusions had been in his mind, though less passionately, for at least a year previously, for it had been the main theme of *Julius Cæsar* and the dominant, if not structurally the main, theme of *Twelfth Night*, both written just before. But in *Julius Cæsar*, though it is handled with a deep and thoughtful gravity, there is not the fierce intensity of apprehension with which it is treated just afterwards in *Troilus* and *Hamlet*; and in *Twelfth Night*, in fact, it is pure comedy. Shakespeare no doubt sympathised with Malvolio, as he did with nearly every character he created. But if he had not thought that "it served him right", he would have given him another name.

have the primary idea, almost unmodified, with an equally simple secondary one derived from it. A woman is false and shallow, and ruins the man who believes and delights in her. Helen, behind her like a figure in a mirror, is another such, ruining not one man but a whole city, which is proud of her and content to fight for her—imagine London standing a seven years' siege for the sake of a Noel Coward heroine! There are decent women, Andromache and Cassandra: but a woman like Cressida, going free herself, ruins them both. (Their tragedy, however, is lightly stressed: Shakespeare's intellect admitted it in justice, but it did not concern his emotions at the moment.) Troilus's devotion to Cressida is as romantically passionate as Romeo's to Juliet: but the lovely speeches are given a horrible counterpoint by the loathsome figure of Pandarus, who looks on.

The discovery which is primarily embodied in the placing of the romantic gallant lover between Pandarus and Cressida, casts a haze over life at large. The truth of the passion of love after all, is Pandarus.* Then the passion of glory, that for Shakespeare, as for many men of his day and others, found one of its major embodiments in the heroisms of the *Iliad*, has its truth, after all, in the lout Ajax, the shrill effeminacy of Patroclus, the sulky boorish vanity of Achilles—and so on: except for Hector (and he is rather stupid), there is not a man in the lot one can respect. If Shakespeare had not loved the tale of Troy as a hundred allusions show him to have done, he would not have guyed it thus intolerably. But he was in a mood to befoul his idols: the glory of life was slimed with humiliation. He had too clear a sanity, even then, to make all love into Cressida and Pandarus, all heroism into Achilles or Paris. He still admits Andro-

* I suppose I had better say explicitly that this is not my opinion. I am merely stating what was, temporarily, Shakespeare's.

A CONCRETE EXAMPLE

mache and Hector, but he sees them broken, *ingloriously*, in a world where Cressida and Achilles survive triumphant. Compare the emotions aroused by Hector's disaster with those of Othello's, or of the end of Hector himself in the *Iliad*.

> Almost all men, reading that sad siege,
> Hold Hector the best knight a long way—

yes, when they read it in Homer: it is better worth while to be Hector and fail than Achilles and succeed. But Shakespeare's conclusion just then was that it was better worth while to be Achilles—whom he despised. There is a certain effort of the will, though: he tried to believe that, he wanted furiously to revenge himself on life by believing it, but being William Shakespeare, he was rather too big to do it, and the touch of shrillness in the play, in spite of its immense and concentrated vigour, comes from the fact that he never really believed it with his whole self.

Now, watch the experience developing. In *Troilus*, it fills his consciousness: except for a shade over gallant ideals generally, there is no more. Then his vision enlarges. He becomes aware of the rest of life again: but this has thrown a new light of darkness on it. He can look away from it to other things, but life is like the shifting columns of Channel fog. There is nobility yet—after all, even in *Troilus* there was Hector: but it wanders blind, and can neither do nor not do what is presented to it: there are no bases for action. He writes *Hamlet*.* I do not mean to

---

* I foresee someone saying at this point: "But Shakespeare took his plots from other men's work. How, then, can they express his own experience, his own conviction?" I shall have more to say about this presently, but meanwhile I will ask the objector to reflect that Chaucer and Shakespeare each wrote a *Troilus and Cressida*, with the same plot. Yet the effect of the two versions is not very similar, to put it mildly. Why? And again, Shakespeare had known the story of Troy for a good many years. Why did he handle it then and not before? And why did he rewrite Kyd's *Hamlet* (if it was Kyd's) just

suggest that *Hamlet* was based entirely on the experience that gave him *Troilus and Cressida*.* It is enormously wider and deeper than that play. But that experience certainly had much to do with it. Probably it precipitated other experience (observed or undergone) into conviction, by colouring Shakespeare's vision of the facts, though the vision itself has now a much larger and deeper content. It is certain, at any rate, that a similar experience is shown to us, explicitly and at once, as having the same effect upon his hero. Hamlet's first free words reveal his whole outlook poisoned by the revelation of the foulness of sex that has come through his mother's conduct—an intimate and indefeasible horror that poisons not only his own sex-relations, but his dealings with life at large, even when he ceases to be conscious of it as such, though in fact he never does escape from it for long at once. In Shakespeare's consciousness, in Hamlet's own, in *Hamlet* itself, this draws round it other images that grow until they dominate it and become more important: but it is always there about their base.

There is a pause then, filled with the mechanical *Measure for Measure*. It was probably a task. Apart from the fatigue of writing *Hamlet* (and though I can believe Shakespeare wrote *The Merry Wives* in three weeks without losing any sleep over the job, I hardly think

then, and not earlier or later? It had been popular when he began to write: he may even have touched it up in 1589, at the same time as its fellow, *Titus Andronicus*. Why wait till 1602—or not wait till 1608? The obvious reason for using it then was that it supplied a vehicle for something he wanted to say about that time. All creative writers do the same kind of thing, though we are less frank than Elizabethans, and sometimes even we deceive ourselves.

* Critical tradition generally takes for granted that *Troilus and Cressida* comes after *Hamlet*. There is no external evidence that it does, and my reasons for thinking otherwise are given at some length in Chapter IV of *The Women in Shakespeare's Plays*. The only external evidence of date is that it was not published till 1609, the year of the Sonnets. But no one thinks it was written as late as that.

A CONCRETE EXAMPLE 49

Hamlet was tossed off in this airy fashion), the man who had just written it and was going on to *Othello* and *King Lear* and *Macbeth* was not likely to feel like romantic comedy. He had not lost his faculty for comedy: Polonius, Osric, Gertrude herself, poor soul, not to mention the grave-digger, would not surprise us in the least if we came on them in *As You Like It*: Gertrude, in fact, might have walked straight out of Jane Austen. (Indeed, there is, properly speaking, only one tragic character in the play: which is, in fact, precisely why it is a tragedy.) He had made a reputation in comedy, and Burbage wanted one for a command performance on Boxing Day. Mr. Shakespeare, the well-known dramatist and useful member of the company, obliged—with the history of Angelo and Isabella.

It is a chilly play. He wrote it, rather obviously, because he had to—to make a living and to oblige his friendly colleagues. He did not care about making it more than an elaborate story in the popular mode, with plenty of effective stage incident and a sprinkling of jokes that he knew would delight the Court. So he looked for a handy plot from his old quarry Cinthio . . . and the one he chose shows a woman—a perfectly, even flagrantly, respectable lady this time, as becomes a heroine of romantic comedy—working the ruin of a very respectable man who comes to desire her. It is slightly worked out, and seldom goes very deep. He was interested in Angelo, though he didn't like him: his imagination—he was a man of the age that built the Renaissance tombs—quickened a little at Claudio's horror of death, and his memory of his own delight in Bardolph woke for a moment over Barnardine. But that is about all, except the mechanical competence of a man to whom the technique of his art is second nature.

Time went on. He was Shakespeare, and his soul was

hard to kill. The enormous life rose up in it again, and burst its negations. Life could betray a man: he admitted that. Yet—leave the betrayal the worst and most intimate, let it lead to irretrievable disaster of circumstance, and a man could rise out of it again, greater than life. His spirit rose from the dust, with the dust upon it, in a more flaming glory than before. When he wrote *Much Ado* or *As You Like It*, he believed in the triumph of life, or took it for granted. He had lived since then through its sheer humiliation, so that now he *knew* the triumph, not only by assumption but by experience. He had to speak out the faith that was reborn in him, make it last in the experience of other men when his should be ended, either by death or by its supersession by other experience. Thus, he had a theme: from this experience had arisen a more or less formed intellectual conviction based on what had been profoundly *felt* and was therefore highly charged with emotion, and this needed a form to embody and convey it—detach it from himself, make it autonomous, to re-create itself in the experience of other personalities.

Now, at this point, there were various possibilities. He might have written the Eroica Symphony. He might have carved the Samothracian Victory, though he would have had to carve her broken as she is to get his effect. But being a dramatist, he naturally turned to write a play: that is, to express his theme by means of a design not of spatial ratios expressed in stone, or of temporal ones in the vibration of air, but of images of human personality, speech, and conduct, presented in his case, not as pure literature—that is, by a setting down of them in words— but by means of people speaking and acting on a stage for a period of about two hours or a little more. This is the worse for us, who seek an illustration of literature: but the next phase would be the same in either case, whether he thought of writing a play or a novel.

A CONCRETE EXAMPLE

This next step, of course, would be to find what we call the plot*—the pattern of conduct, speech, and personality, that should embody what he had to say. There was still a considerable scope about the business: humanity's triumph, in spite of its betrayal by life, could be expressed in terms of various human relationships. He could have shown a man whose religious beliefs had failed him, or his political creed (as already with Brutus), or his friend, or the cause he had fought for, or his followers, or even himself, as with another theme worked in along with it, he was to do later on in *Coriolanus*. But—probably without any very conscious reflection—he chose to keep the terms of his own experience. He himself had undergone betrayal at the hands of a woman he had loved: so should his hero.

Here, then, is the *bone* of the plot. But he might have built a good many tales on that—the story in the Dark Lady sonnets is in point of fact not at all like that of *Othello*. However, he did not use that, though Heywood has a plot not very unlike it.† It was his job, at this stage, to find a pattern of events, with this situation for centre, that should be capable of producing the sort of effect he intended. He might have built one *ad hoc*, from recollections of situations and incidents that he had read of, witnessed, or played part in: but he did not think it needful to take the trouble. After all, there are only so many of the major human relationships, and men have been writing about them for some time; and the more original an artist is, the less he bothers his head about his novelty. There rose to his mind a story he had read, which dealt with a situation of this sort. He had probably, indeed, read scores of them: he had dramatised one before in *Troilus*, and the betraying lover, man or woman,

* = "contrivance", "arrangement", "scheme".
† *The English Traveller*.

has been one of the commonest subjects in literature since there was any—the longest of his own lyrics * had handled it, and probably rather early in his career. But he chose that particular story of Cinthio's for several reasons, many of which we can guess with a fair probability. In the first place, there is plenty of action—the chance of scenes that would hold an audience: an elopement,† a villain tempting the hero to murder his wife, and risking being killed himself in the attempt—and incidentally, in the circumstances, giving Shakespeare a chance to draw the cold Machiavellian villain who was as much in fashion with the dramatists of the day as the Cocktailed Cocotte is in ours: the murder itself, the incidental affair of *il capo di squadra* (Cassio). Already there is the outline of a suitable dramatic action, of a handy size. And it gave him more—things that Cinthio had only had a glimpse of. Cinthio did grasp—indeed, it is his theme so far as he has one apart from "thrill" as such— the dangers of the racial difference between West and East, that helps to make plausible Othello's doubt. (Dramatic critics who consider the Moor simply a touchily jealous fool have never read the play carefully: and on the English stage they have probably never seen it unmutilated: which is their own fault—what would music critics say if we cut Bach about as we "adapt" Shakespeare, whose form is equally important?) Shakespeare saw also that to let Othello experience betrayal by his wife would be all the more effective if later he found that she was innocent: this adds a further betrayal by circumstance, that by deepening Othello's fall, enhances his greatness. Then further, there was the

* *The Lover's Complaint.*
† Much less dramatic in Cinthio, where Il Moro and Disdemona live happily for some time before he is sent to Cyprus. There is no Brabantio, either, only vague kinsmen.

A CONCRETE EXAMPLE 53

possibility of leaving Desdemona a "sympathetic" character. Shakespeare had an instinctive preference for that in any case, since good, being more difficult to achieve than evil, is more complex and therefore more intellectually interesting: and here, too, by making Desdemona lovely, he achieves not only a further reverberation of pity, but avoids belittling his central figure by making him desire what we despise. Cressida, even the innocent and gentle but fundamentally rather common Ophelia, would never have served his purpose here.

So far, so good. He has his theme burning in him like a lamp. He has seen a subject that will embody it.* How is he to tackle Cinthio's mere diagram of events (it is not much more than a newspaper report) so that when it is acted, or it may be, read, it will convey exactly what he wants it to?

Now, he is working in terms of personality and action. The content, if not the outline, of the action is fairly fixed, and with it the external conduct of the persons: he knows what they are to do. What sort of persons, then, if placed in these initial relationships would do just these things so as to give us precisely the emotional effect he requires? In other words, what are the "characters" like? He has to work this out, and the process is a curious and very complex one. I do not wish, at the moment, to do more than suggest it in the barest outline. Roughly, what he has to do is, given certain actions and the effect produced by them, to deduce what sort of people would, in the first place, perform these actions so as to produce this

---

* It ought to be unnecessary to add that you could take the action of *Othello* and make a play of it on a quite different theme—say, obviously, the clash of two racial cultures (this is suggested, of course, but as a detail), or the fact that blunt bad manners are not a guarantee of honesty, or the desirability of an Orderly Officer going on duty sober. Or you could even rearrange it, without changing the data of the plot, and make Emilia the central figure in an effective little domestic tragedy.

effect. Partly it is a matter of intellectual inference: for example, if Othello is a man of large nature, too large for ordinary jealousy, and intelligent enough to be a successful soldier, or whatever he is to be, and if Desdemona has the fine and high-bred chastity without which he would not have loved her enough to stake his soul on her—and the whole point of the play depends on his doing that—then obviously, the man who is to work the disaster must be no common villain. He must be clever enough to make people trust him, and he must have the kind of single-minded egoism that makes a man a wholesale murderer, less from hate than to gratify his sense of power over people who inconvenience him by their existence. The type is familiar to all psychopathologists, and it was fashionable in the literature of the time: hence Iago. In addition to conscious intellectual deduction of this sort, there is a sort of deliberate intuition: he fixes his mind on the thing as if it were real action, and finds it solidifying under his eyes, revealing more and more to him as he looks at it. Gradually his original theme acquires a new body, to which it is transferred, as it were, and which, for purposes of conveyance to others, embodies it better than his own complex, extended, and intangible experience had done, since the latter must almost certainly have embodied a good deal not relevant to his immediate theme, besides a good deal which would need elaborate explanations to be comprehensible . . . to give no better reasons for not transcribing it. He has reached a point, then, where the events and the people of his action have become, as we say, real: that is, they are now objects of as vivid an experience, as "actual", if you like, as Burbage or Condell or Susanna Shakespeare—more actual, probably, when he is thinking about them.

He has now gone the first stage of the road. He has re-embodied the subjective experience which is his theme in a series of imagined objects which can be grasped more clearly, with less explanatory preparation, by the perceptive processes of another person: or to put it differently, he has embodied his theme in a series of imagined objects independent of himself. This is the *creative* part of the affair. Now comes the *constructive*, without which it is useless. He must solidify his vague if luminous perception of these objects to such an image as will enable this other person to grasp them *as he intends them to be grasped*—to gain from them just the experience he means them to hold, and no other. He must therefore determine the *form* of his presentation.

As far as the general kind of form is concerned, three possibilities were open at this point—narrative verse, narrative prose, or drama. It is not likely that he debated the question consciously. Professional habit, general environment, and literary fashion, all made for the choice of a form he was thoroughly and instinctively at home in. Even if he had been writing nowadays he would probably have made a play out of *Othello*, though he might have made a novel of *The Winter's Tale*. As it was, he probably never thought about it. But granted that the general form was to be a play, what next? He knew he must go about to present his subject, the series of people and events he had in his mind, in such a way as to get the emphasis in the right place, without obvious fingerposts. He could not possibly, in two hours' acting, "begin at the beginning" and tell all he knew about Othello, together with the other people in a cast of a dozen odd, or even present, completely, the life of his middle-aged hero, or so much as the whole course of his relations with Desdemona. Obviously, he has to get at the significant points, the things that matter, or that can be made to matter, from his point of view.* But here is a fresh prob-

* In fact, by the end of the performance, we know six people

lem. The significance of a lot of them, of incidents in the experience of a man who has seen some forty years of a life adventurous even for the Renaissance, depends on a grasp of other, past, events, a sense of which has to be conveyed to us somehow. He cannot just begin the play anywhere, and go on presenting everything that happened in chronological order. There has recently been a fashion for this sort of thing in fiction, but even as a novelist, Shakespeare was hardly the man to launch his Argo under such a jury-rig, and to a dramatist who had to succeed in the theatre and not the highbrow bookshops, the thing was a physical impossibility. His next concern, therefore, was a business very difficult in itself, and one in which art conceals itself so well that it is only lately that critics have been aware of it in any but its more obvious manifestations. He has to select from his knowledge of his imagined people and events those aspects which should best convey his theme, and having done so, to arrange them in such a design that the emphasis falls in just the right proportions for giving our experience of them the precise quality he desires that it should have, and forcing us to infer what he desires we should. This matter of emphasis, of course, is not entirely one of general structure: but it depends upon it in the first place. It seldom occurs to a non-writing reader, for instance, that a book or play might have begun somewhere else. *Othello*, for instance, could have begun by showing its hero in "the plumed troop and the big wars", or with the progress of his courtship, or the promotion of Cassio that stirs Iago's hate. All these things are important to our understanding of what comes after, since they are important causally in the sequence of events. But Shakespeare

pretty completely, with a good deal about several others as well. And we see them on part of one evening in Venice and for part of about thirty hours in Cyprus.

A CONCRETE EXAMPLE

began with the incident that knots together all the elements that are to bring about Othello's catastrophe—that is, his marriage. And in showing us that, he allows us, or rather, he forces us, if we give him fair play by listening to what he is saying to us, to deduce what we need to know of past events.* All that actually *happens* in Act I is that Brabantio is told of Othello's marriage to his daughter, that Othello and his wife justify themselves to Brabantio and the Senate, and that he is despatched to Cyprus and sets out, taking with him his officers. Add that Roderigo decides to go there also, and you have the whole of what is actually presented. But its presentation has been so handled that we deduce from it not only the nature and mutual relation of at least six people, but the major facts in the past life of two of them, and those facts about the others that are necessary to our understanding of subsequent events. The whole act is what is technically known as "exposition": it is simply a statement of what we need to know before we can understand the real action of the play, which does not begin until Iago's campaign is opened. It is no part of the actual plot. Yet it serves that, immensely, not merely by giving us the intellectual data for comprehension, but by setting us in the right imaginative atmosphere to *feel* as well as understand what is to happen, and by making us desire keenly to witness it as it does happen. How all this is achieved in so little space is a matter in the main of the actual writing, the final crystallising of the image in the form in which it is to reach its audience†: and I am dealing here only with those parts of the process that take place before the pen goes into the ink.

* Ibsen, of course, is a great master of this type of construction. But he is not the pioneer he is sometimes assumed to be.

† At least it would be if *Othello* were a novel. As it is, of course, there must be another process. The written text, the "score" of the play, must be dealt with by the actors and their producer.

Forming some image of the general lay-out is the last of these. The image need not be a very clear one: by the time the writer is really under way, his *whole* self, subconscious as well as conscious, is "on the job", and he finds himself awakening to all kinds of progressive deductions about his people, their actions, and his method of presenting them, that being largely made in his subconscious mind have to his conscious self the effect of discoveries. In extreme cases he may find that they are leading him quite away from the lay-out of plot that at first seemed natural: the scene that he thought would carry significance may in the actual writing disappear entirely, left merely for the reader to infer: it may even happen that the action itself, or the characters, take a twist, and he finds that after all A did not do so and so, and that the action must therefore change from his first conception. This latter change, as we know, did not occur in *Othello*, for the plot follows closely the action of Cinthio's. We cannot guess whether the former happened or not, but it does not seem very likely. But it would be quite possible, for instance, that as he settled down to deal with *Macbeth*, Shakespeare meant to show the actual murder of Duncan—an obvious *scène à faire* for an Elizabethan—and then omitted it because he found it disturbed his presentation of what was much more important, its effect on the state of mind of the murderer and his wife.*

---

* If I may use the illustration without presumption, I may say that in each of my own four novels, a scene that I had intended—in three of them an elaborate and dramatic scene, that I could visualise clearly—has dropped "between chapters" in this way: it happened, but it happened off stage. In one of the four again, an episode that had originally seemed one of the major *scènes à faire* is merely narrated, rather baldly, by an eyewitness after it has occurred. William Archer has some interesting remarks on this sort of experience in his *Playmaking*.

CHAPTER IV

THE WRITER AND HIS STIMULUS

"The World was made to be inhabited by Beasts, but studied and contemplated by Man: 'tis the Debt of our Reason we owe unto God, and the homage that we pay for not being Beasts."

SIR THOMAS BROWNE, *Religio Medici*

THE foregoing chapter presents a rough but fairly concrete sketch of the pre-writing process as it may be conceived to take place in a particular instance of the most completely depersonalised type of writing—that in which the theme is expressed by means of a projection of the imagined experience of imagined people. Now, with this concrete example as a lead, we may venture to consider the process in terms a little more general, though always as little abstract as may be possible.

First, then, let us look at the initial stage of it, the relation of the writer to the object of that experience from which, in the first place, he derives his theme—in the terms of my suggested formula, which it will be as well to employ henceforth for brevity, the relation of S^1 and O^1. We will take for granted that he perceives O^1, whatever it is, and the general processes of his perception of it, which will be familiar to anyone with some knowledge of the elements of general psychology; and limit the discussion to those peculiarities of the special relation between the subject perceiving and the object perceived when the former is an artist and the latter the object of that experience which serves him as stimulus to the practice of his art. I have already suggested that aspect of the relation on which it would seem that the process as a whole depends—that O^1 provides S^1 with an experience of such vital quality that he is impelled to give it a more permanent being than can be afforded by its temporary existence in his own consciousness. The point has already been considered at some length in Chapter II: a complete discussion of it is scarcely possible, as it leads to regions of speculative metaphysics more tempting than profitable to be explored.

So far, however, O^1 is merely any given objective stimulus to a cognitive and affective experience of the necessary intensity. What qualities, then, must an object possess to function in this manner? It is advisable here to move rather carefully, and to remember that we are considering not objects as such, but, essentially, objects in relation to a subject. To forget this is to find ourselves plunged in a certain ancient heresy of criticism, which like all exploded heresies has a habit of cropping up again, slightly disguised, as another generation's Modern Thought. More than once in human history it has been the fashionable doctrine, implied or even quite directly stated, that only certain properly accredited subjects were suitable for Art,* with the tacit (or at times very vocal) assumption that to treat of anything outside this list was to prove oneself *ipso facto* no serious artist, and sometimes also as corollary, the further assumption that if you wrote about, or painted (or whatever it was), a subject whose credentials were in order, you were, *ipso facto* again, an artist to be reckoned with. It is even possible that this point of view has not completely vanished with the Victorians.

As with all really persistent falsities of doctrine, this has a certain truth about its base. Merely the truth has not been comprehended. It is perfectly true that only a certain kind of object can produce the required effect upon the artist: but the necessary quality is a quality

* Balzac, attacking *Hernani*, actually says "le sujet en (est) *inadmissible*" in so many words. And Balzac is not exactly a sciolist.

THE STIMULUS 61

not of the object itself, but of its effect upon the artist's mind. It must *signify* to him something that stirs some instinctive disposition in himself. This significance conveyed by it may, of course, be simply its own essential nature, as, in a very obvious example, when the object is a noble personality, or a mysterious fact like birth or death. But the essential nature of the object as such may have little to do with its significance. How many men, and not all imaginative, have thrown away their lives very cheerfully to save a square yard or so of torn dirty silk? That an object may mean far more than it is, and affect us in proportion to its significance rather than its actual nature, should be obvious to anyone who has learnt to read. The *Marseillaise* was a sheet of paper with marks on it: but it was worth an Army Corps to France. Nevertheless, it is quite extraordinary how many people fail to grasp this point: and the failure makes alike for idolatry and an ugly iconoclastic philistinism. If I bow my head to the altar on entering a church, an onlooker from Dayton, Tennessee (and from other places as near as the Cathedral of Birmingham), may accuse me of bowing down to wood and stone, whereas in fact the gesture acknowledges the supremacy of "a Spirit infinite, eternal, and unchangeable". The attitude of Knox, of Dayton, and of the present Bishop of Birmingham, would seem, however, to be losing its hold on contemporary minds, for a growing comprehension of symbol-values is increasingly obvious in the popular response to such things as the ritual of Toc H, and the simple and splendid gesture of the Armistice Silence.*

* Both the King and the Prince of Wales owe no small part of their well-merited popularity to their remarkable feeling for the right gesture: e.g., the King's offer to take charge of the colours of the disbanded Irish regiments. It is a notable fact that all great leaders have had this power to find some object which crystallised, so to speak, the emotions of their followers, serving for both their expression and a stimulus to their arousal.

It is possible that the cinema may have aided this: it may for once be credited with some social service. But in any case the recovery was to be looked for by anyone who is not utterly a pessimist, for the man who is fully developed intellectually and spiritually has a natural and instinctive sense of symbolism,* even although, at certain abnormal periods, this sense may be expressed by acute negations. It is only the spiritually sluggish and intellectually arid who ignore these values, and even they are more symbolists than they think. The man who would sneer at his neighbour for lifting his hat as he passes a wayside Calvary would be ill with shame if you forced him to walk down Piccadilly in a frock-coat and a bowler, though he might quite enjoy doing it in pyjamas. We are all symbolists somewhere, even the stupidest of us. If it were not for that fact, there could be no art.

O^1, then, must signify something, whether itself or something beyond itself, by which S^1 is deeply and profoundly stirred—in other words, something that arouses in him some fundamental instinct. It may be as well to remind ourselves here, at the cost of a certain disconnection of the argument, of certain implications of the phrase. As the process of stimulation depends on *two* entities, subject and object, the instinct that is stirred by a given object is not necessarily the same in different subjects, and S^1 may therefore react unexpectedly. Three people are victims of the same piece of incivility. A becomes angry, B is moved to pity for the aggressor, C does not even recognise that he has been rude. All three receive the same sensory percept: A and B receive the same intellectual one, which differs from C's: and yet in A and B two opposite instincts are roused—anger

---

* As, for instance, in the article of good manners, in knowing, as we say, "the right thing to do".

THE STIMULUS 63

(or destructiveness) in the one, protectiveness in the other. The nature of O^1 as a stimulus will thus depend in part on the nature of S^1. There will be more to say of this later on. Meanwhile it is enough to sum up the position arrived at by saying that as long as O^1 possesses, directly or indirectly, this power of stimulating the emotions (or to put it otherwise, of stirring the instinctive impulses) of S^1, it may itself be anything conceivable, even the idea of the inconceivable.

This last phrase brings us to another point. "Object", in colloquial speech, is inclined to mean something material. But since I am using the word in a psychological context, it should be hardly necessary to add (though I fear it is at all events advisable) that since it is equivalent to "anything thought of or apprehended", it need not therefore denote anything concrete. It may, of course, be a person, a scene, a thing, an action, but it may just as readily be an abstract idea of some intellectual or moral principle or spiritual state, or the general and consequently abstract concept of a class of objects material in themselves: we all know the man who wakes up at once at the sound of the word "horse". And, as it need not be concrete, so it need not be actual. The person or the scene or whatever it is, may be actually and physically present to the immediate sense-perception of S^1. But quite as probably it may not: he may remember or imagine it in such a manner that it is more intimately vivid than the actuality which immediately surrounds him—a "form more real than living man". All creatively minded people, and probably a good many others, are familiar with the fact that a memory-image highly charged with emotions may make us

> Hear on Lavernia Scarsgill's whispering trees,

so vividly that a perfectly sane man is startled when

actuality breaks through the vision, and emerges from it with a sense as of being awakened. Indeed, it would seem to be very probable that these imagined objects are a stronger stimulus to art than actual ones. For one obvious reason, the actual object may demand some action to be taken with regard to it: the action may of course be to paint of it or write about it, but a man does not hymn the excitement of an avalanche when he is thoroughly preoccupied with getting out of its way. For another reason, and one less accidental, a memory-image is necessarily selective. It does not recall the whole of an actual experience, but only such parts of it as are relevant to—something or other. What that "something or other" is may be determined by the desires of the subconscious self, or by some immediate external stimulus of which we are vividly conscious: a memory of Queen Mary's ride to Hermitage has just been aroused in me by a sudden drive of rain against the window: the same recollection might have been stirred in the process of answering an examination question, but though the memory-image in either case would be that of the same incident, its dominant factors would differ rather markedly. The image as recollected is, one could say, *prepared*: it has had thrust into low relief, if not eliminated, what does not fit the emotional disposition of the moment. Wordsworth, therefore, was likely to be right in declaring the best basis for poetry to be "emotion recollected", though the "tranquillity" he adds as a condition needs further definition for exactitude. The artist must certainly be "tranquil" so far as irrelevant experience is concerned, but only so far. There must be nothing to disturb his recollection, but if he is tranquil absolutely—if the recollected emotion also leaves him calm—then he is more likely to give us *Goody Blake and Harry Gill* than *Tintern Abbey*. While he is musing,

THE STIMULUS 65

the relevant fire must kindle, or his poetry will go badly "off the boil".

The purely imaginary object is of course only a special case of the recollected one, considerably under the selective dominance of an emotion. Creative imagination is at its root simply memory—but the memory of a man who can fuse and recombine his images, under the dominance of one that masters them. I have only mentioned the point here for completeness, as this process of fusion and recombination *ad hoc* is precisely the subject of a later chapter. Here it is enough to observe that while the man who imagined a creature with a lion's head, a goat's body, and serpent's tail certainly described something he had not seen, yet if he had not seen a lion, a goat, and a serpent, or at any rate pictures of them, he could not have imagined his chimera.

This last point again demands to be dwelt on for a moment. O¹ may be a simple image, the concept of a single undivided act or quality of experience. But in practice it will probably be a compound of several, which may even derive its emotional and stimulative force from this compounding into a fresh and complex image. A man cannot quench his thirst on oxygen and hydrogen if he assimilates them in succession: but if they have been united in a certain manner they form water, and he is satisfied. So discrete images may click together in the mind, with the effect of a sudden powerful stimulation, as when two possible situations that have been dwelling vaguely in the memory suddenly click together as the plot of a book that immediately comes into violent life in the imagination.

There is a point here which may already have suggested itself to the reader. It frequently happens that in such a coalescence of images one factor is what (in these terms) I can only describe as the image of a representation of the data-images, or to put it more concretely, part of the compound image to which S^1 reacts is an image of the manner in which he can fix and perpetuate its other elements: the poet, profoundly stirred by the mortality of human greatness, is stirred at the same time by an ill-defined but powerfully present image of the poem he will make upon that subject. I do not think this element in O^1, as such, is strictly necessary. That it must present itself at some time is so, of course. That it *may* be part of the actual experience of O^1 is obvious: a painter, as he sees "a good subject", may whip out his colours and sit down to it at once: what he saw as he came round the hedge was not a portion of Midlothian or Sussex, but the content of his next picture. But I do not think this is necessarily or invariably the case. In literature especially, a man may live for years with the memory of an experience burning in him, may even desire, quite consciously, to perpetuate it, yet never go about to do so until some day "a voice says 'Write' ", and the conception of the book that is to embody his recollection is suddenly and demandingly in his mind. Thus, while in certain cases (particularly in that of a man who is in the habit of practising an art, or lives among people who do) this derived image of what is practically the O^2 of my little formula may present itself simultaneously with O^1, even as a component part of it, the experiences are really different in kind, and the fact that they are, in practice, contemporaneous, is accidental. A man who is near a gun that is shot off has a compound perception of the flash and the noise. But though the experiences reach him as parts of a whole, they differ in kind and in channel of perception, and if he is a mile away he receives them by two simple acts of perception instead of a single compound one.

This gradual process of perception is not uncommon.

THE STIMULUS 67

O^1, whether simple or complex, may be experienced by a single act of perception, or by a long and elaborate process, covering years, and built up of many apparently unrelated acts of perception which are suddenly seen as synthesising to a whole which is then for the first time perceived in its full significance, and responded to by a single perceptual reaction. The elements of this whole may be of various and disparate kinds—the perception of objective entities, of subjective states or processes, of imagined or recollected objects or experiences; and may blend together, sometimes at the touch of something trivial and almost insignificant in itself, into a sudden and powerfully stimulating unity, to which S^1 reacts as he has not reacted to any of its elements.

Hitherto, in this chapter, we have considered the relation of O^1 and S^1 from the angle, so to speak, of O^1, and discussed what the nature of this O must be to produce the requisite effect upon S^1. We are now in a position to supplement the description of the artist provisionally formulated at the conclusion of Chapter II. To save the reader the trouble of turning back, I will repeat it. "What makes a man an artist in the first place is the innate possession of a 'complex derived instinctive disposition' to react strongly to the emotional significance of objects perceived, by means of a particular activity—the attempt to separate the emotionally charged experience from himself, and give it an existence of its own apart from his."

Now, there is a point to be added here. It is implied in the passage just quoted, and has been fully stated earlier in the present chapter, that O^1 must signify something which stirs S^1 emotionally, and that this significance may be other and greater than its actual self—as, in an extreme case, two bits of stick can signify the nature of God. It follows, obviously, that S^1 must have a perception, perhaps (as indeed is usual) a more than ordinarily developed perception, of the further significance of what is present to his senses. In his conscious or subconscious psychical make-up there must be a tendency to infer, very fully and rapidly, the implications of what he perceives and its relationship with other objects, whether actually present or merely recollected in the memory. In other words, he will have a notable power of *apperception*. In practice, the image of any object to which he attends will stir the images of a great many others and bring them to his consciousness, as in a simple case, the visual perception of our friend's handwriting may arouse images of the sound of his voice, some characteristic gesture, or the day we spent with him on the face of Braeriach: that is, one visual image may arouse a complex one in terms of divers senses, whose components have in themselves no point of contact, but are united by their common relevance to something that is none of them and resembles none of them—namely, our friend himself. All normal people have this power, of course, and to a very considerable extent. But the degree of its possession varies enormously. One man can learn more about a country-side by driving through it once in a char-à-bancs than another in half a dozen years of residence. What one receives from any experience is partly a matter of the psychical mechanism, but even more a matter of the pre-existing content of the mind and its organisation: "In travelling, a man must carry knowledge with him if he is to bring home knowledge." The artist, in common with the scientist and the man of action, possesses in an unusual degree this power of "putting two and two together". It is in fact a quite essential tool, without which art and science are inachievable.

THE STIMULUS 69

The distinction between the artist and those other types of men who are notably apperceptive is that the general disposition of their instinctive tendencies determines its employment in different directions, in (to modify De Morgan's useful phrase) different universes of thought and action. In other words, it is largely a question of the man's dominant interest. If we are intensely interested in any object, we tend to develop a more than normal—perhaps even abnormal—power of apperception with regard to it: it is a commonplace of popular observation that a man who is very thoroughly in love will contrive to relate all experience to the beloved, sometimes in fashions ludicrous enough, and that the man who is dominated by any theory is apt to twist all he meets into a demonstration, as when the Freudian hot-gospeller (I am not exaggerating) discovers a directly phallic significance in the simple act of poking up the fire.

Now, the artist is a man who by some property of his psychophysiological organisation is peculiarly responsive to, and aware of, the quality of human experience as such. It *interests* him, as we say. This disposition is partly a property of the individual intellect: X has by nature an intellectual grasp of the quality of experience, just as Y has an intellectual grasp of the relation of numbers. But it is more than that. An intellectual grasp of the quality of human experience might conceivably make a man a psychologist: but it would not, alone, make him a dramatist or a poet, though the great literary—or any other—artist will certainly possess it to a high degree. What the artist, and particularly the literary artist, needs is an extreme *imaginative* sensitiveness to the quality of states of consciousness. He must not only *know about* them: he must *know* them, know what they are like. He needs this power especially with regard to the state of being conscious of the action of any one of those fundamental human impulses on which is based the process of human living. Now, a consciousness of this sort, a consciousness of the quality of our experience of an instinctive impulse in action, is what we describe briefly as an emotion. It is perhaps some half-conscious awareness of this relation between emotion and the instincts * (i.e., pretty much that of sound to air-waves) that caused, in an age which gave not so much an exaggerated as a wrongly emphasised value to reason, a tendency to misconceive its importance. One of the deepest-rooted instincts of human nature is that to simplify our experience, to reduce it to something readily and tidily to be grasped. The tendency, though necessary to our self-preservation, has dangers, of which the most obvious and disastrous is that we tend to secure this tidiness of the perceived cosmos by eliminating large bodies of relevant fact. One of the chief of these simplifications, and one fashionable through the eighteenth and nineteenth centuries, and still influential, is to reduce the ideal of human experience to a pure activity of reason. Now, no man is so tidily rational as he who suffers from delusional insanity: and it is noteworthy, in the age that admired itself as the Age of Reason, how many men of large and brilliant personality lost theirs. Perhaps the deadliest of all these dangers is that which affects our present generation—the inevitable sequence of a counter-exaggeration that denies validity to reason at all. But in fact, over reason as over other things, one must be reasonable. And the balance would appear to be swinging nearer to the centre. Thanks largely to the brilliant work of Dr. McDougall, modern psychology lays an increasing emphasis on the conative

* The relation is brilliantly studied in McDougall's *Social Psychology* (1908), a book which, in fact, marks an epoch in the study of the subject.

THE STIMULUS

(or "striving") factors in man's psychological make-up. As a result, we are coming to a concordat between reason and instinct, and rediscovering that far from "instinct" in man being a sort of poor relation of reason or a semi-miraculous substitute for it, it is the earth from which springs the whole process of our living, the complex hierarchy of our activities, from the first blind gasp for air to the height of human spiritual achievement. Reason is the necessary tool without which the development of the process with the maximum efficiency and fullness cannot take place. But reason by itself will get us nowhere: it is a chauffeur without either engine or petrol. The result of this rediscovery of a balance between intellect and instinct is the rehabilitation of that Cinderella of psychology, emotion. Emotion is ceasing to be regarded as something not quite respectable, something the ideal man would not permit himself. In point of simple unscholastic fact, a feebleness of instinctive impulse means a deficiency of vitality: and where there is impulse (i.e., specialised *élan vital*) there is bound to be emotion, as combustion is accompanied by heat. To study emotion is to study the quality and effects of those manifestations of *élan vital* that (controlled and modified, if we like, by some autonomous force) are both our reaction to the cosmos and the means of our impact upon it.

To say, then, that the artist concerns himself primarily with the emotional significance of objects perceived by him is not to imply that he is studying an insignificant by-product or vestigial remnant in the ideal process of living. Emotion being the normal means by which we learn the quality and intensity of this process, one could as well call sound an insignificant by-product of the vibrations of air. The "practical man's" scorn of the artist has come from this very mistake: the practical man has fallen into the common fallacy of simplifying the cosmos by leaving out a large part of it. He has less excuse than his fellow-sinner the scientist, who *has* to do this, as one of the conditions of his work—though at his peril he forgets the fact that he has had to do it, as he very frequently does, and argues outside his laboratory in a world where half the data are omitted.

S^1, then, is possessed in the first place of the power of perceiving any given experience (out of a certain class, at any rate—it depends on his general psycho-physiological make-up) in relation to a large number of others—of grasping the significance of its place and proportion in the particular whole in which, for him, it occurs, and responding fully to the whole quality of the experience thus perceived, including that awareness of stirred instinctive impulse that we call "emotion".* Among such impulses, naturally, will be the one whose activity we call "reason"—for reasoning, after all, is as much an instinctive process as anger, or hunger, or lust: and they may also include at this stage of affairs (they certainly will a little later) that instinctive impulse to find some means of arresting and perpetuating the consciousness of significant experience, which is a specialised case of the general instinctive urge to continue in being characteristic of all organic life whatever and indeed the very thing we mean by the word "life".

A good deal of S^1's fundamental quality as an artist

* Notice that this is not the same thing as the derived pleasure in one's own emotions as such that we call sentimentalism. The sentimentalist sees emotion in its reference to one thing only—the self that is his sole or dominant interest. The emotional significance of O^1 for him will be the degree of his admiration for his own reactions to it: it will, in fact, for him exist merely as something for him to feel about. And among those reactions, those which interest him most will, of course, be those which excite the sense of his own delightful superiority to the rest of men. What John Smith, sentimentalist, is moved to write about is not his experience: it is the interesting fact that John Smith is picturesquely, or brilliantly, or obscenely, or otherwise fashionably, experiencing that experience.

THE STIMULUS 73

will therefore depend on the degree and manner in which he may possess these attributes. If the actual impulse to create is not powerful, his work, however adventitiously industrious, will lack vitality. But since this impulse is essentially derived, it will not be powerful unless those others which set it going are powerful themselves: that is to say, a man incapable of vigorous instinctive reactions to at any rate some aspect of life at large will lack the driving-force for effective creation. Allowing that he possesses a reasonably adequate technical skill, the vitality of his work will thus depend directly on his own.

Vitality, however, is not all. It is certainly much: a trivial drinking-song like *Back and side go bare, go bare*, is better art than Blackmore's epic on the Creation, because a living dog is superior in many important respects to a dead lion. But the live lion outclasses the live dog. Given an equal degree of vitality, a reasonable competence of technique, and the work on a great theme will necessarily be greater than the work on a small one—a truism, of course, but one on which depend two or three inferences that sometimes run a risk of being overlooked. One of these is that since the choice of a theme that arouses a man's *élan vital* to creative pitch will depend on what his general disposition is oriented by habit to find of interest, the greatness of his work will depend not only on the force of his personality, but also on its scope and its direction. A great man is not necessarily a great artist, but a great artist—great in the real sense, not a fine technician—must be a great man: that is, he must have a personality so tuned as to respond profoundly and immediately to greatness, to grasp the full significance of whatever experience admits him to contact with what is vitally of moment. His intellect must see first things as first, his instincts react to them most powerfully and most positively.

This is platitude, perhaps. But few things are so often misapprehended as a platitude. A man has not necessarily reacted to a great theme because vanity leads him to sit down and write about it. He may sing, let us say, the creation of a world, because he has *felt* "Omneity informing nullity into an Essence": or merely because he wants to be a poet, and someone has brought the subject into fashion. The latter motive will not take him far: he must choose from his soul and not from the tip of his pen. Further, this caution also must be added, though it is one for his audience rather than himself. The choice of a *theme* is not at all the same thing as the choice of a subject in which it is embodied. The two have as much to do with each other as wine and glass: certain subjects are more suitable in practice for certain themes, just as champagne comes best in an open glass; but champagne would be champagne out of a tea-cup, though the wise man would not choose to serve it so. Jane Austen's invariable subject is the marrying-off of the young daughter of a completely undistinguished country gentleman to a worthy and suitable but not very interesting young man. But her half-dozen repetitions of it have for theme a considerable variety of the manifestations of

> Trouthe and honour, fredome and curteisye,

their opposites, and the delectable absurdities of humanity; and to ignore the fact is to have as poor a palate for literature as the man has for wine who takes Asti for Heidsieck because they are brought up in the same glass. The point seems so obvious as scarcely to be worth a paragraph, but in practice it must be difficult to grasp, for scarcely one in fifty of the professional readers of fiction appears to look through the subject to the theme, unless the thing is such frank propaganda that all its

THE STIMULUS

bones are laid over the surface. To give an account of a novel is to them to give a more or less correct summary of its plot: they seem to think one can know Shakespeare from Lamb's *Tales*, which contain precisely the only part of the plays that is not Shakespeare's, and omit the rest. To take an example of the commonest of all subjects, a book which shows two people falling in love, getting married, and at some stage in proceedings going through various trials in connection with these events, may be a "love-story": but not necessarily. It may, for instance, be a study in the effect of one character on another, with sex no doubt an ingredient in the relation, but not by any means the most significant: or a description of a social environment, of the ironies of fate's impact on humanity, of human powers of self-delusion, of human courage in the face of difficulty, of the absurdities of common life, of the influence, benign or evil, of ideas, or of a dozen or so other things, with which sex as such has only incidental contact. The writer may have chosen that particular relation for the cadre of his story because, in the first place, it makes a fairly radical change in the lives of most normal people, and so helps to give him a beginning or an end: but more importantly for artistic convenience, the relation between the sexes as such is both very common and extremely complex, and consequently, while its external facts can be more easily taken for granted than those of the relation between, say, a poet and his poem, and need less bulk of extraneous explanation, there is plausibly room in it for the play of every major human instinct. If I may be permitted to illustrate from my own work, which is somewhat nearer the average than Jane Austen's, and therefore better as an illustration, I have written four novels, in each of which the main subject is a "love-affair", and planned a fifth whose frame is the relation of a husband and wife.

But in only two of these five has the theme any direct connection with sex-relationship as such . . . and in both these two, by the way, though the action, characters, and angle of vision are different, the theme is identical.

To return, however, to the qualities of S¹. If it is true that great work requires him to be receptive to the stimulus of greatness, it requires no less that he should be capable of continuing to respond to this stimulus when it is no longer immediate. He must have the power of choosing among his possible reactions, of continuing one to which he is not directly urged rather than one to which he has strong motive at the moment. This power of choosing among a man's own impulses is necessary, of course, in other things than art.* The Palæolithic man who wished to satisfy his instinctive impulse to eat had to conquer his instinctive impulse to fear his enemies, although the presence of a sabre-toothed tiger might have the effect of spoiling his appetite. So the man who has reacted to some great experience by the impulse to create an object which will embody it, must not only be capable of feeling that impulse intensely, but must be capable of acting on it when a good many contradictory ones are more immediate. It is not enough that he is impelled to write his poem. He must be able to choose among his subsequent impulses, to act on those which enable him to write it, to reject the others, possibly more powerful, which stand in his way, to focus his present self on something which is already in the past. To put it briefly, he must have a strong will. The strongest engine, the finest petrol, and the most skilful chauffeur will get nowhere unless the chauffeur keeps his hands on the wheel.

---

* The reader will recall Plato's definition of courage, in the fourth book of the *Republic*—"to hold fast continually the right opinion concerning things to be feared and things not to be feared".

THE STIMULUS

To sum up, then, the position we have arrived at, O^1, the artist's initial stimulus, may be simple or complex; actually perceived, remembered, or imagined; experienced by a single act of perception or by a very long and complicated process; material, immaterial, or a blend of both. But it must convey to him something which sets in motion a powerful and deeply rooted instinctive impulse, with its concomitant emotion. In other words, it must kindle life in him. The force of that life first of all will determine his primary quality as an artist: and the importance of the art which he creates will also depend, in the long run, on the evolutionary value of the instincts thus aroused, and of the direction and quality of their reaction. The man whose self responds most accurately, powerfully, and profoundly to the stimulus of the greatest theme, and whose will is able to keep his being thus focused, will necessarily be the greatest artist . . . if some failure at a later stage do not cripple him, as Hercules might be maimed and lose a hand. Even then one might know the cripple for Hercules, though that is not to say he is stronger lame.

CHAPTER V

THE NATURE OF THE PROBLEM OF CONVEYANCE

"Faire entrer dans la même forme vivante toutes les puissances contradictoires qu'il s'agit pour nous de concilier."
ÉLIE FAURE, *La Danse sur le feu et l'eau*

HAVING considered the general aspects of the relation between the artist as such and the object that stimulates his art in any given case—between S^1 and O^1—we have now to concern ourselves with the main subject of this book, which will be the material of the next six chapters: namely, the relation between S^1 and O^2—between the artist and the object which re-embodies and conveys to a fresh subject the experience he has received by means of O^1. As the art-process with which we are dealing is the specific one of literature, O^2 is thus what S^1 sets out to write, as the result of some specific process of experience.

Now this relation of S^1 and O^2 does not arise *simpliciter*. It is derived. The stimulus which begins the process of its existence is the initial relation of S^1 and O^1. The object or series of objects we describe as O^1 has aroused in S^1, through some harmony between them, an unusually vigorous action of his *élan vital*. This enters the consciousness as an unusual intensity of living, derived from his experience of O^1. He therefore assigns importance to that experience. It has value: it represents an act of full living: therefore he desires to preserve it, in its essential quality. To describe the facts as we ordinarily do, he has come on something that he wants very much to "get down". Now, we assume S^1 to be a writer:*
"getting down" a thing, to him, means writing about it.

* This is, in fact, assuming rather a lot at this stage of proceedings. But a discussion of its implications must come later.

THE PROBLEM OF CONVEYANCE 79

I have used the widest phrase that I can find. "To write about" O^1, or rather about his experience of O^1, is to create a new object, in this case a body of words, which can produce in someone else as nearly as possible the same experience as O^1 has caused in himself. This body of words, so devised, is our O^2. O^2, then, is a symbol of O^1, and the task with which S^1 is faced in creating it is to make the symbol embody as perfectly as possible that which he intends it shall convey.

Now, language is itself a series of symbols: that is, of things which convey to the mind the idea of something unlike in nature to themselves. "A black cat"; "un chat noir"; "felis nigra". Those are three sets of marks on paper. The marks are not like each other; they are still less like the sounds they represent; and neither any of the sets of marks nor their corresponding sounds is any more like a furry animal of a particular colour than my right shoe is like next Wednesday morning. Nevertheless, to anyone who is familiar with the three conventional systems of auditory and visual signs we call the English, French, and Latin languages, the three sets of marks convey each a more or less definite image of certain sounds, and *also* an image of the furry beast in question . . . which in turn, in the time it has taken me to write this phrase, calls up a variety of other images, from the sinking of H.M.S. *Hampshire* to the Pyramids.

Now, this curious power on the part of a set of arbitrary marks or sounds is the phenomenon on which literature is based. This violently genetic quality in the written or spoken sign is that which makes it on the one hand very difficult for S^1 to convey his experience of O^1 by means of it, on the other possible for him to do it at all.

He has the problem presented to him: how is he, by means of such signs, to convey the given experience? And it is not as simple as it sounds. For the time being we can afford to ignore the fact that the written sign is in effect only the sign of another sign, the spoken word, and treat the written and spoken languages as if they were the same thing. But even with this simplification, we find ourselves faced with a fairly complex process.

The phrase "to convey an experience" is not one we can take very literally. If I want to convey to my friend in Dingwall my pleasure in a fine day in Surrey, I cannot send him the fine day in a box. Still less can I send to him my pleasure itself, tied up with string and a wrapping of brown paper. What I do send him is an image of the day as I have experienced it. This image may be conveyed in various ways, of which writing is one. I have, then, to produce a piece of writing that will arouse in his mind the image that is in mine.

The obvious thing to do, of course, is to describe that image as it stands—describe the fine day exactly as it has been to me. But then there is trouble at once. To describe the fine day exactly as it has been *to me* will almost certainly mean a reference to other specific fine days, or days not fine, and to half a hundred other images, some of which have nothing to do with either weather or landscape. If I know my friend very well, and especially if we have a lot of memories in common, I can say: "It was like that day in the Cotentin when", etc. I can give it him, that is, in terms of our common stock of recollections. But suppose he was not there that day in the Cotentin?

Suppose, now, that the image we desire to convey is something a great deal more complex than that received in contemplating a particular landscape in particular conditions of weather. Suppose, further, that it is not of an actual experience at all, but rather of a possible one to which some combination of actual and imagined experience has given the key, and that our friend is not

THE PROBLEM OF CONVEYANCE 81

our friend but an absolute stranger, and several thousand absolute strangers at that? We cannot begin to explain to them all the peculiar modifications of our individual percept that depend on past experiences not otherwise related to that which we are trying to convey. It is attempted, I know. We have all met Miss Bates in real life, of both sexes and of all social classes, and recently her characteristic method invaded fiction itself, though the mode is passing. And in fiction, at least, if you want people to say things about you, it is very effective, while the novelty lasts: but if you merely want to say something yourself, it has the disadvantage of being cumbrous. One is wiser to reduce the experience to be conveyed—I will call it the *experiend* for convenience—to an image which will convey it without a lot of elaborate parenthetic explanations to cast a cloud of fog over its outlines.

In certain cases this is not difficult. If the experience, for instance, is a purely intellectual concept, varying not at all from man to man, but the same to anyone who can grasp it at all, it is not difficult, especially if there already exists a body of technical terms with a precise and definitely limited connotation and no haze of ambiguity round their edges. If a man wishes to convey to another that the square of the sum of two quantities x and y equals twice their product plus the sum of their squares, he has only to write down $(x + y)^2 = x^2 + 2xy + y^2$, and the idea is conveyed without possible ambiguity to anyone who is capable of grasping it at all. But even in mathematics, though our terms are precisely univocal and we are working by means of the pure intellect, uncoloured by any individual emotional association (save that one assumes and experiences that concomitant with the exercise of the instinct to reason)—even in mathematics, one is really presenting the image of the experiend in terms of other images present in the mind

F

of S^2. It is no use attempting to convince a man (by means of Pythagoras's Theorem, at any rate) that the square on the hypotenuse of a right-angled triangle is equal to the sum of the squares on the remaining sides, unless there is already in his mind an idea of the equality of the base angles of an isosceles triangle. Given that he knows this fact, however, one can convey exactly what he should apprehend, and do it very neatly and economically.

A direct and economical statement—that is to say, a statement as easy as possible to grasp completely and as hard as possible to grasp amiss—of the experiences we receive from observing, say, a highly complex relation between two people, not itself possible to state directly through the rather clumsy medium of words, and depending through a complex system of contingencies on their circumstances in the past, their relations with several other people, their physical and psychical make-up, and half a hundred equally complex and impalpable things, reacting and interacting on various intersecting planes—such statement is not so easy. To trace the genesis, development, and consequence of such a situation is less easy still. To do it for a number of people is still more difficult. But it can be done, is done with a good deal of competence every day of the week, because, by sheer instinctive "intuition", by deliberate intellectual analysis, by experience of our own and each other's practice, we have built up a technique for the process—one capable of innumerable modifications and grades of quality, but radically the same, whether used by the *Daily Mirror* or by Shakespeare. An image is constructed which is not an image of O^1, but which when perceived by S^2 will produce upon his mind (taking "mind" in the sense of his whole psychical make-up) the same effect that O^1 has had on the mind of S^1: and (since we have limited our universe of discourse to literature)

THE PROBLEM OF CONVEYANCE 83

this image is projected by means of words. We can now describe a little more fully the process summed up in our previous formula, $O^1 \to S^1 \to O^2 \to S^2$. An object or series of objects, O^1, the stimulus of the whole process, arouses I^1, an image of the experience gained from it, in the consciousness of S^1, the first subject of that experience—i.e., the writer. (Let us say, for example, the Dark Lady's treachery, O^1, arouses in the mind of Shakespeare, S^1, an image, I^1, of his experience of it.) S^1 develops from this a second image, I^2, which by means of an assemblage of words, O^2, is conveyed to the consciousness of another subject, S^2. (That is, S^1—Shakespeare—derives from I^1, his image of this treachery, a second image, I^2, which is his idea of the plot of *Troilus and Cressida*. Now to embody this image he creates an object, O^2, which is the completed play, and which arouses his own experience of treachery in other subjects, SS^2, his audience.) We have already considered the relation of S^1 to O^1. We have still to see what is his relation to I^1, in what way he derives from it I^2, and how I^2 is projected by O^2. More concretely, one man has undergone an experience he desires to write about. What happens next?

CHAPTER VI

THE WRITER AND THE APPREHENSION OF HIS THEME

(The writer must be) "no *automaton* of genius, no passive vehicle of inspiration, possessed by the spirit, not possessing it."
S. T. COLERIDGE, *Biographia Literaria*

GIVEN that the relation of the image conveyed by O^2 to that received from O^1—of I^2 to I^1, that is—is simply that it should convey a like experience to the subject perceiving it, it is obvious that there is room for a good many degrees of complexity in the process of discovering the second image. O^1 may be the fact that two and two are four, O^2 a simple arithmetical formula, $2 + 2 = 4$. But also, O^1 may be a five minutes' interview or the chance glimpse of a place seen from the train, O^2 a novel in 150,000 words, with scores of characters and an action comprising the fortunes of several people for a score of years: Dante described all Heaven, Hell, and Purgatory to image the effect upon his mind of a few chance meetings in the streets of Florence: and he was not by way of wasting words.

Obviously, before S^1 can create O^2, the object which projects the experience he wishes S^2 to receive, he must know two things. He must know what he desires S^2 to experience—what is to be conveyed to him by O^2; and he must have some idea in his mind of the image itself that can project this. In other words, before he writes his book he must know what he is going to say by means of it, and have some idea also of what the book would be like that would say just that: he must know what the experiend is, and have some idea of I^2 that is to convey it. This sounds, in fact, too obvious to be worth stating:

THE APPREHENSION OF THE THEME 85

but as a publisher's reader with some training in the analysis of literature, I can assure the reader who feels it so that many people have not noticed it.

Yet both of these two points are of some importance. A large number of competently written and very intelligent books have failed as literature because, though the writer knew what he meant to put into his book, he did not know what he meant to convey by means of it. His work is like a pleasant voice articulating very clearly and carefully a series of unrelated words. We have seen already that S^1 must be capable of what one can only call the deep and powerful reception of the stimulus afforded by O^1. He must be capable of, and undergo, a profound and intense experience of some kind. But this, though vitally necessary, is not all. A passive submission to experience is not enough. There must be that: he must be willing to undergo, without any drugging to his perceptions, a *passion* of some kind, in the strict Latin meaning of the word. But before his experience can be of use as a theme, he must do more than that: he must *know* the experience.

The phrase demands a certain examination, for "to know" is rather an ambiguous word. "To know an experience", even—a much smaller thing—"to know its meaning", is not necessarily to be able to describe it in a sentence or two. If human living were as simple as that we should not need either poetry or fiction: and indeed one notices that people who proclaim they have no use for either commodity are rather apt to simplify their perception of life down to what will fit within a few neat formulæ. The knowledge I mean is larger than intellectual perception—that is, it is not wholly a matter of reason. Reason has part in it, and a very important part, of testing and co-ordinating and delimiting: in its negative aspect always, and in its positive generally, it is most vitally necessary. But to attempt to apprehend any human experience by reason alone, though it may be necessary in certain circumstances, is always to falsify it to some extent. The extent may be fairly negligible, of course. If we take the experience usually conveyed by $(x + y)^2 = x^2 + 2xy + y^2$ or by "If no S is P, then some not-P is not not-S" and regard each as a perceptual act of pure reason, our experience will not be distorted at all, and very little may be omitted from it. Yet even then, the exercise of this pure reason is not after all quite the whole of the experience: there will be a faint aura of emotion round it—of bewilderment, perhaps, of bewilderment overcome, or the perfectly definite pleasurable emotion that comes of apprehending something clearly.* If it were not for this element of emotion, humanity would never have troubled to create the sciences of mathematics and formal logic.

It is true that in these two sciences one does come as nearly as possible to apprehension by the reason pure and simple. But that is simply because, in both of them, one is dealing with a carefully abstracted field of fact. And abstraction, no doubt, is necessary to learning: we must study the skeleton by itself before we can know very much about bones. But we shall not know the most important things about bones unless we realise that they are more than parts of a skeleton. The femur on the anatomist's table is very useful, but its normal place and function, quâ femur, is inside somebody's leg, helping him to stand; and to think of it only on the lecture-table is to be more truly ignorant about it than the man who has never thought of it at all. Abstraction is an invaluable servant, but cocaine is safe in comparison as a master.

* This emotion is not necessarily faint. It can rise to a passion capable of dominating such powerful primary instincts as hunger, fear, and sex.

THE APPREHENSION OF THE THEME 87

To know an experience, therefore, is more than to schematise it by the reason, more even than to apprehend it by the reason as in relation to a larger scheme. It is to be acutely aware of the whole quality of it, quâ experience. This means, of course, that our "intellect", the purely cognitive aspect of the mind, is acutely and elaborately aware of its relation to the whole body of other experience, actual and possible: but it is also to be no less acutely and elaborately aware of the quality and nature of its impact on our sense-perceptions, and—from the point of art the most important of all—to react to it by some definite exercise of élan vital, *and to be precisely aware of the quality and implications of this reaction*. The artist must apprehend, as fully and profoundly as possible, both the essential nature of the object experienced and the essential quality of its subject's —that is, his own—reaction to it. And since ex hypothesi this reaction is fairly intense, and therefore likely to be reverberant, this process is not so easy as it seems.

We have seen already that to achieve it at all he must have a considerable—in fact a more than normal—power of both perception and apperception with regard to those variously directed streams of *élan vital* whose tides and interplay are the human life-process. Interplay: for they seldom work very simply, and never for more than a little time at once. As a conductor is simultaneously aware of the action and quality of every instrument in an orchestra of forty or more, so S^1 must have this power with regard to a symphony of instinctive impulses in action. All normal men have some degree of this power. A man knows, say, that he is surprised and angry and ashamed at once, and he can tell that the violins and the kettle-drums are both in action. But Sir Henry Wood knows exactly what each player is doing, and yet is intensely aware of the one unified thing that the combination of them together is producing, and of its relation to an imagined concept. S^1 has that power with relation to human experience.

Now, if you asked Sir Henry Wood, "What is the meaning of X's Opus 48?" he would not say to you, "Birds singing at dawn"—though possibly the programme might. He might tell you, if he knew the history of the piece, "What X felt when he heard birds singing at dawn". But if you asked him, "What was that?" he could give you no answer except by playing Opus 48: which of course *is* the answer. So our S^1, though he may know what his experience is, cannot tell you what it is—cannot tell himself, in fact—except by transposing it to something else, through which, if we like, we are able to perceive it. It is only then, by the way, that he can be really comfortable. To be face to face with a chaos of experience and not be able to apprehend it firmly may not be why a baby howls when it is born. But it is a painful situation for the adult, and one to which he commonly reacts by vigorous signs of anger and discomfort. Indeed, that very need to apprehend reinforces the intensity-value of the experience, that makes it a stimulus for art. The man has to force himself on it until it burns him. It is partly this very friction as he forces himself into and upon resisting experience that makes the flame that he feels as life more abundantly, that dares him to let it die or to keep it living. Hence he struggles to compress the challenging experience, as it were, to something he can get hold of with his mind. The thing is so vast and so impalpable that he cannot clasp it until it has been trapped into some image that appears to be—for the experience is rather deceitful— more fully within his grasp. There is this underneath all great tormented art: something that mocks perception has been dragged by sheer resolution within the scope of

THE APPREHENSION OF THE THEME 89

it. *Hamlet* is a case of that, and *Lear*, I think, and the violent intellectualisms of Donne. One has it in the great intellectual mystics, Teresa de Ahumada and John of the Cross, in the fierce and smoky work of Webster and Marlowe.

Now, to achieve this grip upon experience needs the qualities of perception I have described. But it needs something more, needs it essentially. If it is anything great enough to be not easily grasped, it needs resolution, needs that stringency of the will that can hold the personality focused on a chosen end, whatever temptations come to turn aside. It needs courage, in fact, for courage is very precisely this resolution. It is easy for a man sensitively organised to feel a sudden vivid flash of interest as he comes across something that promises great experience. But it is like the flash of burning straw unless he is willing to devote the time and effort that are needed to let him get a full hold of it. If the theme is great, there needs an expenditure of both that can only be achieved by not spending these elsewhere. Unless, perhaps, the artist has a volume, richness, and intensity of personality that are rare in even the happiest of ages, he must vow himself to a merciless ascesis. An ascetic is a man who canalises the whole of his energy in one specific direction, so that, in that particular direction, he can use all that he has of it without any leakage. It need not always be the same direction. Often it is, but not always. A man like Leonardo could fling his whole life at one thing after another, grip each with an almost fantastic rapidity, and without waste of himself swing his whole gigantic force to a fresh object. More commonly, as in the type of saint like Louis of France or Catherine of Siena, who have a tremendous influence on the life of a generation in half a dozen different directions, the forces are canalised to a single end, but allowed to pass through different means of attaining it. The artist needs a volition of this kind if he is to grasp anything that is not within easy reach of every day. He must be able to hold himself steady, as it were, to the furious impact of a greater thing than himself: and in this be not merely passive to its print, but seize it with his whole self and refuse to be diverted, until he has achieved what he willed of it. This terrible marriage of the soul and theme, in which he must play both bridegroom's part and bride's, is that from which great art is begotten on him, and it is one which no coward can consummate.

This is large language. But I am using it of large affairs. The process, however, varies enormously, though only in degree, never in kind. When a tremendous theme mates in this fashion with a mind equal to it, that is the greatest art. But not every lover is capable of knowing what Donne knew in Anne More, or Dante, in another fashion of love, in Beatrice: and not every man who is truly religious can grip on God like the great mystic saints. Yet there are honest lovers and good men, whose love and religion are real and effectual. So with the artist, whose work indeed has its base in that which is the end of both love and religion—the fusion of the self with something greater, that results not in its loss but rather in its fulfilment, whether in one aspect of being or in all. He also mates with a theme in proportion to his mind: and his mind and its power vary from time to time. It may be a theme that needs stringent focusing of the whole personality through months or years of an agony of effort. It may be one he can apprehend at a touch, with a smiling easy relish as he perceives it. The same man may do either at different times: the man who wrote *King Lear* wrote *Come unto these yellow sands* and Autolycus's fooling, and had delighted in Bottom and Dogberry. Even Our Lord was not always on the Mount of Transfiguration,

THE APPREHENSION OF THE THEME 91

but came as a pleasant guest to a country wedding and played with the children by the Lake of Galilee. The mind must grip upon the theme, that is all.

When it grips a small theme very perfectly, and the artist's technique can mirror what his mind holds, we have the small perfect art, like Austin Dobson's or Herrick's. (Indeed Herrick takes great themes at times: but always it is as if one saw them reflected in miniature, caught very tiny and clear in a convex mirror.) But great art needs a great theme to beget it, and a greatness of mind to mate with such a theme. Perhaps indeed very great art cannot be perfect, because the greatest of men cannot be more than human, yet, since he *is* human and therefore is part divine, he reaches out beyond his scope, "above and through his art, for it gives way", so that in all the very greatest art the man is necessarily handling something he cannot completely possess.

One must add a caveat to this, of course. The obverse proposition is not true. Art is not great because the artist has chosen something he has not the capacity or the resolution to grasp. If mere perseverance will not make a man an artist, still less will laziness. He has to go through with the business to the end, shirk nothing—and take the risk of being too small. The price of too great audacity will be failure, but if he does not risk that he achieves nothing. In other words, art is like life at large.

But art is not all a matter of great themes. For "art" in general and unspecified, it is enough that the mind and the theme should be capable of this transfixion or transfusion—transflammation, one might almost call it—of each other. They may be great or small: it does not matter, so long as they are capable of this. Whether the O^2 that gives the process its result is the *Divine Comedy* or "There was a young lady of Riga", if it is art at all and not what the excellent American idiom would call "near-art," there is always this marriage-union at its source.

S¹, then, we take it, *knows* his experience, and the sign that his union with it is consummated is a crystallisation in and beneath his consciousness of some image that is *what his book is to convey*. He has been gradually made aware of the complex of components that make up O¹. Suddenly he becomes aware that they are no longer a complex of discrete or even unrelated fragments of experience, but a whole. The process is familiar in many fields: in fact, I have come on two excellent descriptions of it within a few hours of each other, one in an old *Hibbert* article and the other in a detective-story: I cannot better them, so will quote them as they stand. In the one case, the hero of the book is puzzling over a complicated problem: "And then it happened—the thing he had been half-consciously expecting. It happened suddenly, surely, as unmistakably as sunrise. He remembered not one thing nor another thing, nor a logical succession of things, but everything—the whole thing, perfect, complete, in all its dimensions as it were, and instantaneously. . . . He no longer needed to reason about it or even to think about. He knew it."* The second description supplements this somewhat. "There are days of incubation when the data seem formless and elusive, like a heap of dry sand; when the wheels of the brain seem to turn creaking slowly in a void, and bite on nothing; when reason maintains that something is bound to come out, but one cannot feel as if it would be anything but some dressing and patching up of old unsatisfying forms. Another day comes when all at once, without any effort, a ray of light falls on the scattered grains at an unexpected angle, and they are crystallised

* Dorothy L. Sayers, *Whose Body?*

THE APPREHENSION OF THE THEME 93

into stones, and take shape as a structure, and one feels not that one has made it so, but that it was so all the time and only waiting to be seen."*

In short, S^1 has *apprehended* O^1, as such. It is no longer $o^1 + o^1 + o^1 \ldots$ discrete fragments embedded in a mass of other experience. To use the homeliest of illustrations, it is as if I took a piece of silk bought last week at Liberty's, some ribbon acquired this morning at the Stores, and a metre of lace bought a year ago in France —things with no logical connection with each other. As they stand, they are three completely useless objects. A little treatment, and behold, they are useless no longer, but have synthesised into one very useful garment. And in the same way, S^1's meaningless memories have suddenly become one, highly significant.

Now this single percept or image of O^1 may be fairly simple. But it is more likely to be far from that. It may in point of fact be enormously complex, built up of interwoven parts and stresses, reaching out and living —for it is a live thing—in and by relations with what is not itself, but fully self-existent for all that. It cannot live without the man whose mind holds it. It takes life from him, as an unborn child can only live through its mother: but like the child, it has an entity.

Quite possibly, however, this is the most that can be said of it as yet. S^1 may know that the image of it exists in his mind, and that this image is of something that matters, rather as one knows that an unread letter in one's hand is about something very important, without as yet knowing its actual content. He may have yet to

---

* Sir Frederick Pollock, *Mystic Experience and Philosophy*. Hibbert 1913. Reprinted in *Outside the Law*. He adds the very sound caution: "Of course, it by no means follows that a result so presented is right, or even the best that can be had with the means then and there available. It is conditioned by the worker's capacity; but if I mistake not, it is likely to be the best of which he is capable."

learn the content of his image, as there is a stage where one has yet to read the letter one is holding. It is possible, of course, that the first perception of O^1 as such may bring the whole content of the percept to full consciousness, though I doubt this, for no idea, however clearly grasped, is quite without some delicate strands of connection with the subconscious content of the mind. It may certainly be *mainly* in consciousness, as, in the most obvious case, when O^1 is an abstract concept, as of, say, the economic principles underlying the Industrial Revolution, or a simplification of the proof of a theorem. S^1's clear consciousness of this concept is the image of his complete experience of O^1 as such—that is, it is the I^1 of my enlarged formula.

But in a very considerable number of cases, the perception is not even mainly in consciousness. The greater part of it, "as a great Prince in prison lies", may be held at first in some subconscious layer of his mind, and be aware of it only as some deep emotional disturbance, that will not let him rest, but whose cause is out of reach of his conscious cognition. The more fully it has flooded his whole personality, the more deeply it has gone down to the very source of his *élan vital*, and the more deeply that stream flows in him, the less likely is he to be able to form, at this stage, while the perception is still active in him, a clear intellectual idea of it. What happens is what occurs in all similar states, when some powerful stream of activity is at work in the subconscious levels of personality. When his conscious mind is passive for a while, as in sleep or in that suspension of voluntary mental activity that comes to most of us at some time or other,* there rises into it some symbol-image, that may be, indeed, apparently unrelated to any particular important experience, but which he will recognise as

* "Sometimes I sits and thinks, and sometimes I just sits."

THE APPREHENSION OF THE THEME 95

being causally connected in some way with the disturbance or tension of which he is already aware. This image will most probably be in terms of sensory perception of some kind—of what kind will be determined by his prevailing perceptual habits, but it is likeliest, it would seem, to be visual-motor, most people being of that class, as their dreams show.

It is the "crystallisation" of his experience. He perceives in this case, as the image of that experience (as the I^1), not an abstract intellectual idea—i.e., a concept—but a concrete perceptual symbol. The reason why it reaches consciousness in this fashion is that before it can rise from the instinctive levels which are not at present in direct external action but in which none the less it is working powerfully, there must be a sort of lull in the conscious activities, in the higher reasoning faculties of the mind, which may have been directed in some other direction in response to present external stimuli. And when these activities are in abeyance the mind reverts to the older mode of thinking, and drops verbal abstraction for the pictorial image.

The symbol is not a conscious perception of analogy, as when one describes Edinburgh as "the northern Athens", but arises spontaneously from the deeper levels of the mind—from levels so deep, indeed, that its intellectual significance may be as hidden as that of an ordinary dream-image. Yet it is recognised as having power, as being connected with profound experience whose quality cannot as yet be otherwise expressed. It is possible that the symbol may be able to *convey* this quality, in which case the I^1 of our diagram becomes also I^2, and S^1 can set to work at once to project this symbol exactly as it has come to his consciousness. If he is a painter, sculptor, or musician, he may be able to do this in most cases: suppose his experience of newly consummate transient freshness of beauty—derived, perhaps, in the first place, from a spring morning—is crystallised in this fashion in a vivid image of a beautiful youth, and he reproduces this image in a statue: the image embodied in the statue (I^2) is identical with that first formed of the experience—i.e., with I^1. But if he is a writer, he will probably find, in the majority of instances, that though his vision may *express* what he feels, it will not *convey* it. It merely signals to his conscious mind that there is something to be conveyed—something that shall be affectively equivalent to his vision, that shall rouse an identical complex of emotion. He must set about to find a second image, deliberately harnessing both conscious and unconscious self to the task.

But even when he has achieved the second image and projected it with no direct reference to the first symbolic vision, the power of the first may persist in a curious manner. I will give two instances from first-hand experience. One is concerned with a recent novel of my own. When the first idea of it came into my head, it came as a very clear and potent visual-image of a wide bare landscape, black and dark green and grey, seen in uncoloured light that cast no shadow and had a most peculiar quality. I knew I had seen light of that quality: but it was no kind of daylight or artificial light that I could recall. Now, no landscape of the sort is described in the book—certainly nothing is described as in that light, for as I say, I did not know what it was, and was even uncomfortably unable to find any form of words that would describe it. But a friend of mine, Miss Nan Shepherd, remarked to me, after having read the finished book, "It reminded me of a landscape *seen by lightning*". Now, there is no mention of lightning in the book: but that is exactly the light in my symbol-landscape. I did not recognise it as such, because the vision had no dimension of time: but the

THE APPREHENSION OF THE THEME

quality of the light was the peculiar one of lightning and of nothing else. And some undercurrent of this vision of mine had struck through the images of the book to my friend's mind.

The other story is not mine, and therefore I cannot give the name of the author and book, but it is even more remarkable. It was told me by the well-known woodengraver, Miss Clare Leighton. She was commissioned to design a cover for a novel. The author told her she had taken the idea for the book from something told her by a woman in Africa, who she hoped would not recognise it. Miss Leighton, having read the book—a commendable proceeding in a designer of covers—drew a woman's figure. The author, when she saw it, exclaimed, "That's exactly like the woman who told me the story!" The preimage had evidently taken the form of the woman who was the story's source, and was powerful enough to get itself into the book in solution, as it were, to be precipitated in the reader's mind.

It is fair to add that in each of these rather spectacular cases the reader was a person of more than average æsthetic sensibility. Miss Shepherd has written two fine novels herself, Miss Leighton's work is well known, and I have other instances of her sensitive perception of atmosphere: she had previously designed two covers for me (one is the design now in the British Museum, catalogued as *The Crinoline*), and in each case the landscape setting gave a true and vivid impression of actual places mentioned but not fully described, which she had not seen. Both places were very well-known to me, and were strongly present to my mind as I wrote, though I cannot recollect whether either of them played any part in a pre-image like that mentioned above, which I should have forgotten if the light had not puzzled me so.

I do not think that the actual appearance of a symbolic

pre-image of this sort is a necessary preliminary to literary creation. What first comes to consciousness may conceivably be the direct beginning of the book itself. I might, for instance, in the case described, have imagined not my symbol-landscape but the group of persons in a specific relation which was the initial datum of my plot. But if a book is to be of any real æsthetic value, it must have beneath it those deep mental processes of which such an image is an evident sign: it must be based on a perception, an experience, which has gone down below the surface layers of conscious cognitive activity, and soaked into those on the deep instinctive level. A mere apprehension by the tips of the personality, so to speak, is inadequate. This is not to say, of course, that a book founded on such deep apprehension is necessarily good, let alone great. My own that I have cited is a case in point. There was certainly such apprehension beneath it: but I am far from pleased with the finished work. Between the first definite conception and the last touch to the proofs a book goes through a pilgrimage of dangers, and may weather the first and fall victim to some later one.

Yet none the less, though this deep apprehension is not all, or nearly all, it is rather considerably necessary. The reader may have noticed, possibly, that there are, for example, two different kinds of novel. Any novel takes a certain time to read. It cannot be perceived in a single *coup d'œil*, as a statue can: one has to walk along it, so to speak, as one walks along a frieze in order to see it. But when one has come to the end, two things may happen. One can remember it as one remembers the frieze, as a *sequence* of experience, alive or dull, ably or clumsily projected: and this is what happens with the majority of novels, the ordinary competent commercial article. But in others it is as if, when one had come to the end of the frieze, it drew suddenly together and fused

THE APPREHENSION OF THE THEME 99

all its shape and meaning into a single group of statuary, that one saw all at once with a single stroke of the eye. In the first case, the book has been a record—it may be an able, even a brilliant, record—of the experience that is its content. In the latter, it is, as well, an experience itself. What matters most in, for example, *Wuthering Heights*, is not what it tells us about Heathcliff and Catherine, but the book itself. Its "meaning" is not what it says, but what it is. What we receive from it is not, primarily, a record or interpretation of the experience of its characters as the author observed them in imagination: it causes us to have an experience of our own, or rather to enter one of Emily Brontë's. In other words, it is not science, but art. It is these books that one remembers, by the way—remembers as books, and not, vaguely, as the source whence we derived such-and-such information. I recall of Miss Kennedy's *The Ladies of Lyndon*, a "frieze" book, that I thought it capable and entertaining: but I have no image of itself as such, though I recollect vaguely "what it was about". Of the same writer's *Constant Nymph*, which I read much earlier, I remember its content only rather vaguely, and would be sorry to have to summarise its plot: but I have a vivid image of the book itself, not as a sequence of parts but a unified whole: a group of statuary, not a frieze. There is exactly the same difference between *Jane Eyre* and *Shirley*. I suspect that in the case of *Shirley* and *The Ladies of Lyndon* the author wanted to write a book into which she could put certain things. In *Jane Eyre* and *The Constant Nymph*, she wanted to write, or rather could not help writing, a certain book. And between the two is a very profound difference.

It is not simply a question of technique. *Shirley* is a later book than *Jane Eyre*. But as Charlotte Brontë was not a brilliant or careful technician—she is greatly her sister's inferior on that point—I will take another example, Miss Clemence Dane. Nobody who was not a very careful and deliberate artist could have handled a piece of technical virtuosity like *Legend*. But her first book has this unitary quality, while *Wandering Stars*, written much later, has not, in spite of a sensitive care in the construction and, one cannot doubt, an equal sincerity on the conscious level. The difference is not one of technical skill or intellectual perception, but of the presence or absence of this deep and fundamental reaction in the writer's personality.

Lacking that, the theme cannot achieve the preliminary crystallisation without which the book has not this self-existent entity. I am not chemist enough to know how crystals are formed: but I fancy that in this metaphorical case it is very largely a question of the temperature, so to speak, at which the fusion of the writer and his theme has taken place. The eugenic theories of Shakespeare's Edmund are equally applicable to æsthetics: a piece of art "got betwixt sleep and wake" of the greater part of the writer's personality has not enough heat of life in its composition for it to crystallise in such clear self-existent being as to find expression in a unified image apprehensible by a single act of perception.

CHAPTER VII

THE WRITER AND THE DISCOVERY OF HIS SUBJECT

"The vision of dreams is of this thing against that, the likeness of a face over against a face."
The Wisdom of Jesus the Son of Sirach

WE may take it, then, that S¹ has some idea of what he wants to say. This idea may take the form of a clear but abstract intellectual concept. It may, again, be a vague consciousness, blurred and relative and contingent, yet powerfully affective none the less, of experience on deeper levels than the cognitive. Or such deeper experience, being, as it were, thoroughly digested—and being based probably on clear intellectual and sensory perception in the first place—may throw up a symbolic image of itself, so clear that he perceives it at a single glance. This image, if analysed, would be found to reflect the implications of the consummated experience, in the manner observable in the imagery of dreams.

Logically, I suppose, to convey the experience and its significance it should be enough to describe—to convey a percept of—this pre-image in which it crystallises. But in practice, it is nothing of the sort. If, in the case I have already given, I had described a country seen by lightning, I could not have got into the description what it signified to me. I could only convey that body of significance to someone else by creating a much more elaborate and complex image. Apparently I succeeded in projecting it on one person's mind at least, as what I had conveyed to her recrystallised in her mind in the same symbolic image as in mine. But I could not have so projected it by merely making her aware of that pre-image.

This necessity for a more complex image is not, however, invariably present. If the experience is psychologically simple and its percept clear and relatively self-contained, it may be possible to describe it directly. By psychologically simple, I do not mean that the experience itself is necessarily a simple matter to grasp. The theory of relativity, for instance, puzzles people who are trained mathematicians: but Dr. Einstein's apprehension of it, however elaborate the process of its achievement, is a good deal less complex in itself, as a psychological process, than, say, his apprehension of his relation with his mother. It works practically on a single well-defined plane. So also, to turn from science to poetry, Wordsworth's experience at dawn on Westminster Bridge is on this comparatively simple plane. The perceived image and the projecting image (I^1 and I^2) are alike, for the elements of the first, though seen more intensely than is customary, have nothing in them that cannot be made self-evident. Such contingency as they have is upon experience generally familiar, and again what is required is no more than simple description, though here it must have not only clarity and a definite focus, but a certain degree of intensity if the projection of it is to be truthful. This is gained, however, not by any modification of the image itself, but by the method of projecting it—i.e., by the writing, the choice and arrangement of words—and so does not concern us at the moment.

There are, in fact, a good many kinds of experience where, as I have expressed it, the image of the content of O^2 coincides with that of the experience derived from O^1—where I^2 and I^1 are the same. Literature based on an image of this sort will be a direct statement by the author in his own person, or very frequently in some imagined or semi-imagined rôle of that person. It will be completely expressible in those terms, whether it is *The*

THE DISCOVERY OF THE SUBJECT

Fundamental Principles of the Metaphysic of Ethics, *Eothen*, *Tintern Abbey*, *The Essays of Elia*, or the works of Euclid. These are all direct formulations of the writer's real, imagined, or semi-imagined experience, in terms primarily of itself. All scientific writing belongs to this kind, all critical and nearly all historic, including biographic and autobiographic, and the various types of prose we know as belles-lettres. So also does lyric poetry and all those intermediate varieties of verse where the presentation is cast in the direct first person. So long as the content of O^2 is either comparatively simple, contingent, in ways reasonably direct, on experience that is generally familiar, or, though complex in itself, yet dependent on a clearly defined body of pre-experience, which (as in a treatise on the higher mathematics) the audience can be assumed to possess, this direct presentation may be possible.

But this is not always the case. The experience derived from O^1 may be a very complex affair, where several planes of experience, intellectually cognitive, instinctive-emotional, and subconscious, are combined, not in parallels either, but in an interplay as complex as a tide-roost: it may be contingent in a hundred directions on individual subtleties of pre-experience, and its appeal may be to a complex of perceptions that includes, importantly, other channels than that of a purely intellectual apprehension. The only thing that can be done here is to present the experiend indirectly, in a form which projects its content on different experiential planes and whose contingencies are as far as possible within itself, and are so contrived that when their reference goes farther it is to the common human stock of experience, or at least to one common to the probable audience.*

---

* Dr. H. J. C. Grierson, in his brilliantly suggestive lecture on *The Background of English Literature*, speaks of "the varying and

To put the thing a little less generally, O^2 will project its content by showing it re-embodied in a phase of experience devised to the sole end of its complete portrayal, and consequently freed from the adulteration of irrelevancies and contingencies found in its first experiencing as received by S^1 from O^1. It will be shown, then, by means of the imagined experiences of imagined people, created *ad hoc*, and thus be perceptible in its full quality. "By means of", not "as": the point is of some importance. The experience to be conveyed need not be undergone by any character in the book. The experience conveyed by *The Pickwick Papers* is not Mr. Pickwick's mainly, but Charles Dickens's. The experience conveyed by *Hamlet* is not only Hamlet's, but Shakespeare's of what he presents to us in the court of Elsinore. The two can coincide, of course. The presentation of fictitious events through the direct experience of one participant—the novel in the first person—is not uncommon. And Miss Matty's niece saw as much of Cranford as Mrs. Gaskell did. The coincidence, however, is sometimes more apparent than real. Esmond tells his own story, but we, through Thackeray, realise more of it than he appears to do. As a rule, the author sees more than is grasped by any of his characters. They are elements in a pattern, not all of which they can divine: while the author, seeing the whole, can grasp and present the full meaning of its interplay and juxtaposition of elements, and convey them to us.

This method of projection, though the most complex psychologically, is the most useful in practice for dealing with themes of any subtlety. It is most useful because

---

yet for long periods the enduring character of the historical, philosophical, and scientific, but especially the literary allusions which an English writer could assume that his audience would understand, and on the understanding of which the full appreciation of his work depended". He has some valuable remarks on the effect of the loss of any such generally common background of knowledge.

THE DISCOVERY OF THE SUBJECT 105

most inclusive and elastic, and also because it has the strongest impact on the imagination, since general principles are most vitally apprehended by means of some particular example. To quote a young French writer, whose own work contains some notable examples of the clear projection of a complex and impalpable experience, "Les evènements massifs, les souffrances en bloc, ne frappent l'imagination ou la pitié qu'imparfaitement et d'une manière abstrait. Pour être vivants, notre tendresse et notre effroi exigent un exemple singulier."*
The forms of literature to which it leads are the tale in verse or prose, the drama, and those forms of lyric where though there is no direct narrative element the speaker is an imagined character, as especially in that form which Browning well described as the dramatic lyric. The technique of presentation in these and their sub-forms varies considerably, but the formation of the image presented is always by means of the same kind of psychological process, which it is now advisable we should consider.

I quoted, a few lines back, from M. Kessel's *Les Cœurs purs*. A little earlier in the same preface occurs the illuminating sentence, "(j'ai) inventé le conflit qui me semblait le plus propre à mettre en relief une figure et une atmosphère que je connaissais". That is, to show the *"figure"* and the *"atmosphère"* which are his O[1], he has imagined for them circumstances in which they can be seen more truly and more vividly than if he were to try to present them in those in which he actually had seen them. Now, it might not have been the *"conflit"* (or "action") that he invented. He might have seen that, and invented actors and setting through which its quality might be better perceived than through its actual ones.

* J. Kessel, *Les Cœurs purs*. Préface.

Or, aware of an atmosphere alone, he might have created persons and an action to convey it, as Mrs. Gaskell, for instance, did in *Cranford*, Joseph Conrad in *Heart of Darkness*, and Emily Brontë in *Wuthering Heights*. Stevenson (who knew more about writing than his idolaters have left us willing to admit) has in fact divided all fiction in these three kinds: that in which the author begins with the plot, that in which he begins with the characters, and that in which he begins with the setting. Which is perfectly true, except that in point of fact he begins with none of them. He has to start earlier, with an attempt to find whichever of them happens to be the bone from which he boils his soup.

"I thought of Mr. Pickwick", said Dickens. And that was that. Having thought of him, he deduced *The Pickwick Papers*. Now, Minerva sprang full grown from her father's brain: but as with other infants less illustrious than Pallas or the President of the Pickwick Club, there were certain necessary preliminaries. Zeus does seem to have taken all the credit, but as a matter of record the goddess would not have been manifest thus abruptly if he had not previously swallowed her mother. And the author of Mr. Pickwick's immortal being had swallowed (and digested) a good many things. I have already spoken of the way in which the received experience derived from the object or series of objects O^1 may crystallize, as it were, into an image in the artist's consciousness. It would seem that the initial idea of Mr. Pickwick's personality took rise in this manner, and it would therefore be as well to consider more closely the method of formation of such images.

The process is mainly a subconscious one, and for that reason has always been considered something of a mystery. In fact, any given case remains mysterious enough: we may guess at it by a laborious process of psychanalysis,

THE DISCOVERY OF THE SUBJECT

but unless the writer is his own analyst, and a very laborious analyst at that, it is all but impossible to find the full truth of any specific instance, though we may, after search, come on the main ingredients. But as Gascoigne says (and he knew more of letters than the average psychanalyst) "the occasions of inventions are infinite".* But the process of invention is another story. "Time and Education beget Experience: Experience begets Memory"† —and memory has a way of recombining in new images, by processes that are something more than the shift of hazard. We have lacked for long some insight of the process that guides and determines their reintegration, but (thanks to Professor Freud more than to anyone) we are beginning to understand—not why, to be sure, and not very clearly by *what*,‡ but *how* at any rate these forces work.

It is a very well-known fact that under normal conditions of consciousness it is impossible to rouse the activity of any psychical disposition without at the same time rousing to some extent that of others connected with it. Suppose O^1 has stimulated a given disposition in S^1: "these dispositions are connected with one another with various degrees of intimacy to form systems; these again, with less degrees of intimacy to form larger systems . . . and so on, until we reach the most comprehensive system, which is the whole of the central nervous system. . . . While any one disposition predominantly active is . . . the central focus of excitation, those most intimately connected with it are in a state of sub-excitement."§ Dr. McDougall is speaking here from the point of view of

* *Certain Notes of Instruction* (1575).
† Hobbes, *Answer to Davenant* (1650).
‡ The famous "Censor" is a little mythological, though he seems to have been swallowed whole by various people who are pained at the idea of a guardian angel.
§ W. McDougall, *The State of the Brain during Hypnosis*. *Brain* vol. xxxi.

neurology: but the statement holds good also, of course, for the changes in consciousness or subconsciousness parallel with the changes in nerve-structure he describes. Now, these activities are not all, by any means, on the conscious level. They may be near it, of course: "the subconscious activities may be of various degrees of remoteness from waking consciousness, or as it is generally said, . . . there are in some subjects at least, many strata of submerged or subconscious mental life".* But in any event, whatever activity, on whatever level, is stirred in anyone past infancy has pretty certainly been stirred before in some fashion or other: and the disposition which is active retains, in some manner of whose mechanism we know next to nothing, some print of the past experience which is liable to cause that emergence of an image of such experience that we call "memory". The emergence of this image may in turn serve to guide or stimulate other activities of the same disposition or of others connected with it: yet the whole process may take place below the threshold of consciousness, even though it involves a complex activity of reasoning. This latter statement may perhaps be a little startling to a reader who has not chanced to be trained to the observation of psychological processes: I have known a learned professor reach the edge of apoplexy over the very phrase "subconscious reasoning". Yet we are all as familiar with the fact as with the continued pressure on our bodies of a weight of something like fifteen pounds to the square inch—the weight of the atmosphere. Suppose I am fencing. My opponent attacks. That is, at a pace so rapid that the untrained eye can scarcely follow, he goes through a complicated series of movements of which I cannot foresee anything but that he intends to hit me. I have to comprehend the precise significance of his actions before his point, some inches off my

* W. McDougall, *An Outline of Abnormal Psychology*.

THE DISCOVERY OF THE SUBJECT

body, can touch me, and devise a set of complex movements of my own, that will not only counter his attack, but leave me in a good position for a thrust at him: he parries my ripost in turn with a fresh set of actions, and I have once more to perceive their implications and contrive a fresh defence against fresh attack, and, if I parry it, a fresh riposte—all this to be reasoned out on well-defined intellectual principles, in the time it would take an onlooker to count four. Am I conscious of thinking elaborately, "That thrust is coming on the outer low line: I will parry in octave and ripost in sixte—he has sprung back out of reach—very well, as his blade comes up again, closing that line, I cut over to quart, disengage as he changes line to meet me there, and take him under the sword-arm with a lunge——"? much less do I think, "I will parry by dropping my point and moving my hand to the right," etc., etc. The whole process has to be reasoned out, with the aid of a complex system of memories, and acted upon in the space of a couple of seconds. My actions show that it has been so reasoned and that the intentions formed as result of this reasoning are carried out: but all I am *conscious* of is an intention of landing my point on a given area of white canvas in front of me, and, more vaguely, a desire to preserve the integrity of my own jacket. Yet it is impossible to doubt the existence of a very complicated chain of perception, recollection, and reasoning, the latter both inductive and deductive: and I may become conscious of this process later on, if I talk over the bout with my antagonist, or the maître d'armes comments upon the play.

Now we are all accustomed to react to our surroundings with similar subconscious processes of perception, memory, and reasoning: and yet, although all three are violently active, we may be conscious of them only as a sense of conation, or even a vague emotional disturbance. Indeed, there may be even less than this. A little while ago, uncertain of the next point in my description, I got up and began to "quarterdeck" the room. I was conscious of being, as it were, focused, that my personality was in a state of directed tension. But all the images in my conscious perception were in two parallel streams, neither of which had anything to do with psychology. I was humming an old song and keeping time to it, and at the same time "thinking" such complete irrelevancies as the pleasantness of an open fire, the precise shade of stockings to wear with a new evening-dress, and the arrangement of the flower-beds in the Luxembourg Gardens—ideas completely irrelevant to my work, and apparently, though only apparently, to each other.* After a little of this, I sat down again, and found that I could go on with what I was writing, and had recalled what I wanted to remember. What had happened was that I had let my mind go its own way, wasting no effort on the conscious level: it had already a powerful impulse in a given direction, so that, when I freed it from my conscious control, it went on subconsciously in that direction, co-ordinating my unarranged memory-content so as to make it bear upon

* Their connection is worth noting down in the present context. On reflection (though not at the time) it appears as "fire—flame-colour"—a dress I once had and liked—a new one and its accessories (I had seen it earlier in the day)—Paris, where I had just bought it—in Paris, flowers of the colour of the fire—and of these, their arrangement in a co-ordinated scheme, *as I was then trying to arrange a scheme of ideas.* My apparently unconnected train of images is thus guided by my conscious perception of the fire and by the subconscious effort I was making. But it is to be observed that for anyone else to interpret this chain correctly he would have to know I had had a flame-coloured dress and had seen the Luxembourg in early October. Without this knowledge, the sequence would seem merely arbitrary, or at best with an invented connection determined rather by the content of the analyst's mind than by that of my own. Suppose him a Freudian, it is Lombard Street to a China orange he would get in some sexual imagery somewhere, and in any case it would be quite a simple and natural guess to proceed "stockings—pink—roses—garden". Only the stockings happened to be silver!

THE DISCOVERY OF THE SUBJECT

the point at issue—in other words, bringing forward those aspects of it which had a common relevance to my theme.

Now, any strong stimulus of an instinctive disposition of impulses is apt to guide our processes of ideation in this manner, on both the conscious and the subconscious level. When a man is thoroughly scared, "how easy is a bush supposed a bear": when he is obsessed with the idea of sex (see the works of Mr. D. H. Lawrence *passim*) a Marylebone lamp-post becomes a phallic symbol: if he has a profound sense of "the numinous"

> The spacious firmament on high
> And all the blue ethereal sky
> Their great Original proclaim:

and if he has a strong and pleasurable interest in his neighbour's sins, Mr. A cannot walk down the street with Mrs. B before he is hot on the trail of a promising scandal. This discovery of occulted associations of ideas —see the footnote preceding, in which my conscious perception of the fire and my semiconscious effort to schematise vague ideas cause my idea of a pair of silk stockings to call up the memory of a fine morning in the Latin Quarter—is not only on the conscious level. Whatever the dominant interest, at the time, may be, it works also in this way in the subconscious self—works even more fully, for then it is not (directly) inhibited by the will.

It is in this way that the apparent irrelevancies of our dreams are formed. The dominant urge of the personality, which may be suppressed by the will in waking life (as fear, in many cases of war-neurosis) tends to recall all memory-images with which it has been directly associated. And the awareness of the play of this instinct—i.e., the emotion (of fear)—may rise to consciousness through the emergence not of an image of an object that directly arouses it in the present, but of some other which has once aroused it in the past, of something which has been perceived when it was aroused in the past, or even of something associated with one of these objects. This substitution of a remoter image for the present one is because, in some manner which we as yet comprehend very dimly, some other disposition of the self is working to inhibit our consciousness of an image which directly arouses the emotion, but is less on its guard, as it were, against the substituted one, which thus comes to the surface of our consciousness, particularly in dreams, where our conscious direction of mental processes is in abeyance, or in "day-dreams", where we allow our minds to wander freely without deliberate direction.

Now, S^1 has ex hypothesi been aroused to a powerful activity of élan vital—that is, to the activity of an instinctive impulse or impulses—by the perception of O^1. The apperceptive processes thus aroused include a profound sense of the intensity, and consequently of the value, of his experience of O^1, whence ensues a desire to perpetuate it. Ex hypothesi, again, the means his psychophysiological nature determines him to adopt for this are to write something that has power to convey an image productive of the same experience, arousing the same kind of reactions. And he discovers that to fulfil this purpose he needs a better image than merely his recollection of O^1—that is, he needs an image more readily apprehensible by the other subject or subjects (SS^2) whom he wishes to perceive it. Now, his whole organism is alert to the content of this yet undiscovered image: he is, so to speak, reacting to it before he knows what it is, as a hungry man with confidence in his cook may think with satisfaction of the meal that will be waiting for him when he comes home, though he does not know what it is going to be. His psychical processes are dominated and guided by the urge which the undiscovered image is to convey. Accord-

THE DISCOVERY OF THE SUBJECT 113

ingly, all of his memories that can have any bearing upon the experience—that is, which have any association with the presently active instinctive impulses—are sensitised, as it were, brought into a state of potential recollection. We will suppose that he continues in, or can recall, the particular equilibrium of the instinctive processes that has begun the whole affair—that he continues, as we say, in such-and-such a "mood". Now, a mood is "a persistent sub-excitement of an affective-conative disposition"—or dispositions, for there are extremely complex moods as well as simple ones: and such a sub-excitement renders us particularly liable to the full re-excitement of the disposition and consequently of its corresponding emotion, just as warm water boils sooner than cold. In a simple case, if a man begins his day with a quarrel, he may be made to laugh at a funny story, or to feel anxiety about his business, but he will remain more than usually ready to show bad temper on the slightest provocation. So S^1's mood over O^1 has roused a variety of recollections, all of which, as he remains passive from external disturbance (i.e., from any drainage of his élan vital to a fresh channel) tend to bring up images which by cross-association further excite it. He gropes among these (with a conscious expectancy as a rule) until he comes on one which in itself or with a little modification excites in him the kind if not the intensity of emotion aroused by O^1, or more likely, by some factor of O^1. In the latter case, the different factors of O^1 may each be "equivalated" in this way by separate images, and in addition there may be more than one image to a given factor, or again the same image may refer to more factors than one. In my own fire–dress–garden chain quoted above, my perception of the colour of the fire and of my own pleasure in it are *both* expressed in the image of the flame-coloured dress it gave me pleasure to wear: and again they are *also*

H

expressed in that of the garden where I had again felt pleasure in colours resembling those of the fire: and the ideas of the dress and the garden have a fringe of others behind them, with no sensory similarity, but with the same affective tinge—my black-and-silver dress, its stockings, Paris generally . . . all pleasant things, or at least I am in a mood to hope so!

If the dominant mood of S^1 continue undisturbed, the complex of aroused images tends to draw together in a system, which (since the mind never rests) will be active within itself, establishing new relations between its elements. Suppose, after vaguely noticing my pleasant fire, I had fallen asleep. The play of the images would be unchecked by my conscious reason, and I might have gone on from the ingredients I have mentioned to, say, an image of myself walking the Luxembourg Gardens in bright sunshine, clad in the black-and-silver evening-dress, and accompanied by someone else in the flame-colour one—and been amused when I woke at such an "inconsequent" absurdity, wondering, "Whatever put that in my head?"

But S^1 is awake, not asleep. The interplay of recollected images is checked by his reason within certain bounds of probability or at least of plausibility—within the limits of what might happen, or perhaps between those of what might happen *if* so and so—something rather unlikely, like an invasion from Mars—were to take place. Within these limits, however, if he still remains undisturbed, the play of them goes on with an accompanying process of abstraction. It is not the *whole* of any recollection he sees, but that aspect of it consonant with his mood: and it is what is most consonant that he sees most clearly, as a depressed man is conscious of wet pavement where a happy one sees the lights reflected from it. Eventually, the process reaches a point where its matter stands out so clearly as a

THE DISCOVERY OF THE SUBJECT 115

whole that he can see it as a single image. This image may be comparatively simple—a pure recollection of one act of experience: it may be a most elaborate recombination of a number of elements from different sources that have nothing in common but their association with the idea of O^1. But whether simple or complex, it is at all events something in which is seen reflected as in a mirror the emotional complex derived from O^1 as he experienced the latter. Those images which produce the same effects as the various factors of O^1 have come to the surface, because they correspond to the present direction of his personality. He is conscious of some unity binding the factors of O^1: so he tends to impose a similar relation on the discrete recollections that supply their parallels, and so to produce a *new* image, which, *taken as a whole*, is not of anything previously experienced by him. Some ancient Greek felt the horror of human faculties guided by blind desire like a beast's and with a beast's strength beneath their exercise. Human faculties—a man: a beast's blind lust and strength—a bull. The horror of the two combined projects an image for their combination, the bull-man Minotaur. In the same way with my landscape seen by lightning. I had in my mind an instance of Hegel's famous "conflict of the two goods"—in this case the tragedy of a swift clear passion, noble enough in itself, but clashing irremediably with responsibilities ignoble to break. The idea of such a situation, of course, had been familiar to me for many years: it is in every folk-lore in the world. The various chains of experience by which a sense of its implications was arrived at are traceable over years. At a given time some balance between stimulus and disposition enhanced the cumulative perception of this so as to produce a deeper reaction than the mere intellectual perception of the various possible causes, forms, and consequences of such a situation. There was, of course, the usual stirring of associations: the relevant recollections, over a wide apperceptive sweep, would no doubt be seized and tested and flung aside, but the process was mainly subconscious, and I was aware only of that sensation of strain and discomfort which is the precise analogue, on the psychical plane, of an indigestion on the physical. As far as I can recollect, the first thing that rose to the surface was an idea of high wind ($=$ my own stress, I fancy, though it may have been symbolic of the drive of emotion I was "thinking" about). This, by immediate association with the East Coast, was probably what determined the landscape pre-image which was the first crystallising of the diffused experience. The lightning (clear, high, sudden, heavenly) and the landscape of walled fields (earth, security, everyday food and duty, with the walls $=$ the network of their obligations) are obviously the passionate impulse and the obligations which it suddenly reveals in face of it. The dark green and black, the clear uncoloured light, represent the emotional colours of hard clear tragedy. Apart from the association of high wind with the East Coast landscape, the extreme simplicity of the image, like a lithographed poster, represents it as involving the plain fundamental necessities of human life. Thus I had evidently focused my perception of O^1 to the point of forcing it into a simple image, receivable in a single coup d'œil. The perception was not yet, however, on the intellectual level. I did not—as yet perhaps I could not—analyse the image as I have just done: I knew it stood for something that caused a strong emotional reaction, but what that was, out of the various objects actually or imaginatively present to my mind about the time, I did not know. In fact it is only now, when the book based on it is finished and published, that I have analysed its symbolic content in this way. Presumably I could have done so before that, in the way

THE DISCOVERY OF THE SUBJECT 117

in which one may analyse a dream: but there was no occasion, and I certainly did not do so at the time. What I was conscious of was merely a very vivid visualisation of this image, the fact that it aroused, or was charged with, considerable emotion, and an impulse to write something (writing being the only art that comes natural to me) which should convey these emotions.

S[1], then, we take it, is finding his crystallised experience emerge as some such concrete symbol-image. This may take many forms. It may be a person or a situation, a place, a social group, or even a thing. But its appearance marks a phase in the business. S[1] has at last got conscious hold of his subject. This does not mean, of course, that he has never had any conscious perception of O[1] or of the experience arising from it which is his theme. He has almost certainly had that some time ago—even years ago, it may be. What he has now got hold of is not a mere idea of O[1], or even of its effect upon himself, but an image which reflects a sort of condensation of the quality of his own fairly profound experience of it. I say "fairly profound", because if it is not that, if it has not soaked into his essential nature, there will not be the drive for a real creative process—it will not have aroused sufficient of his *élan vital*, supposing he has sufficient of that in the first place. If, as sometimes happens, the only real emotion that has been stirred is that specialisation of the self-assertive impulse which takes the form of wanting to be a writer, this also may crystallise in a pre-image of a likely-to-be-successful book: but the impulses to be symbolised in that case will be merely those involved in the pleasing idea of the writer's self as successful novelist or poet—a theme that is usually a little shallow, as most people with selves worth conveying as such want to convey something larger than the self.

Now, as I have said already, S[1] may find, at this stage

of the process, that the image into which his experience has crystallised is not as it stands of any use to him. In the case I have just mentioned, of course, where the image is of the self as writer of a successful book, it is obvious that the writer must do something else—i.e., think of the ingredients of a successful book, according to some current estimate, and put them together. Which in fact is done, with various degrees of skill, every day of the week, with results that are often sufficiently like the real thing to pass in the market. Again, my landscape was not much use to a novelist, unless perhaps as a background to some episode: as which, in point of fact, I did not use it, for nothing resembling it occurs in the story, though it probably determined me to place that story in a countryside that had more points in common with it than the Hebrides where I first meant to place it, and so did a good deal to form its atmosphere.* Where the pre-image is a situation or a character (as with Mr. Pickwick) the author is already a stage farther. His problem is already mainly on conscious levels. "Given Mr. Pickwick, find an action and setting to reveal him perfectly." The answer = the content of O^2—i.e., the content of *The Pickwick Papers*.

In the case of such a purely symbolic pre-image as my landscape, the matter is rather more elaborate. "Given the image, like a Wilkinson poster, which represents an otherwise unformulated complex of emotions, devise place, action, and character to convey these latter." Some further brooding is required: by a continuance of the

* I knew I wanted flat country swept by sea winds. I could have got plenty of that, with Atlantic gales to sweep it, in the north of the island where I was born and bred: but I wanted, for some obscure reason (which, now I have analysed the picture, I can guess), cultivated land, not the moor and machair of the Isles. So I chose, not the Buchan that the image actually most resembled, but the Kincardineshire coast, which has the same general character, and with which I have more personal emotional associations.

THE DISCOVERY OF THE SUBJECT

previous process a fresh image is thrown up, as one dream succeeds another with the same latent content. In this case, the image was a vague outline of the "Hegelian conflict", of which, as a matter of fact, I had been consciously thinking. Vague and general as the image may be intellectually, it rises now not in the already familiar form of an abstract idea, but charged with a similar quality of emotion to that contained in the image of the landscape. I had thus, as data, a skeleton situation, and the emotions it was to arouse in the onlooker. It might not have been the situation that I saw, of course: I might have come first on my principal character, or (though not very probably here) the social background. (I suppose I had seen the geographical one.) I might even have seen the course of an action in progress—with some sorts of theme this is very probable, and in fact it was at a very early stage in proceedings that I began to have a notion of definite people doing definite things in a certain order determined by causation. But in any event, the problem would have been the same. Having seen one of these elements in a piece of narrative, I had to reduce it from a general abstract image to a specific concrete one—in this case, imagine a definite individual instance of this particular situation that would serve as the basis of a reasonably interesting story and would not take me too far out of the terms of my own general experience—using this last word in the widest sense, of course, to include imagined experience that I could check by observation or reading.* I chose terms of the ordinary domestic relationships: or rather that possibility was the first to come to mind, as for many reasons the most natural—I knew where I was

* For example, I can easily see my initial situation in political or military terms, or in those of scientific work. But I know very little of the machinery of either politics or science, and nothing at first hand of war, so I should have been a fool to try to use any of these.

with it, I could easily contrive a complete "case" of my situation, with a clear set of issues and a narrow field of action that would add in various ways to the intensity. And I was appealing to a wide body of actual or vicarious experience on the part of possible readers. As a matter of fact, this version of it had such obvious advantages that I pitched on it first of all, guided in part, perhaps, by the fact that not long before I had come in contact with a similar situation in real life, though neither its persons, its circumstances, nor its conclusions were in the least like those I drew.* It was only later that I really "considered" the choice of it, and then for the purely adventitious reason that the subject lacked novelty, and consequently would certainly be charged with lacking originality, whether it did or not—and I was, of course, in no case to be sure that it would not. Reflecting, however, that all the good themes and most of the good subjects have been handled rather frequently already, and that no one (least of all myself) could know until the book was finished whether my handling would have the originality that consists in a vigorous and individual vision of common facts, which I had to risk proving in the negative—reflecting on this, I saw that to aim at an adventitious novelty would make no real difference one way and would seriously cramp me in the other, and so stuck to my initial conception of the thing as in terms of domestic relations. I wanted a case with the issues clearly cut, so took the old triangular arrangement of husband and wife and the other woman—a situation which in fact recurs fairly frequently in life as well as literature, if not quite so often as certain young writers believe. But this, of course, was not the only datum. I had already, besides,

---

* For the manner in which actual experience is transmuted in the process of creation, cf. Wordsworth's *Leechgatherers*, and his sister's account of the incident on which it was founded.

THE DISCOVERY OF THE SUBJECT

a very clear image of the emotional effect that I wished the portrayal of this situation to produce. And this second datum is quite as important as the other. I could have treated the situation as it stood from the emotional angle of *Antony and Cleopatra*, of *Pelléas et Mélisande*, of *Aaron's Rod*, of *The Man of Property*, of the last books of the *Morte Darthur*, of an American musical comedy, or of a French farce—works whose treatment of that particular relation of three individuals has not much resemblance. I could even have treated it from the point of view of my own attitude towards it at some other time, which might be anything from abstract sociological interest to sardonic amusement. But what I had to do was to convey the precise emotions I was then experiencing over the vivid imaginative realisation of what it might be like to be in such a position. I had a fairly vivid notion of these, and of a concrete situation that might arouse them: in other words, I had the start of my plot.*

S^1's experience, then, the experiend that is to give the content of O^2, will crystallise in some image which represents its most important factors. If these latter are on a deeper plane than the cognitive, then the image may tend to be symbolic rather than conceptual. This image, if it can be conveyed *in all its implications*, will project the experiend upon other consciousnesses. In the case of an abstract idea whose significance is almost wholly on the cognitive plane (e.g., the central idea of *The Metaphysic of Ethics*), or of the idea of some phase of experience whose contingencies are either within itself or readily comprehensible (*The Essays of Elia*, *Epipsychidion*), or

---

* A "concrete" situation is not necessarily an "actual" one, though of course it would have been possible for me to acquire this concrete perception through experience, either as observer or as participant, of some actual example of such a situation. In the latter case, however, I hope I should not have made a novel out of it, even in these "daring" days of apologies *à haute voix*.

again of a definite personality (as in *The Pickwick Papers*), or of a definite series of events (as in Shakespeare's plays), or of a definite setting (*Heart of Darkness* or *Cranford*), it is possible to deduce from it a projection of all the implications necessary to reveal its full significance. But where the image that first emerges has implications that cannot be so deduced, the process of "digestion" of the theme will have to continue farther, until some image is produced which *can* serve as datum for the deduction of a fuller one, which fuller one will be the content of O^2. In other words, whatever the planes of consciousness which receive the original experience, it is not until the idea of the experience has crystallised on the intellectually cognitive level as well as on that of pure imagery—that is, to put it crudely, until it is not only perceived as an image associated with certain sentiments, but as one which can be "thought about", as we say—which can be actively considered as well as passively contemplated— that it can become the germ of a piece of writing. I may have seemed, to the hardened intellectualist, to undervalue the part played by intellectual cognition and the ratiocinative processes in the earlier stages of the process of literature, though I ask him to do me the justice of observing that if I have shown that part as small in comparison, I have also called it vitally important. But once this initial image of the content of O^2 has risen above the threshold of consciousness, then the intellect is in charge thereafter. Mere "brains" will not produce a live book: there must be the drive of instinctive impulse beneath it, even though it be a treatise on logarithms. But an impulse as strong as a man may feel and live will produce no book —no, not the most transcendental poetry—that is worth the paper and ink that print the words of it, unless there is a clear directing intellect. And neither will serve, either alone or together, unless there is the will that can make the intellect keep in the saddle when the impulse it rides is stretched to its hottest pace. No man, whatever his gifts of apprehension, can achieve greatness in art unless he has the power of holding himself steadily focused on what he chooses.

CHAPTER VIII

THE WRITER AND THE DEVELOPMENT OF HIS SUBJECT

"Many inventions are good, and yet not finely handled."
GEORGE GASCOIGNE, *Certain Notes of Instruction*

S^1, THEN, has conceived within his mind a general image of the content of O^2. That is to say, he has not only apprehended his theme: he has also conceived a subject to embody it. He has thought of Mr. Pickwick, who stands before him as the image of a certain experience: or he has conceived certain reactions of a man's soul which can be brought about by events similar to those in a tale of Cinthio's he remembers reading. He is also aware of an impulse to create an objective entity which shall make other men (SS^2) think of Mr. Pickwick, or of the reactions he can imagine for Il Capitano Moro, and so experience the things of which Mr. Pickwick or Cinthio's captain are so far merely his own private symbol: that is, he has thought of a book or play, non-existent as yet, of which Mr. Pickwick or the captain's adventures shall be the subject. He wants to write—in fact, he feels he must write—*The Pickwick Papers* or *Othello*.

Probably, at this point, the thing feels easy. There is a glorious moment when after a space of vague mental discomfort he knows so exactly what he wants to do that for a little while he can see it as done. The image is so clear and vivid to his mind, so highly charged with emotional significance, that it seems impossible that other men should not see it and react to it as he does. But in hard and brutal fact, this is not the case. There is a temporally long, psychologically complex, and volitionally fairly difficult process yet between the first vision of a

THE DEVELOPMENT OF THE SUBJECT

gaitered figure and correcting the press proofs of *The Pickwick Papers*. This process it is now our business to describe.

The pen has not yet gone into the ink-bottle. S[1] has only just become aware of what is to be the subject of his book. But he is at any rate aware of that—so much so that just as Mozart used to say that when he conceived the idea of a piece of music he could "hear" every note of it *simultaneously*, so he has become so keenly aware of his subject and of its possibilities for literature that for the moment he feels as if he "saw" the whole book in a single coup d'œil. What is really the case, however, or a good deal nearer it, is simply that he is intensely conscious of his subject as having a great many implications, some of which he can already image vividly—e.g., if he is about to write a play or a novel, he will find that he is already surrounding his primary image, of Mr. Pickwick's personality or the situation of the Moorish captain, with other images of characters and episodes connected with it, which rise from the subconscious to the conscious level of mental activity in exactly the same way as the subject has done already: Mr. Pickwick is no longer seen alone, but appears to be haloed with a larger vision— more vague, perhaps—of the Pickwick Club, of inns and roads, of Christmas at Dingley Dell, of a ghostly Sam and Jingle, perhaps a faint adumbration of Bardell *v.* Pickwick—none of them clear as yet, but all somehow "real", known to exist, if nothing more as yet. The mythopœic power of the subconscious mind is casting up a cloud of subordinate images to represent the implications of the main one which is already gripped by the consciousness.*

---

* Some of these implications may be representable conceptually. But it is highly probable that some of them will not. Conceptual

From now onwards, the conscious and subconscious activities must work in harness, and the process of their working, though easier to perceive than those which have preceded it, is yet sufficiently difficult to describe, since they work not only simultaneously with each other, but on overlapping and intersecting planes. A book takes a considerable time to write: there was a point of time in which Shakespeare knew, of *Hamlet*, that he had a general notion of such a play, and was trying to write a play that when performed would embody for him that notion: he knew its subject, had a rough outline idea of most of its characters (probably not of Osric or the Gravedigger, perhaps not of Rosencrantz and Guildenstern) and of the general lay-out of the action as a whole, and he knew very precisely just what he wanted the effect of the whole to be, though he could not have told you that except by showing you the finished *Hamlet*. He had, let us say, already got the first act on to paper, though probably at this stage it would need some touching up before it represented what was in his mind: he would have (if he was not in a cursing interval of impotency)* a pretty detailed notion of how the action was going to run from Hamlet's arrival on the battlements to the play-scene or thereabouts. Of what was to come thereafter, he would have a clearer image of some parts than of others: he might, for instance, have a very clear one of the play-scene, of the one in the Queen's closet, and of the last, with only a hazy notion of some of the intermediate episodes that join them, and perhaps none at all as yet

thinking is a very accurate machine. But its meshes are coarse: it cannot handle the finer and more subtly compounded percepts. It is for this reason that Dryden very properly declared that "imaging" was "the very height and life of poetry" (*Apology for Heroick Poetry*).

* He probably spared himself a good deal of this by looting the outline of his subjects ready-made, so that he always knew in advance the next major episode of his action.

of the part Ophelia was to play in motivating Laertes's share in the denouement, far less of the effect of the mad scenes in the general impression of the play as a whole.

All this amounts to saying that practically all the processes which succeed the discovery of the subject (and some of those which have preceded it) are in action simultaneously till the very last stage of the actual writing is reached. It is theoretically conceivable, of course, that a man might work out every detail of plot, character, incident, and presentation before beginning to write, though if he did he would probably be sorry for it. But it seldom occurs that books are written in this way, and I am pretty sure no live one ever was. Nevertheless, for the sake of being as intelligible as possible, we may take the liberty of handling these processes in an order based on their logical development from each other rather than on their actual interplay in practice. It must never be forgotten, however, that to consider the layers of process separately in this manner is as purely artificial an arrangement as the dissection of a hand to show the vascular or the nervous system. It is necessary: but it is not nature.

If we look at the processes in this manner of logical division, it is obvious that they fall into two groups. On the one hand, the writer must decide just *what* of his subject he is to present in order to give its full significance, on the other he must determine just *how* the presentation is to be achieved. It is, in fact, a repetition of his former problem. He has already had to decide what is his theme (i.e., to apprehend its essential significance, divorced from the irrelevant experience contemporary with its primary apprehension) and to determine by what means (i.e., through what sort of an image—his "subject") he can present it. And the same problem will present itself now at each stage of proceedings until he has finished putting his stuff on paper—he is lucky if it does not continue after that! Up to the present, however, it may, and in "creative" work almost certainly will, have worked for the most part on the subconscious level, but from now onward the conscious, "intellectual" layer of his mental functions is at least as active as the subconscious, though their periods of maximum activity may be alternate rather than coincident.

At present, then, his problem, in concrete terms, is to measure the implications of his subject; to lay it out for presentation; and to find the best means of presenting it.

S^1 has found a "subject" which can convey his theme. The subject may be a system of abstract concepts, an attitude of mind, a situation, a course of action, a person, an atmosphere, or the relation between any two or more of these. In the first of these cases (which belongs to science rather than to art proper) it is necessary to break it up into the related ideas of which it is composed, and so dispose these that their relations of interdependency appear most clearly. This is naturally a matter of intellectual analysis: and the nearer the process can be to pure conscious reasoning, the earlier the stage at which it is likely to be completed. For example, in a book setting forth some scientific or philosophic theory, the writer can hardly make a beginning at all unless he has a pretty clear idea of the various major aspects of his subject that will be his "heads", and of the order (determined by their logical relation) in which he intends to treat them. This process, of course, may continue as he writes: he may find that what seemed one facet of his subject is really more than one and must be divided—for example, in this present book, this chapter and the next were planned as one. But in its main lines he can complete the whole process

THE DEVELOPMENT OF THE SUBJECT 129

before he begins to write: and this is probably the only case in which, if he is wise, he will so complete it.

The presentation of a state of mind, as in a lyric poem or an essay, is such a constant "detail" in larger-scale work that it is unnecessary to discuss it separately. What gives it its power of separate existence is simply that it happens to be complete within itself, or comparatively simple in its contingencies.

The typical "creative" form of literature is that which contains an element of narrative. This includes the novel, the short story, the verbal part of drama, the epic, the narrative poem, and even certain kinds of lyric poetry, from the ballad to such things as *Andrea del Sarto* on the one hand and *Mariana* on the other—the narrative element in the last being purely implicit. Now, all kinds of narrative have common elements, implicit if not actually presented. A narrative must have action, it must have actors, and if it is to be reasonably convincing, it must give some idea of their circumstances. To put it as we usually do, a "story" needs plot, character, and setting. If it is to signify anything more than a mere arabesque, it must have a certain logical coherence—that is, it must show some causal relation between its elements. And finally, if it is to have any real effect upon the mind, it has to aim at producing a certain total impression, which of course is that of the underlying theme.

The relative importance of these elements will vary, of course. In *The Egoist*, for instance, there is very little external action in proportion to the amount of room devoted to the direct portrayal of the characters. In *Treasure Island*, the external action is what counts—action and atmosphere, at all events, for Stevenson was too much of a Scot not to have at all times that keen sense of place, of human life as rooted in the soil whence it springs, that is the chief specifically Scottish contribution to the

I

literary uses of our common tongue. At the same time, this excess of one element over another will in work of much quality be more apparent than real. *The Egoist* has little external action; but the internal, the processes going on in the minds of the chief characters, is continuous, elaborate, and interesting: while in *Treasure Island* the external events would have little power to grip any but the most unsophisticated mind if they did not befall people so completely real as Long John, Hands, the Doctor, the Captain, and the Squire. It is true that in the one case the emphasis is on what Sir Willoughby and the other people are and become, in the other on what Jim and the rest do and undergo: but in all narrative, even the barest journalistic report, there will be something of the first four elements, while in all that has any claim to be called art, there will be something of the fifth to master them.

It is not very likely, however, that S^1 will have come upon these elements all at once. The last he will certainly have had before now if his book is to have any vitality: he must know what he wants it to mean when it is finished. And he must have at least one of the others before he can know what its subject is to be. But the subject may appear to him at first in terms of only one. Which it will be depends principally on the nature of the theme, which, of course, depends again on the writer's temperament. Certain themes (that is, the experience of certain given objects by a particular temperament) will crystallise naturally in an image of a situation or a course of action, others in a personality, and so on. The distinctions are not hard and fast: there are many cases where the determining factor will be less temperament itself than the body of other experience which forms the apperceptive mass to which the initial experience is related; and this, of course, depends on circumstances in the past. Suppose

THE DEVELOPMENT OF THE SUBJECT 131

two men react in rather the same way to the idea of difficulties and hardships confronted with resolution. One is a quiet scholar, whose most stirring experience is a politely contested election: the other has seen hard service in the War. The milieu of the former is London, and he has the intense parochialism of the Londoner: the other has knocked about three continents. Both may be aware of their theme with equal intensity, and react to it in much the same manner: but one will tend to see it in terms exclusively of the interplay of character and character, or of character and more or less static circumstances, the other in terms of character and action; and external action will thus play more part in the second book. This is only the very roughest illustration, of course—a mere diagram. The actual facts are in practice not so simple: the quiet scholar may have the invalid Stevenson's joy in violent action and have filled his mind with images of that, the soldier may be a passionate devotee of Jane Austen, *Cranford*, and the *Annals of the Parish*; and these internal circumstances rather than external supply the determining range of apperceptions. But none the less, it is something on these lines that does in a general way determine proportion. A man's past interests make certain kinds of image take a more prominent place in his mind-content and render them readier to form apperceptions.

Whatever the initial element may be, the others have in their turn to be deduced from it. As we have seen, the problem arises in perfectly clear shape. Given this situation, what sort of people would have got into it, how would it arise, and how would they react when it had arisen? What would be the consequences? And in what sort of setting and atmosphere would these things pass to produce most fully the effect the finished work is desired to possess? Or again, given these people, set in conjunction, or against such-and-such a background, and what would happen? Or again, given such-and-such a setting, what people, in what circumstances, will express its emotional (or emotional and intellectual) significance, and what action will reveal them most clearly?

Obviously, it is in part a matter of deliberate conscious reasoning. S^1 thinks (i.e., reasons), "the man who would do that must have certain qualities"—and at once, since ex hypothesi his image-making power is well developed, there arises in his mind an image of a man possessing not only these qualities but those which he associates with them, and *also* others which would justify S^1's own attitude to the part played by this imagined person with regard to the theme. This figure, A, emerges as a clear idea. But it is more than an intellectual concept of a certain human type. The image is that of a particular man, possessing certain definite qualities, having done or about to do some specific action, and associated intimately and in a particular manner with some definite idea or complex of experience which at the moment is powerfully stimulating some deep instinctive disposition in S^1, and is therefore highly charged with a specific emotional quality. A therefore becomes associated, and intimately, with the causes of this emotion, so that the idea of him is also charged with it, and—since he can stir the vital processes of S^1—he is felt as having a sort of real existence. S^1 may not know much about him yet. But as the projection of the action goes on, as episode after episode goes through S^1's mind in extension, the latter comes to perceive and apperceive his image of A by precisely the process through which he does that of a "real" man, Smith or Jones. He is seen to act in certain ways, which bring him into specific relations with other people, who have been divined in the same fashion as himself: he is seen in these relations: he reacts to them in a manner we know, since

THE DEVELOPMENT OF THE SUBJECT 133

the primary outline of the action has made us aware of it: he acts upon and is acted on in turn by a particular setting: all this until we have a quite clear and definite impression of a personality which in turn, if we are of a visualising habit of mind, we see embodied in a personage, who will be swarthy, with eyes of a certain shape and a long chin, or fat and rosy with a bowler hat, and—if our sense of word-values is strong—have a certain name, which could not possibly be anything else. In short, A has become as real, in all experiential planes but that of the possibility of physical contact, as the man who has just sat next us in the bus ... and we know in fact a great deal more about him.

It looks like a miracle. But—like all miracles—it is merely a completely natural process whose mode of functioning is unfamiliar. The key to it is that though we know more of A than of Mr. Jones next door, the more we know of Mr. Jones, Mr. Smith, and Mr. Robinson, the more we are likely to know about A. We may have this knowledge by direct observation, by a mixture of observation and inference, or from books, for there is no book so bad but it tells the truth about one thing at least—its author: but in practice it is usually derived from all of these. So the image of A, in all its living reality, has been produced by a web of conscious and unconscious inferences and apperceptions whose warp is the *conscious* perception of certain data—to wit, that A played such-and-such a part in a given action which causes the onlooker certain definite feelings. The intellect, working on this, makes certain inferences, by means of a complex process of induction and apperception. But along with this, more or less *subconsciously*—"more or less", for the images leap and fall like salmon going up a river in the spring—there is a further and even more elaborate process of apperception and re-apperception, guided and determined as the similar process in dreams is always determined, by the instinctive dispositions that happen to be active at the moment. The apperception-masses touch and coalesce and interlace, as it were, on both the subconscious and the conscious planes: and naturally, the richer the content of the mind, the more scope there is for this apperceptive process, just as the more thoroughly that content is organised the more completely it will be set in action and the farther will drive the reverberations of the original idea. In brief, the more knowledge S^1 has accumulated of men in general, or of certain types of men at all events, the more he will be able to infer about A, supposing him capable of such inference at all.

But A is not the only personage demanded by the action. There are others, who are being divined in the same way by a similar process: and all of them are seen in contact with each other, throwing light on each other. "A does so and so to B: but a man who would do so and so to B is", etc., etc.—so that we know a little more of A, and consequently of his relations not only with B but with C and D and the various actions all of them perform. When a scientist deduces the whole anatomy of a pterodactyl from a couple of toenails and the lower half of the beak, he is doing exactly the same kind of thing: he reaches true conclusions in proportion to the amount (*a*) of his power of correct inference and (*b*) of the organised knowledge in his mind of objects which have any quality in common with that which he is trying to divine.

When the original datum is other than action, the problem and the process of its solution are very similar. Given that "I thought of Mr. Pickwick", the primary question is, "What would be the most characteristic *action* for such a man?" and then, "Contact with what sort of people would produce it?" and, "What is the setting

THE DEVELOPMENT OF THE SUBJECT 135

most natural and appropriate to these?" The whole of the content of *The Pickwick Papers* is implicit in that gaitered benevolence.

When setting comes first, the terms of the primary equation are rather more complex, but they are still possible to state with some concreteness. The problem is now, "This scene (or whatever it is) produces a certain definite effect on me. What sort of people or action would be most likely to reinforce that effect if I should see them there?"—after which it goes on as before.

The whole process, it is important to note, is neither conscious nor subconscious, but *both*. At one time the one layer is dominant, at another the other. Generally speaking, it is the part of the conscious mind to analyse ideas, and of the subconscious to grope apperceptively for their "symbolic" equivalents and bring these together, emitting the result as an image which takes its place in a growing complex of imagery: but this is only a very rough general statement. The process, however, has two fixed determinants, on which its efficiency largely depends. One of these is the conscious rational intellect, which must test every image as it appears. Its function here is largely negative. It may not be able to determine à priori that A should be a dark and rather heavy Civil Servant of thirty-three: but if the first image of A is of a fair slight priest of sixty, then it must know if this is wrong—if it will not fit convincingly with other data. If it is alert enough to test such an image at the moment of emergence, so much the better: but it must do it at some stage of proceedings, or the sequence of consciously and subconsciously perceived causations that produce conviction on the reader's mind will run a serious danger of being broken. The logical intellect must test the whole process sleeplessly and without mercy: and the finer it is, the more sensitively alert to the relations—particularly the causal relations—

between entities and events, the less likely is S¹ to permit a breach in the intimate parallelism of theme and subject. But it must be noted that this effect, immensely important, is yet mainly negative. The intellect will keep imagination —the creative image-making or mythopœic power of the mind—from going off the rails: it may even aid it by certain conscious positive inferences. But it cannot take the place of imagination. The purely intellectual structure (if such is possible) will remain on the purely intellectual level. It may be exquisitely clear, but it will not have within it the drive of life. A man without a skeleton is no good: but a skeleton is no substitute for a man. A good deal of brilliant work in contemporary fiction has failed as art for just this very reason. It is conceived both neatly and lucidly on the intellectual plane, but has never gone deeper, for the simple reason that there was nowhere to go. Our type of civilisation is a little apt to produce persons of clear and active, if shallow, intellect, singularly alert to all fashionable ideas, but very anæmic in point of instinctive impulse,* and consequently half-educated with regard to humanity, with the typical closed mind of the half-educated to anything outside their own experience.

The other of the two guides is the counterpoise to this: it is the directed drive of the instinctive disposition which is active in S¹ since its arousal by O¹. This, working strongly on both conscious and subconscious levels, dominates the direction of his perception as it plays among the memory-content of his mind,† recalling relevant aspects of these memories, so that the various ideas implicit in that of A are associated with their appropriate external

---

* They sometimes mask this fact by a weakness of will which they like to consider proof of their "strong passions".

† For a brilliant study of the manner in which this memory-content is used, see Professor Livingstone Lowe's *The Road to Xanadu*, in which the imagery of Coleridge's poems is traced to its (sometimes very unpromising) sources.

THE DEVELOPMENT OF THE SUBJECT 137

symbol, until the bare diagrammatic idea of certain people or happenings becomes a fully perceived section of life, through which appears a dominant concept of some kind.

And now, too, a rather interesting thing begins to happen. Again and again, *within* this process, as it were, the whole business is repeated in miniature. In the past, S^1 has been moved in a similar, though less profound and far-reaching fashion to that produced by O^1 by several other objects, less important to him, which we will call oo^1. As the recollection of these is drawn into contact with the image I^2 he is striving to create, it is quickened and elaborated, so that the content of his experience of oo^1 crystallises just as the content of his experience of O^1 did, into an image or images ii^1:* and these sub-images or their equivalent symbols ii^2 take their place now as parts of the general image I^2. A good many degrees of this subordination are possible. Just as S^1 tried to create i^2 within and as part of I^2, he may find that i^2 in turn has a further web of sub-images crystallising within it and derived in turn from some minor experience. As a concrete example, suppose S^1 is thinking of his plot in relation to the general image I^2. He wants a personage. By association with what he already knows of his subject, there arises in his mind an image of X, whom he used to know at the University—or more probably, an image of certain factors in the personality of X, which suggest the type of person he is looking for. His recollection of his experience of X may be vivid and intense, but it has not been sufficiently so to demand an absolute objective existence—i.e., to become the object of a separate piece

---

* This may have happened earlier, but the o did not rouse S^1 sufficiently for the experience, though memorable, to demand a separate objective embodiment. We see this sort of thing happening when a painter goes round sketching fleeting impressions. He would not show these sketches (ii^1) in public: but he may use them later on as elements in a finished picture based primarily on none of them.

of writing. Swept into contact with the larger experience derived from O^1, it suddenly acquires a more powerful significance, and claims a part of the object embodying this experience—i.e., it demands to become *part of* the book in hand. In fact, it may even be roused so thoroughly as to take up more than the place strictly appropriate to it, and distort I^2 into something quite different from what it was originally meant to be. It is possible that something of the sort happened with Shylock.

This process may be repeated again in a fresh degree of subordination, and probably will be. As contact with I^1 as a whole has crystallised some image derived from X, so contact with the latter image in turn may crystallise and make significant S^1's experience of some incident or characteristic connected with another man Y, which in turn takes its place as part of the i^2 he has derived from his i^1 of X . . . and so on and so forth. The whole business, though its results may be simple to grasp, is in itself of a complexity that when we look at it, seems unbelievable until we examine, say, the psychological and physiological chains of process involved in typing the address on an envelope or vamping the accompaniment to *Yes, Sir, that's my Baby*.

The whole process, looked at thus, throws a good deal of light on what has always puzzled non-creative intelligences (and indeed even the creative themselves)—the fact that a writer may describe with perfect accuracy an experience he cannot possibly have had himself, or perhaps even watched anyone else have. There is a passage in Mrs. Gaskell's fine *Life of Charlotte Brontë* that refers to this phenomenon. "I asked her whether she had ever taken opium, as the description given of its effects in *Villette* was so exactly like what I had experienced. . . . She replied that she had never, to her knowledge, taken a grain of it in any shape, but that she had followed the

THE DEVELOPMENT OF THE SUBJECT 139

process she always adopted when she had to describe anything which had not fallen within her own experience; she had thought intensely on it for many and many a night before falling to sleep—wondering what it was like and how it would be—till at length, sometimes after the process of her story had been arrested at this one point for weeks, she wakened up in the morning with it all clear before her, as if she had in reality gone through the experience, and then could describe it, word for word, as it happened." This shows the same process at work. The writer "thinks intensely" on what he already knows of the image he is seeking to form—i.e., reawakens in himself the emotion, the activity of instinctive disposition, that charges it, and then, either in actual sleep or in the passivity of mind we call reverie, allows this absolutely free play among the content of his mind at large, where it draws to light whatever is implicit in the data, whatever is analogous to them, what may be inferred from them, and so on, till they crystallise in an image which the conscious intellectual judgment accepts as being that of a probable experience in the circumstances.* The accuracy of the divination is sometimes remarkable: but it is to be noticed that this will not be the case unless S^r has *some* experiential data (vicarious or direct) to go upon. If he has had no contact at all with the experience whose quality he is trying to divine, he will not make very much of it. Charlotte Brontë had never taken opium herself: but she had seen her brother under its influence: and from that observation she could create an image of *his*

* Charlotte Brontë's trick of "thinking over" before sleep is an old and common one: a good many writers also use other means of inducing this "active passivity" of mind, such as a warm bath or the condition of mild hypnosis produced by a steady tramp or by tobacco. The use of the rosary shows another means of producing a similar state, conducive to meditation: a means so effectual that it is used by all the higher religions of the world, with the exception of Protestant Christianity—whose strongest side has never been psychology.

experience so vividly that it became as her own. But when she had less than this to go upon, the process often failed her: in fact, when she goes outside her own direct experience she is very unsuccessful as a rule. She cannot even use that derived from books.

This dual process of intellect and imagination may move with an extraordinary speed, unrolling before the apparently passive mind like a dream, and as rapidly as those dreams where the dreamer goes through a whole series of adventures between his landlady's knock on the door and his own reply. On the other hand, to complete it, at any rate—or even, as in Charlotte Brontë's case described above, to complete a phase of it—may require days and weeks or even months of this brooding, through a process of trial and error, as incompletely satisfactory images emerge, are tested, and then thrown aside. Many men, who like to think of themselves as mute inglorious Miltons, do not go through with it. They give the whole thing up, or content themselves with a set of images that are at best but semi-satisfactory. To carry the whole thing out to the most perfect conclusion possible to S[t] demands a certain hardness of the will. He must be able to go on in spite of discouragements, and also to keep his personality still focused on the theme and subject without permitting it to be distracted. And what is sometimes quite as hard as either, he has to be able to recognise when he has turned to the wrong channel of activity, check himself, and remain passive until his subconscious self throws up some indication of a new one—and it may keep him waiting for a much longer time that he enjoys. I have said already that no coward can be a great writer: and no man of weak will can be even a fine one, which is a rather different affair. It is true, of course, sometimes with sad results, that a man's will works in a patchy sort of fashion, and he may show iron resolution in one

THE DEVELOPMENT OF THE SUBJECT 141

direction and be more than usually will-less in another. A man may drive himself through danger and discomfort —both which he feels acutely—like a hero: and go to pieces over a casual petticoat. In which point artists are like other men. Yet if they are artists, they will have this stringent will where their art is concerned, however Gauguin may rot in the Pacific, or Baudelaire fill himself up with dope. Those gentlemen who try to follow their example by an imitation of their general conduct will leave out the essential if they omit their steely resolution in matters of art. And it may be said that they will be completer men, and so have the chance of a completer content to their art, if they cultivate a little more will all round. Ceteris paribus, the less a man has of what is usually called "the artistic temperament", the better artist he is likely to be.

CHAPTER IX

THE WRITER AND THE CONVEYANCE OF HIS SUBJECT

"Un écrivain organise et dirige son récit. Il le soutient de son intention, de son arbitraire, de ses qualités, de ses défauts."
J. KESSEL, *Les Cœurs purs*

THE development of I^2 (the full image of the book's subject-matter), which is the *complete* symbolic equivalent of I^1 (the image of that experience which was its theme), and which is capable, therefore, of conveying the whole significance of the writer's experience of his initial stimulus O^1, does not as yet bring S^1 in sight of his book. He may have gone through the major part of it before he so much as permits himself the rather exciting act of laying in a stock of MS. paper. To be sure, like Dauber, he "can see it all", now. But Dauber, poor lad, was not the only artist to learn how much lies between vision and accomplishment.

I have said just now that S^1 has "gone through the major part" of the process of development of the image from its first rough vivid outline to its full content. In the case of work of any size at least no more is possible yet, or even desirable. From mere circumstantial necessity, it will take him some time to get his image on to paper. Even Mr. Noel Coward admits that it takes him a fortnight to write a play, and Mr. Edgar Wallace does not publish a new novel oftener than about once in seven weeks. Less favoured mortals require a little longer as a rule. After all, an average seven-and-sixpenny novel contains from 75,000 to 100,000 words, and the draft of it, if the writer is conscientious, may have been easily half as long again. If, too soon, he lets his image crystallise

THE CONVEYANCE OF THE SUBJECT 143

fully on the level of a completely conscious possession of all its details, he may lose his first keen-edged perception, and—since the creative impulse will have worked itself out—will not be able to recover it: this means that the image will be detached from the profounder levels of impulse, and "go dead", as we say—will have no more driving-power. What the creative writer usually has in mind when he tackles seriously the actual writing of his book is simply a vision of the main lines of his image. He will have a pretty vivid impression of the chief characters and their relation, of the main outline of the action, the general setting, and of the interrelations of all these. But he will not know all the detail of them as yet, including the detail of the interrelations. He will know that Macbeth is going to have Banquo murdered, at what stage in his career the murder comes, and its general effect upon his fortunes. He may even visualise the episode of the murder. But he probably does not know yet *exactly* how it is to be brought about: he will not have invented the murderers, or that dialogue between the King and his parting guest. He will leave these, as the children say, to "make up as he goes along".

None the less, he has now a rough but very vivid general impression of I^2 *as the content of* O^2. The new evocative image he has conceived appears now, specifically, as the content of a book. It does not merely signify his own experience to himself: it is capable, if it can be rightly perceived by S^2, of making him also to share S^1's experience. S^1 has his tool for that conveyance now. But he has yet to sharpen it and use it.

The sharpening consists in the fining down of the image so that it can be perceived by S^2 with the maximum of fullness and the minimum of addition or distortion: the using in the presentation of this proposed image so that having come within range of it, S^2 must attend to it until it is perceived. This fining down of the image already created is what we call the *construction* of a book: the presentation of it is the *writing*.

Now, it is important to notice, before we go any farther in discussion, that so far as the book *as a whole* is concerned, these processes go on simultaneously. They do not, it is true, run *pari passu*: they must overlap each other to begin with, and both overlap in turn the previous process of expansion and development of the subject. A man does not (if he is writing a live book) imagine its content down to the last detail before he lays out its construction in his mind, and in turn determine that, completely and finally, before he begins to put it down on paper. In theory, it is possible. In practice, it may happen at times: it would account for some things I have reluctantly read. But normally, all these processes, though as distinct as respiration, digestion, and the circulation of the blood, go on together just as these do, and like them have a necessary interdependence—if we look at all events at O^2 as a whole. Only, in any given part of it, there is a certain necessary precedence. A man must have *some* idea of the content of a chapter and of the lay-out of that chapter before he writes it, though the idea may certainly be rather dim, and only come fully to light as he writes it out.

The specific problem of construction may be stated thus: S^1 is aware of the content of I^2—of the image that is to be perceived by S^2, his reader. He has to find for that content the *form* which will best enable (or enforce) S^2 to perceive it also. From the psychological point of view, the "form" of a piece of art $=$ the order and the relative emphasis with which its subject-matter is perceived by the audience. That is to say, form is not an arbitrary addition to content, but an important and inseparable

THE CONVEYANCE OF THE SUBJECT

part of it, that gives us the temporal, spatial, and causal relations which affect the concurrent factors of the content, and which may include some of its profoundest significance. To present the "content" in some other "form" is not to present it at all, but to show something different. To pull about Shakespeare's arrangement of his scenes is to present something equivalent to showing the *Discobolos* with one leg hung round his neck ... which may, of course, improve on Myron's intention, but scarcely represents it truthfully.

Now, when S^1 is seeking for the right form, the most obvious and natural thing to do is to describe the whole content as known to S^1 in the temporal order of its imagined occurrence, omitting nothing. This is, in fact, how a child or a savage goes about the business: it was the manner of the weaker medieval romancers, and indeed has been attempted recently in more or less civilised modern art. Such an attempt, in our time, was sure to come, as it is merely working out to an extreme a fundamental principle of the Romantic Revival—a proceeding which is the foundation of nearly as many recent "novelties" as the slavish inversion of Victorian conventions.

In practice, there are serious objections to this method. On the one hand, it is psychologically unsound, because we do not normally perceive things in this fashion. When we look at a cube, we perceive three sides of it, and infer the rest from their perceived relation and our past experience: and if it is desired to convince us that we are seeing a cube, it is better to show us three sides in their typical relation (which is as much a part of the cube as the sides themselves) than to present us, as a child does, with a simultaneous vision of all six. It may be objected, of course, that since the writer's image includes the dimension to time, what really happens is that we see the six sides successively, and so have a truer idea than if we saw the three by a single *coup d'œil*. This is true, however, only of *simple* objects, and the objects with which creative literature deals are far from simple. If we examine successively every face of a hundred-sided polyhedron, we dull our perception of their mutual relation, and consequently our perception of the polyhedron as such, and of the relation of individual sides to that. In the same way, to include in a narrative everything one can infer about its characters is tempting on account of its intellectual easiness, and if we are young, its display of our own knowledge: but it blurs the reader's (and the writer's) perception of the relations between the different sub-images, relations which are probably the most important and significant—certainly the most intellectual—element in I^2 as a whole, since the parallel between I^1 and I^2 consists precisely in a series of like relations between unlike but corresponding factors.

Now, this parallel between I^1 and I^2, between S^1's image of his own experience and the image that is to arouse a similar experience in S^2, is precisely that through which the subject reflects and so conveys its underlying theme—by no crude collocation of concept and parallel percept as in allegory, but with the conceptual element (or theme) so inseparably fused in its perceptual field (or subject) that it cannot be stated otherwise than by means of that field. Accordingly, anything that blurs our perception of this field as a whole unity of related parts will *pari passu* falsify S^2's apprehension of what is inherent in it, and lead him off on irrelevant lines of apperception. It follows, therefore, that if S^1 puts down all that he can infer about his hero X, he runs the risk of distorting that very image of him he is anxious to clarify.

It was no doubt some perception of this fact that induced the classical critics of the Renaissance to claim that art should only paint "the general", omitting the par-

THE CONVEYANCE OF THE SUBJECT 147

ticular and individual. I have no wish to re-enunciate this sufficiently exploded doctrine: yet there is a truth below it, none the less—that the artist, if he is wise, will confine himself to portraying only those details of his subject which bear directly on its presently significant aspect, omitting the rest. What he omits *may* be "the streaks in the tulip": but it is quite possible that the streaks and their arrangement may be the very fact which is significant. A very small detail may "mean" a great deal—i.e., have a great deal to do in determining the precise quality of the percept received from the object of which it is part— even though its meaning cannot be precisely stated as an intellectual concept. We perceive things and people by a process of synthesising, more or less justly, a variety of details, small in themselves, and it is S^1's task to present his readers with the data for forming, justly, such a synthesis.

What this amounts to is a need to produce the illusion that they see I^2 as a whole wherein certain parts are more important than others: and that they so perceive it of their own vision, the latter point being necessary partly in order to prevent the process of suggestion from becoming one of contra-suggestion, a form which it readily takes in people who are aware of being very suggestible and resent the fact,* and partly because in almost any case an image perceived at first hand is stronger than one seen at a remove—in other words, we tend to respond more profoundly to being shown a thing than to being told about it. Now, if S^1 desires that SS^2 should receive a certain impression from the events and personages he presents to them, he must select from his total knowledge of such events and personages those aspects which will

---

* We all know the type of "strong silent man" who can always be induced to go to X by the simple process of telling him that of course he will naturally go to Y.

be of most service to his impression: and this selection is the first element in the process of construction.

From the general mass of images which, perceived as a whole, form the "final" image, as we might call I^2 considered as a unity, he therefore selects those having most significance—in other words, those characters or episodes which have the directest bearing on his theme. These give him the main features of his "plot" or lay-out. As he deals with each of them in turn, the same process is repeated: each major episode breaks up into sub-episodes, each character is perceived as having various aspects or phases, among which he must choose those most expressive of its significance with regard to the whole, omitting those which are not thus significant. In dealing with each of these sub-episodes or phases of character, again there must be a selection of the same kind among the speeches, reflections, or actions which are implied in it, and even among the sensory elements implied in the perception of these images, which (projected on the imagination of S^2) convey an image of such speech, action, or whatever it is, to his consciousness.

As a crude instance, suppose that S^1 wants to indicate that John has been badly startled by something said to him by James. He can say that, of course. But if he prefers to put a direct image of the startled John before his reader, he says, "John turned and looked at him with a face like clay", or something of the sort. He does not add that John was wearing a morning-coat and white spats, or sitting with his back to the window, though to an actual spectator of John both facts would be as visible as his movement and complexion, if not more so. He selects the two points that the spectator would not only *see* but *notice* if he happened to be concerned to know John's state of mind . . . and it is with John's state of mind that S^1 desires he should concern himself.

THE CONVEYANCE OF THE SUBJECT 149

Stated thus baldly, the whole affair sounds very mechanical. But it calls, in fact, for considerable tact, for "importance" or "significance" of this sort belongs not only to those images which convey the theme, but also to those which produce upon S^2 the effect of an objective reality of the subject—the sense that he is witnessing something which actually happens, but seeing it rather more lucidly than usual, with a deeper understanding of its meaning. S^1 desires him to undergo certain experience, as a result of perceiving certain images. He can only accomplish this end if he succeeds in convincing S^2 that these images are of things that exist, or at least of things that given certain assumptions, could reasonably be conceived of as existing. And (especially if these preliminary assumptions are rather unlikely in themselves, as for instance in *The First Men in the Moon*, or *Still She Wished for Company*), S^2 can only be so convinced, with the full cognitive and affective conviction required, by making him feel as he would if the thing were actually present to his senses—i.e., by creating in his mind just such an image as he would have if it was. To this end come in a good many details like the description of a room or of a character's dress. John's white spats do not help to impress upon us the idea that John is startled. But they may help to impress upon us that John is John: and if an image of them is aroused simultaneously with one of his white face, they may produce an impression of the fantastic contrast between his primitive emotion of fear and his civilised and ceremonious exterior, which may be of great importance in conveying the precise affective and even cognitive quality of the scene in which he happens to play part. Too little of such corroborative detail, and the theme will remain insufficiently embodied: it will not fuse properly with its perceptual field, and sticks out from its surface as a naked concept, an abstract and fleshless statement of a generality. Too much, and the theme is blurred and smothered by it. And as "too much" or "too little" is so relatively not to S^1 but to S^2, the business is none too easy for the writer: he can only fire into the brown, and aim at fitting the average of his intended audience . . . who after all are not humanity at large, but a certain section of it, of whose perceptive powers he has some idea. Shakespeare, for instance, did not write about high politics for the benefit of the boys of twelve who are forced to read *Julius Cæsar* and *Coriolanus*, and thereby convinced for life that both plays are dull. If a man's work goes much outside the kind of audience he has in mind, there will probably, in fact, be trouble, but he has got to take his chance of that, as well as of being wrong absolutely, which is never an easy matter to decide. The most he can do is to aim at the best balance he can, between hiding the wood in trees upon the one hand and leaving it a bare clearing on the other. If he has got essentials in true proportion and they happen to go deep in human nature, his audience may go wider than he counts on. I once had the pleasure of meeting a young Chinese gentleman who had had the singular good fortune to read *Macbeth* for the first time at twenty-three or thereby, and there was no doubt he had missed nothing of the play's significance—nor that it had reached more deeply than intellect alone, for it takes a good deal to make a well-bred Chinaman show excitement. He made me feel, as I have often felt, what an excellent thing it would be for the English-speaking nations if the reading of Shakespeare could be prohibited by law to everybody under twenty-one.

This process of selection among images is naturally a matter in which the conscious intellect plays considerable part. S^1 can "reason out" a good deal of it, especially the broad lines, the selection of the main elements in the

THE CONVEYANCE OF THE SUBJECT 151

design. But even here to some extent, and increasingly as he goes down the scale of the subordinated systems of sub-images, the drive of the subconscious or semiconscious disposition of impulses will determine his choice. The process which determined the general image of his subject in the first place, and then, as it grew and developed, of its parts, can be reapplied, as it were, *by his conscious volition*. Whether deliberately or by semiconscious impulse, or even on one of which he is totally unconscious until it acts, he closes his mind to other perceptions than that of the idea of I^2 or of some element in I^2. This image, thus allowed to fill his consciousness, has a remarkably and apparently mysterious potency.* There is the usual interaction between the image and the instinctive impulse which has given rise to it: each reverberates upon the other, so to speak, and so long as nothing interrupts this process, both the image and the impulse are strengthened mutually. Now, when, as in the dreams of normal sleep, an image rises into consciousness as result of the subconscious play of instinctive impulse, that image is always composed of *remembered* sub-images. And those remembered will always have some relevance (direct or indirect) to the play of that impulse. Accordingly, as S^1, allowing himself to be dominated by the impulse roused originally by the object reflected in I^1 and now transferred (or at least also attached) to I^2, broods patiently upon this latter until it is perceived as clearly as possible, those elements in it which he sees

---

* Dr. McDougall's theory of hypnosis, as expounded especially in the chapter on that subject in *An Outline of Abnormal Psychology*, throws a good deal of light on the curious compelling power of such images. In fact, the cases are more than merely analogous, for the process of "composing oneself to write" is in practice the induction of a mild auto-hypnosis: indeed, not always a mild one, for the images perceived in it may have almost the vividness of actual hallucination. [See, however, McDougall, op. cit., p. 92, opening paragraph on "negative (hypnotic) hallucinations".]

most clearly—the high lights, so to speak—will be those most strongly charged with the impulse at work in him, and so most significant for its revelation.

This sounds as if the selective process were easy—a thesis difficult to maintain in view of the current literature of any age. But in fact, even the achievement and maintenance of this stillness of the mind are not in themselves particularly simple, for it consists not of mere stillness, but of a very delicate and perfect equilibrium, so sensitively balanced as to move at a touch. It is largely, of course, a matter of natural gifts developed by practice; one man can do it more readily than another, just as one man shoots straighter than another. It is partly also a matter of circumstances: my own train of thought has just been violently interrupted by the lady in the flat over my head, who puts on her coals with a good deal of expression. But the business of keeping at bay external stimuli, of concentrating attention on a given image in the mind and allowing it to form itself uninterrupted, is largely a matter of will-power and of patience, which after all is simply the same thing.

If the original impulse has been dissipated, or has not, in fact, really been very strong, the resultant images will lack clarity. They will not compel the mind to attend to them. Thus a man whose impulses, though vivid, are fleeting, will find it difficult if not impossible to produce creative work of real vitality, at all events on more than the smallest scale. The image must live to him before he can make it live to anyone else, and unless his impulse lasts till the image matures, that will remain incomplete and uncompelling, a feeble and shadowy reflection, lacking true form.

When the mind succeeds, either voluntarily or involuntarily, in reaching this semi-hypnotic state in which its perceptions are bound within one image (ex hypothesi

THE CONVEYANCE OF THE SUBJECT 153

one produced by an impulse initially strong) and can maintain itself so focused for a while, the resultant effect is very curious. It has been thus described by Charlotte Brontë, in one of her letters. "When authors write best, or at least when they write most fluently, an influence seems to waken in them which becomes their master—which will have its own way, putting out of view all behests but its own, dictating certain words, and insisting on their being used, whether vehement or measured in their nature; new-moulding characters, giving unthought-of turns to incidents, rejecting carefully elaborated old ideas, and suddenly creating and adopting new ones."

All writers are familiar with this phenomenon. At such times, one simply sits and watches the words form by what almost seems a process of "automatic writing". This guiding-power seems so completely external to oneself that it is not surprising it should be personified as a muse or daimon or the shade of one's departed Aunt Eliza. I am not going to affirm that there is never any possibility of any such external factor. As a Catholic Christian I believe in the Holy Ghost, and that all true art, science, and philosophy must ultimately derive from Him through such human channels as become suitable: and I do not see any convincing evidence for the non-existence of other discarnate intelligences interested in mankind, who, if they existed at all, would find it easiest to exert direct influence on a man in the passive condition I have described.* But to explain the phenomenon as generally experienced—as I have frequently experienced it myself in writing the usual undergraduate quantum of

* I suppose I had better make it clear that I do not affirm the existence of such beings. I should think it highly probable, à priori, and there is certainly no valid negative proof. But the positive evidence is both incomplete and remarkably hard to come by, as to evaluate when one comes on any.

bad verse—it is completely unnecessary to hypothesise anything of the sort. In the case of the writer in a state of "inspiration" or of the medium under "control", the guiding impulse, on examination of results, is seen to appear external to the subject precisely because it is so intimately internal. The images it creates appear autogenous, as the images in a dream appear autogenous. But we know that the dream-images are linked by a definite causal relation to the general content and habitual processes of the mind: and the same is true of the "inspired" images, in the case of both the writer and the medium.*

It is because of this fact that the writer who has any power of looking at his work objectively becomes familiar with that unpleasant experience, the next-morning shock. One has the same experience in dreams. I recollect one of my own, which culminated in a sentence of such amazing beauty and wisdom that I woke repeating it reverently, thrilled to the marrow. It was: "The taxi-man will bring the cheese sandwiches." Now, this absurdity had a real relation to the dominant desire in my mind. I was in the thick of a book at the time: and the dominant impulse guiding most of my thoughts was to convey the idea contained in it as lucidly—i.e., as quickly—as possible. Hence the taxi-man, who *brings* me something—i.e., the vehicle for my idea comes easily and quickly. The cheese sandwiches, with the important part, the savoury and nourishing cheese, shut in between two flat pieces of bread, are the idea pinned down between the covers of a book: and I happen to like bread and cheese. In fact, the sentence conveys (in a form a little Delphian, no doubt)

---

* In the case of the latter, however, it seems to be definitely established that there may be a certain telepathic "contagion" now and then from other minds. It is possible that these might be discarnate: but I should want very strong evidence to believe it in any individual case.

THE CONVEYANCE OF THE SUBJECT

an assurance that my book would be completed easily and quickly, and would be a pleasantly satisfying piece of work—a statement which I naturally found agreeable. Unfortunately, the assurance was not only lacking, to my waking mind, in authority: it was also inartistically expressed, and my strong sense of its beauty and wisdom was therefore purely subjective.*

All artists have had somewhat the same experience. There is the glorious rush, when the thing simply flies ahead, easily and without apparent effort, and in a single evening you cover more ground than in the whole previous week. Then follows the cold douche of the next morning, when you realise that your mind has been running down the line of least resistance, that two-thirds of what you have written is completely irrelevant to what you wanted to write about, and the rest must be rewritten from the start. That is, of course, if you happen to be a fairly modest person, with some sort of critical eye for your own work. Otherwise, the warm comfortable feeling is apt to persist and is responsible for the publication of much bad poetry, and a deal of soulfully pretentious prose.

The reason for this disconcerting phenomenon, of course, is that since such "inspired" writing is caused by the play of a complex instinctive impulse on the latent content of the writer's mind, the absolute value of what is produced by it will depend on the power and value of the instinctive disposition at work and on the richness of the mind-content its material. When the impulse is itself intensely powerful (when its subject's vitality is strong, that is) and proceeds from a disposition of the self which blends harmoniously a series of major instincts, and when, further, it plays on a mind-content which,

* The odd choice of symbolism was probably determined by going to bed late after an early dinner, and the presence of the taxi in the rôle of Phibbus's car by the fact that I am sufficiently poor to make taxis a good deal of a luxury.

being rich in scope and completely organised, offers a wide choice of delicately discriminated images, then the compound image produced will be clear-cut and have intimately associated with it a considerable power of arousing similar instinctive dispositions, and therefore of arousing profound emotions. When in addition, the content of such a mind includes a wide range of delicately discriminated images of the activities required to present such an image truly—in other words, when the subject is completely master of his technique—then this image, so formed, will be truly presented also, and the result may be, for instance, *Kubla Khan* or *La Belle Dame sans Merci*—both of which are known in fact to have been written in this kind of "creative trance". When, on the other hand, the impulse, though strong relatively to the subject who experiences it, is absolutely feeble, shallow, or unimportant, and plays on a scanty and imperfectly assimilated mind-content, the result is more likely to be Ella Wheeler Willcox, or the ecstasies of the late Miss Marie Corelli. And sometimes there is a curious third case, accounting for such odd phenomena as that a man who could write the *Ode on the Intimations of Immortality* could also publish, and with perfect seriousness, poems as astoundingly bad as Wordsworth's worst. What happens is that the impulse compelling writing is simply the force of habit. The man is used to writing, feels comfortable and occupied—himself, in fact—while he is doing it. So this impulse plays on the images most usually and easily present in his mind (the mechanic side of technique being one of them), and the result is a parody of his real work: and if his power of self-criticism is not only originally rather to seek, but has also been as carefully extinguished as Wordsworth's was by his wife and Dorothy—why, then, he will complacently publish the work. Or, if he is not quite foolish enough for that, but not wise

THE CONVEYANCE OF THE SUBJECT 157

enough to destroy it, posterity may, as has lately happened to many unfortunate artists, whose ghosts must now be cursing on Parnassus.

It is necessary, therefore, that the conscious intellect must play its part, and work alongside this creative activity of imagination. The manner of co-operation varies. In some individuals the subconscious processes are themselves so ordered, coherent, and logical that the critical judgment appears to work in and through them, as it does in people who have "presence of mind", as we say—that is, who can act reasonably on the spur of an emergency that does not give them time for conscious reasoning. The most probable cause of this, I should imagine, is simply that clear self-critical judgment is so habitual (with regard to creative activity, at any rate) that it acts as unconsciously as any other habitual activity. In other cases, there is a curious sort of what I can only describe as "double consciousness", where one is a critical and completely detached spectator of one's own intense and genuine experience. I have noticed this in other things than writing, and in fact a good many soldiers have recorded a very similar phenomenon as occurring during occasions of very intensely emotional (i.e., instinctive) stress, when something had to be done that was not in the direction of the most powerful impulse, and was done, in spite of a consciousness of this impulse. Again, in every case, whatever may have happened during the period of "inspiration", once it is ended and the emotional stress is over, the critical judgment can regard the result, and if the image then perceived does not satisfy it, can often see not only that something is wrong, but even what is hindering true perception, and decide how it should be modified. To take a case in point, suppose the instinctive urge which is at work picks up a memory-image, X, as an element in what it is creating. X, at the moment, is seen purely in this capacity, as which it is satisfying. Its relevant associations fit, and S^1 is not at the moment conscious of any others. Then later, the critical intellect, regarding and testing the completed image, becomes aware that this component X has *other* associations, normally stronger, that suggest, for instance, a second-hand banality, or something else equally likely to overpower its positive value as an element in I^2. So on reflection he changes it for something less charged with irrelevant suggestion. A poet, with his mind strongly charged with the image of a garden, might conceivably write about "a blooming rose": but he would have rather a shock when he came upon the phrase next morning.* So again, while X may serve well enough with the immediate image i^2, it may fail to harmonise with the rest of I^2 of which i^2 is in turn a component part . . . though this error, of course, must be pretty carefully distinguished from the use of contrast as in much of the tragic irony of Shakespeare, where various mechanically minded editors, who like their kinds of literature neatly labelled, have scolded him for mixing comedy with tragedy, or have even failed to see that he has so mixed it. Ben Jonson has a vigorous passage somewhere on those who "miscall all by the name of fustian that their grounded capacity cannot aspire to".

Before we pass on from this process of selection among the combined implications of I^2, there is another point that may be remarked. Charlotte Brontë, in the passage quoted above, speaks of the manner in which, during a spell of "inspiration", images that have previously seemed determined may be greatly modified. This phenomenon

---

* Cf. the unfortunate first line of *Itylus*: "Swallow, my sister, O sister swallow." It is all right if one does take "swallow" as a noun. But unless one is very well up in Ovid, there is nothing at a first reading to prevent it from being read as a verb. Recently in a MS. novel I came on the sentence, "He came to her dancing-lessons, and was astonished at the strides she made".

THE CONVEYANCE OF THE SUBJECT 159

is one familiar to all writers in some degree, and very familiar to those whose impulse is powerful, but who cut short the preliminary "cartooning" in their impatience to get down the subject. One intends one's characters to do so and so, and behold they insist on doing something else: or one's scène à faire either does not take place at all, or drops out of sight between a couple of chapters. And one seems to have no control over the thing . . . or at all events, that is what it feels like. As a matter of fact, if we analyse the feeling, A's obstinacy is merely an image of our perception that this second possible course of action is the right one, is what A would have done in the circumstances, rather than what we originally thought he would do. A further acquaintance with those of the elements of the complete image, of which A is part, that precede in time and in causal relation this particular action of his, causes us to see its determinants more clearly, to have a fuller grasp of what they imply. As the time arrives for us to focus our immediate attention on this action of A's it appears to us now as the consequence of other preceding elements of the plot which have had their turn in the spotlight of attention, and we see it now more accurately than before, in relation to a clearer grasp of the data. Our conscious critical judgment is aware of the greater "rightness" of this new version, but the data may be too elaborate or too subtle to be readily formulated, and we simply have to act on the intuition. In fact, it is at our peril that we neglect it, even if it overthrows, as it may, the whole balance of the plot. There is nothing in the experience, however, to be particularly vain about. A book where the characters do this is ipso facto alive, and so will be readable. But it would be a better book, for all that, if the author had laid more leisurely foundations, and allowed the main lines to take shape before he began to write. This "cartooning" of the book is a very different matter, when it is properly done (that is, allowed to develop from within), from the lifeless and mechanical patching together of a plot with which people who are too lazy for it sometimes confound it. At the same time, in the case of minor details, within the major lines of the cartoon or primary image, this phenomenon may play a valuable part in deciding changes, not in the substance of an episode, but in the manner of its presentation. One sees a scene happen *so*, with the events in such-and-such an order. And then, writing it down, one finds it ought to begin, say, in the middle, or that X's interruption of the dialogue between Y and Z comes much earlier or much later than we thought, or we hit on a more plausible way of getting A off the scene before B, who must not meet him, is due to arrive, or find that the scene between C and D would be better in the garden than in the drawing-room. On such detail of technique the writer is best to keep an open mind till his proofs are passed. But if he finds that the saintly M is a first-rate villain, or his vamp has an unexpected heart of gold, then either his characters are being shoved to fit his plot, or his "fundamental brainwork" has been inadequate: and in either case, "he will get what is coming to him".

So far, during the present chapter, I have looked mainly at the process of *selection* among the different implications of I^2—of choosing which of these are actually to be presented to the reader, and which, on the other hand, may be left for him to infer, or even omitted as irrelevant to the theme. But alongside this, so intimately that I have already had to assume it more than once, is another process, that of the *arrangement* of the elements thus selected, so that they form a significant design. Now, the original meaning of the word *design* was "to set apart for", which became specialised to connote "an adaptation of

THE CONVEYANCE OF THE SUBJECT

means to ends". It is precisely in that sense that it fits here. S^1 has an end in view—the transference of an experience to another subject. He has his means—the images he has discovered. And he must adapt them as far as possible to that end.

We have seen already that the sub-images of which I^2 is built up correspond roughly, as stimuli to experience, to the sub-images composing I^1. The common factor between I^1 and I^2 is the system of relations obtaining between these sub-images,* and it is obvious that in grouping ii^2 to form I^2, the more clearly these relations are marked the more satisfactory will be the equivalence between I^1 and I^2. The chief of these relations are those of causality and of relative importance, and ii^2 must accordingly be set forth so that these relations are clearly to be perceived. When ii^2 are intellectual concepts this is not difficult, as their relation then will itself be a concept as near the sphere of pure intellect as may be, and may even be stated directly *as* a concept like another. But when they are sensory images highly charged with emotion, whose conceptual content is latent, it is less easy. One can *say*, of course, that the fact X is a consequence of A's having done Y. But to give its due emotional significance to this causal relation as such, we need an image rather than a concept—that is, we need to *show* rather than state that X is the inevitable result of Y. And this can only be achieved by arranging the images which make up the percept of X and the percept of Y in such a way that those relevant to their causal relation are conspicuous.

* As illustration, $\begin{smallmatrix} & o & \\ o & & o \end{smallmatrix}$ and $\begin{smallmatrix} & x & \\ x & & x \end{smallmatrix}$ are groups of signs which do not resemble each other—one set are circles and the other crosses. But the circles bear the same relation to each other as the crosses do, so that although the groups are of dissimilar signs, they produce, as groups, a similar effect—each strikes us as an equilateral triangle.

The problem is thus subsumed under that of showing the relative importance of the elements in I^2, which includes, of course, that of the causal relations inherent within it. S^1 secures this end by endeavouring, so far as he can, that the more important sub-images shall make the stronger impact upon the perceptive processes of S^2. It is naturally a somewhat hit-or-miss affair, as S^2 may have an abnormal apperceptive power for something of slight importance in the design, and so see it with quite disproportionate emphasis, or on the other hand be so completely unaccustomed to one of the other elements that it strikes him as merely odd, or is missed altogether. But—speaking generally, at any rate—the means at S^1's disposal are, roughly, those of space and juxtaposition, both of which can be applied, of course, either within I^2 as such, within any of the system of images that compose it, or within the systems of which these in turn are built up.

With regard to space, it is obvious that the more important images will be given their proper value by being presented at length, in rather copious detail, with the others much more briefly and slightly handled, or even left to be understood. There are times, however, when this method can be inverted with good results, and an important climactic image may gain in vividness by being left to the reader's prepared imagination to project for itself. This, of course, is one of the strongest weapons of the short-story writer.

Again, the special quality of the image X may be made more vivid by juxtaposing with it the image Y, of something completely contrasting, or containing explicitly something that is latent in X. A good deal depends on the subtlety with which this is done, and particularly on the economy. A capable writer who brings in an image to serve as an adjuvant to another will generally see to it

THE CONVEYANCE OF THE SUBJECT 163

that it serves more ends than one. Technically speaking, of course, the ideal of writing is to get into every unit composing the work the maximum charge of relevant meaning with the minimum of irrelevant suggestion. It is a useful object-lesson in this to study carefully the precise function of the secondary characters in Shakespeare's plays, taking them in relation to the play as a whole: Emilia and Kent are good examples.

The manner in which this process is performed is the same as the concurrent one of selection. In fact it could be considered as simply a subdivision of the same process, since to "arrange" anything is to "select" among possible relations. There is here the same reciprocating action of subconscious imagery and conscious intellect. It is probable, however, that the part of the latter is relatively more important, as relation, being a categorical concept, may be supposed to appeal primarily to reason. But I am not sure of this, as in actual fact one does image relations, as such, to a certain extent, though this, however, varies with the individual.

S^1 has now done more than merely discover what is the image I^2—that is, he has done more than find out the *subject* of his book. He has perceived the implications of that image within itself: that is, he knows the content of his book—what in a narrative we call the *plot*. And further, he has selected and arranged (though roughly as yet) the sub-images conveying these implications—that is to say, he has thought out the main lines of the *construction*. All these processes, of course, will be repeated on a diminishing scale with ii^2 and with the systems of sub-images which each of these contains in turn within it. The tool has thus been not only discovered but sharpened. It remains to use it—to project this prepared image on the consciousness of a fresh subject, S^2, so that he in turn receives an experience equivalent to the original experience received by S^1, that has set going the whole complex process. And that is the business of the actual writing.

CHAPTER X

THE WRITER AND HIS WRITING

"If they say that if they go that way the king is their cousin they may say they can they will say that both a day and a half and a half a day and a half without doubtless in soon."
GERTRUDE STEIN, *Three Sitting Here*

WRITING is of itself a somewhat mysterious business. In its early stages, wherever we come on them, it always seems to go hand in hand with magic. The word *rûn* that stands for the first Germanic letters means equally "a letter" or "a spell", and it may be that the very swastika, that widespread sign that has puzzled all ethnologists, is the monogram of the primitive uncial alphabets, and owes its potency to its power of holding all letters within itself. And primitive man was right about the magic. A mere telepathy is a simple and rational business to the fact that by looking at a marked sheet of paper I can know what a man thought and did four thousand years ago in a place that I have never set my foot in.

The immediate function of writing, of course, is to represent speech, and so to convey it farther in place and time. We have recently attempted other devices for this, the gramophone and the wireless telephone. But although they reproduce the actual voice, which may in some cases perhaps be an advantage, and although some combination of the two—as in the "talkie" films—is feasible, they can never take the place of writing as a means of transmission of speech, however they may restrain a lost sensitiveness of aural perception. For combined efficiency of both record and reference, no conceivable combination of machinery can take the place of a well-organised library, though I can easily imagine a time when Miss Ethel Dell will dictate to something that carries farther than a dictaphone, and cease to use the printed word at all. When that time comes, we shall have got back to the conditions of the Middle Ages, when the severance of "popular" and "learned" literature was marked externally by the fact that one was oral, the other written—one came through the ear, the other through ear and eye.

Writing as such consists of a series of arbitrary symbols, whose original forms, however, may have some visual association with what they stand for. The process of development appears to be: first, pictures, increasingly simplified, of concrete objects, such as a man or a house: then ideograms, signs that are not so much pictures as diagrams, like our mathematical > and < for "greater than", "less than": then phonograms, or signs representing the actual sounds of the language: and finally, as the sounds change and the signs remain fairly constant, a mainly phonogrammatic but partly ideogrammatic system of writing, like that which I am now using to convey the system of articulate sounds we call modern English.*

In the case of the mainly phonogrammatic languages the system simplifies its notation to a series of phonogrammatic symbols not for words but for the individual sounds which compose them, and which are infinitely less numerous, in any given language, than their possible combinations into groups. *But these symbols are not essentially visual.* 𝔄.а.A.a.*a*. are five different visual signs for the same *idea*—that of a letter representing certain sounds (at least three in English) and called for convenience "ay". In practice, indeed, the idea of a symbol representing the vowel-sounds in *as*, *gate*, and *all* has a

---

* The mistake of our spelling reformers is in a failure to recognise that in written English (and still more in written French or written Gaelic) this ideogrammatic element is strongly present and of great psychological importance. Italian and Spanish, on the other hand, are almost purely phonogrammatic—i.e., they have (practically though not with logical completeness) a phonetic orthography.

great many more visual signs than these: my script *a* is not very like my sister's, and neither is like the Roman uncial A. Yet anybody who can read English can identify all these signs as standing for the idea of the symbol (= letter) "ay", which in turn stands for the vowel-sounds to be heard in *as*, *all*, and *gate*. In practice, however, we read not by letters but by the groups of letters associated with entire words, or still more, by the groups of such groups that make up phrases and sentences: we certainly write by words and not by letters, as anyone knows who has tried to transcribe on a typewriter long technical terms familiar to him in handwriting. We learn the complicated system of visual signs that parallels the aural signs of our mother-tongue exactly as we learn another language, with the rather important difference that the idioms are of course precisely parallel. We can learn more than one set, as parallel to one language: most of us do in fact learn to read upper- and lower-case print and various sorts of script, and sometimes other alphabets as well. I have stood on the bridge of a coastwise steamer and watched the mate flash Morse almost as fast as I could have written the words. And to complicate matters a little further, some of these signs may be perceived *aurally*, as with Morse on a buzzer.

From the "receiver's" side, however, writing is normally a set of visual signs. But from the "transmitter's" it is mainly motor. Writing, from the writer's point of view, is the graph of a gesture—indeed, it can even be the gesture without the graph, as in semaphoring or the deaf and dumb alphabet. It is this motor quality in script that makes it so characteristic of the individual that his signature is considered as a token of identity.

Besides the motor-visual quality of words as written, and the visual quality, with a certain motor association, of words as read, there is with each a more or less powerful set of *auditory* associations, linking the visual-motor sign to the spoken, and so intimately that I am fully conscious of the sound-value of what I read at the rate of 350-400 words a minute—a rate at which I could not possibly speak. To read faster than that—which I do not as a rule—means to lose consciousness of these, however, and to grasp only the meaning, and that with some effort. Yet reading MS. examination-papers at the former pace, I am sufficiently aware of the individual words and letters to correct the spelling and punctuation.

The psychological processes involved in the interrelations of spoken and written language are rather elaborate. Let us think for a moment what is involved in writing down "John Smith". One has the idea of John Smith the man. By a process of association which is not very simple in itself, two groups of sounds "stand for" this idea in our minds. To hear these two brings up some sort of image of the man. To utter them conveys to other people that some image of John Smith is in our minds, and will arouse some image of him in theirs in turn—perhaps only such a vague general one as that of a male human being, probably British or American, perhaps a most elaborate complex of images and associations. To write the name means recalling nine distinct signs (themselves with scores of visual-images apiece) combining them into two groups, and tracing them by a gesture whose graph will arouse (*a*) an exogenous visual-image of those nine grouped signs, (*b*) an endogenous auditory image of two complex sounds (*c*) an endogenous image, conceptual, visual, motor, auditory, or all four combined, of the man John Smith. Any of these may be consciously perceived almost to the exclusion of the others: or we may even perceive them all subconsciously, and recall the fact later, as when going up an escalator I become aware that *I have just read* an advertisement. And the most astonishing part of the whole performance (of which I have only given the barest outline) is that it does not surprise us in the least.

The psychical mechanisms underlying the complexes of visual, auditory, and motor images that convey our thought in writing, are very interesting, but here I think we are justified in assuming them, as we assumed the initial sensory perception of O^1. They are, in fact, accidental to creative literature as such: the primitive folk-epics needed none of them, yet much of orally transmitted "literature" (the ballads and the Gaelic songs, for instance) is undoubtedly creative art using words for its medium. The actual writing down is no more essential than the binding of the book that is the embodiment not of the experiend itself, but of the words that in their turn embody it. The material book—ink, paper, and binding-case—is not the outward sign of I^2, but merely the sign of that sign. It is thus in reality not the O^2 of our formula, but, one might say, an O^3. The object by which Jane Austen conveyed the experience of which the story of Anne Elliot was the image, was a series of imagined *sounds*. This series of sounds is recorded, and so conveyed in turn, by each of a large number of rather dissimilar objects, formed of ink, paper, glue, strawboard, and other substances, and my copy of *Persuasion* is one of these.

The other arts show parallels to this. In music, of course, the doubling of O^2 is more obvious. O^2 as such is a pattern of sound and time. But this pattern may be recorded in a score, a gramophone record, or some other device such as the system of verbal notation or *canntaireachd* which transmitted the elaborate structure of the *ceòl mòr* or classical Gaelic pipe-music. And this device may be considered an O^3. The player receives from his perception of O^3 an image of O^2 (the sounds) which (imagined or actually perceived by the senses) conveys to the hearer the I^2 of the creative process—i.e., an image of the experience the composer had it in mind to convey. And here again, O^3 is inessential. In sculpture, again, I^2 is conveyed directly by the statue, which is O^2 ... though of course there may also be a cast of the statue, which would thus be an O^3, and one can even add an O^4, in the shape of a photograph of the cast!

To return to literature, however: although the actual putting down of words on paper is not an essential part of the art we call "literature", it has come to be, in the case of most civilised writers, a completely inseparable accident, as is proved by our use of the word *writer* and the art of *letters*. In practice, it is not so much a case of the visual signs representing the auditory, which in turn represent the thought. The two systems are so familiar to us that when we are using the first we are not immediately conscious of the second, but use the visual-motor signs, the written notation, as the *direct* equivalent of thought, just as although, when we learn French, we are apt to think in English and then translate, we come in time to think in French directly, and often form perfectly correct French sentences we should have difficulty in translating to our mother-tongue. We all make a certain distinction between the written and the spoken language. I myself (and the same thing is true of many other people) can express myself much more freely and clearly in writing than orally, and in lecturing from notes I have more than once had the edifying experience of finding that the word I had used quite naturally and correctly in the notes was one I did not know how to pronounce. Too complete a severance of this sort is to be avoided very carefully, as it leads to a serious weakening of perception with regard to the rich and delicate auditory associations which—as will appear later on—are of very great importance in writing and reading, particularly in

THE WRITING 171

a language like English, with its glorious many-coloured range of them. None the less, it is probably true enough that a compound perception of both sets of symbols at once (i.e., of the visual-motor *with their full range of auditory associations*) is richer than that of either system alone. It is not only that they sing to the spiritual ear, which hears the perfect image of the sound, but that in many languages, English and French and Gaelic for example, the graphic sign conveys associations that are not conveyed by the phonic alone and as such—of the etymological background, for example. The *simplifid spelin* movement ignores this fact, as well as the impossibility of achieving a phonetic spelling of English without large extension of its present alphabet—or deciding whose phonetics to reproduce.

The proportion of auditory and visual-motor elements in script-perception varies with the individual: a predominantly "auditory", a "visual", or a "motor" type of percipient will naturally perceive them in different ratios. But it seems possible that this variation is less in the whole perception than on the conscious level. I am myself a markedly visual-motor type. Consciously I *see* words and *feel them move* rather than hear them: but when through fatigue or haste I make mistakes in writing, the form they usually take is to use a wrong word whose connection with the right one is by means of a purely *auditory* association. Nor is it merely a case of writing down a more directly phonetic equivalent: I often write *two* for *too*, but not vice versa, though *too* is much the easier to write, and I am quite as likely to put down "my knew hat" as "I new the way"—and would certainly not write "my nyu hat". So apparently I have more sense of the auditory relations of words as such than I consciously feel I have. I have also noticed that in writing dialogue I have a very distinct auditory image of the voices—their difference in pitch to a slight extent (I have a poor ear for pitch in actual sensory perception), their difference in intonation, rhythm, and pace most markedly. I am certainly quite as aware of these things as of a character's actual choice of words or sentiments, though of course I cannot be sure how far I have succeeded in conveying the distinction in my writing. This in the case of one who appears to herself almost purely visual-motor in general perception (I have a poor memory for tunes or voices, and am hardly ever aware of sound in a dream, though I sometimes am of silence) suggests that unconsciously one perceives language more widely, as it were, than seems to be the case. But since I have no opportunity for systematic investigation of the point, I do not desire to lay much stress upon it.

I think we may consider, at all events, that the material substance of which, in literature, O^2 is composed, is a sequence of articulate sound-images, agreed on as conventional symbols of ideas, and arranged (these points will be dealt with later on) with regard to the relation of their content in the first place, and in the second with regard to such factors of quality, pitch, duration, and emphasis, as may help to bring out the significance of that content. These are the medium's primary characteristics. But in the case of most civilised writers, there are further sensory associations which can also be invoked, and these will be not aural but visual, arising from the associative interactions between the actual spoken speech as such and the recording device, or written speech, with which it is very intimately associated in the past experience of both S^1 and S^2.

The medium of literature, then, its material body, is not a substance of homogeneous texture. It is a highly complex synthesis of related units, the basis of which, in

THE WRITING 173

practice, is the word. I say "in practice", because the word itself is of course a synthesis of sounds and signs, and even of "syncategorematic" elements with a definite significance of their own—e.g., syn-categorem-atic, extrem-ism, extreme-ly, extrem-ist, etc.: and it is true that, in certain kinds of writing especially, one is often clearly conscious of it as such. (It is possible that before orthography grew fixed, this consciousness may have been more intense: Dr. Grierson's observations on Milton's spelling almost suggest this.) None the less, it is probable that we can fairly consider the word itself as the tessera of the mosaic pattern, for though it may be changed for another and a better, it cannot (normally) in itself be altered.

A word is for practical purposes a fixed group of sounds, which by a process of association has come to signify certain ideas. Notice, "ideas"—not "a certain idea". There is a class of words, generally technical terms or such parts of speech as prepositions or conjunctions, whose meaning is limited to one clearly defined idea: and these, especially when the content of the passage in which they are used is a purely or almost purely intellectual concept,* are valuable tools of thought: abstract conceptual thinking is of course impossible without the use of words: and as compared with, say, botany or physiology, the sciences of psychology and ethics have always been seriously hampered for lack of a set of terms of this description to express their fundamental notions, and prevent X from thinking he is talking about the same thing as Y when in fact he is merely using the same word.

The majority of words in the working vocabulary of a

* I repeat that strictly speaking there is no such thing in human psychological process: there is always an affective aura, however faint, or we should not be capable of thought at all.

language are not, however, as strictly defined as these. One word comes to be associated with several different ideas, in a very complex and elaborate fashion. It may denote the genus of which they are species so slightly distinguished that the generic term will indicate them fairly well alone: or through accidents of orthography we may find two words originally different in their meanings have adopted the same form while the meanings remain— e.g., to *let* him go without *let* or hindrance, from O.E. *laetan* and *lettan*. In any case, the "central" or primary contents, whatever they are, stretch out antennæ of association with other ideas, while the word as such has other associations with others resembling it in sound or spelling, which may displace its original connotation either completely or for all practical purposes. "Blooming", for instance, is impossible to use attributively in what everyone still knows is its literal meaning: you may say, "The cherry-trees are blooming", but you dare not talk about "those blooming cherry-trees" in any serious context, since the word, first by a mere sound-association and then by an association of frequent usage, has come to be regarded as a mild equivalent for the favourite proletarian intensive particle.

This multiguity of the elements in the ordinary working vocabulary can be a serious impediment to their use in presenting a precise and delicately shaded meaning. The words used may mean what the writer wishes to say: but they may also include some things he does not wish: "A blooming cherry-tree" and "a cherry-tree in blossom" do both denote exactly the same thing—a tree of a particular species in a particular stage of growth. But in practice they are not at all equivalent, and the first might be fatal where the second would be perfectly appropriate. The "right" word is always that whose most prominent content for the time being (what that is will be determined

THE WRITING 175

by the context) is completely dominated by the major factors of the idea, and whose overtones of association are either so overshadowed as to be latent, or else are completely relevant to the desired presentative aspect of the content. For instance, if I say "the heart beat faster" and "the cardiac action was accelerated", I am obviously describing the same facts. But they are described from different points of view, in relation to different chains of apperception, and with a slight difference of emphasis. Each is perfectly correct in its appropriate context, and the latter at least would be completely absurd in that of the other, while the first might be slightly less precise in that of the second. If these associations, in addition to being relevant, are also rich, various, and vivid without being intrusive enough to blur the main idea, then we have the finest kind of writing, that which conforms most closely to the actuality of living consciousness in a man to whom life is a rich, intense, and organised activity.

It is overrunning my immediate subject a little, but since the "figures of speech" are simply an extension of this use of associations, it may be as well to make mention of them here. Mr. G. M. Trevelyan, in one of his pleasant essays, remarks that "much of literature is allusion". He could have said "the whole", and been justified. There are always, in practice, these associative overtones of the actual words to reinforce the direct content, as harmonics to the melody their "meaning".* And not infrequently these harmonics, instead of being a frail obbligato, come

* This is true even of a purely technical term like *femur*, *rosaceæ*, or *polyhedron*. The overtones here are simple but quite perceptible. Each of these words conveys an atmosphere of precise and dispassionate intellectual apprehension and statement of facts, shut off from more than a certain immediately relevant aspect of living. Their emotional association, apart from one of interest or the lack of it, is completely negative: and they all imply that the thought has been confined to a certain specific universe of discourse.

out like a full crash of orchestration. Milton may say "in ruin reconciled", where he intends *ruin* to have not only its English meaning, of something broken past use, but a decided relish of the Latin one, of something crashing downward violently. He is using, and very gorgeously using, the intellectual and emotional overtones of the word's associations—he is *alluding*, that is, to other meanings in both languages, and doing exactly what he would have done if, instead of keeping to the associations of ideas possible within the word itself, he had enriched its meaning by drawing in analogies from outside the word, analogies only to the idea it contained. In

> He, above the rest . . .
> Stood *like a tower*. His *form* had not yet lost
> All her *original* brightness . . .

he does both these. "Stood like a tower" has exactly the same thought-process under it as "in ruin reconciled" or "her *original* brightness" or the use of *form* both in its English sense and with the reinforcing Latin one of "beauty", pointed by the *her* which suggests *forma*: but the reinforcing associations in the simile go outside the denotation of the word which conveys the idea to be reinforced. Metaphor is the same process as simile, but with the link—the "like" or "as" of the overt comparison—thrust into subconsciousness by its omission in the presented image, so that the union of idea and reinforcing association is more intimate. The danger, of course, is that when the idea A is associated thus with the idea B on account of some common factor X between them, what may happen is that in B the factors Y and Z are more prominent than X, so that instead of reinforcing our perception of X in A the arousal of B serves rather to blunt or distort it, as in the famous image of Tennyson's drunkard in *The Last Tournament*, who fell.

THE WRITING

> As the crest of some slow-arching wave,
> Heard in dead night along that table-shore,
> Drops flat, and after, the great waters break,
> Whitening for half a league, and thin themselves
> Far over sands marbled with moon and cloud,
> From less and less to nothing.

Perhaps the greatest safeguard against this danger is never to seek for an image, or be too eager to use one from the cold-storage of a notebook, but to take only those which, having risen spontaneously into consciousness, prove thus that they have a real association with the point. "Des métaphores cultivées en pots" *may* serve, but the probability is that lacking organic union with the subject, they will lead thought away from it rather than towards it. Even those which arise of their own accord need a certain care, especially in a language like English, whose idiom is strewn with them in any case. A student of mine once wrote in a class essay, "The real meaning is somewhat *veiled* by a *strain* of *lighter vein running through* the work". But it was a very wise professor of literature who once warned his class, " When you *get on to* a metaphor, be sure you *carry it out*".

The full significance of any word, however, depends upon its place within a context. In practice, words are never used alone. Even in a univerbal speech like "Yes", "Here", "John", other words are understood, though not actually spoken. Speech is always *combination* of words, whether actual or implied—combination in the strictest sense, too, not mere collocation. The words are fused in an organic unity, and only become organic when so fused. A word is dead till it moves among other words, for the reason that a word, as such and alone, is static, and the thought-process essentially dynamic. Give it the word "man" as an object; it cannot rest on that, but must go

M

off on some indefinite track determined by casual association. Give it instead, "The man walked down the street", and you have determined that the thought shall be guided as it runs along a specific channel of progression.

Few single words, too, would be capable of conveying the whole of a complex image to our mind, though they may convey more than the image rather than less. The image, whatever it is, is of a synthesis of objects having certain qualities, doing certain things in a particular manner: and these objects, their activities, and the qualities of both, stand with regard to each other in various relations. To convey the image in words it is necessary to present a synthesis of images of all these factors, with the just proportion of emphasis on each: in other words, to choose the precise noun, adjective, verb, adverb, conjunction, and preposition for each element—of entity, quality, action, or relation—that makes up the whole significance of the image in that particular universe of discourse, and arrange them with the proper relative emphasis, so that the most important factors are the most conspicuous. In addition, these words and the sound-pattern of their arrangement must be so chosen that the apperceptive overtones they possess as such may deepen and reinforce the particular affective and cognitive processes it is desired to stir, and eliminate, as far as may be, the possibility of stirring any other processes which would impede in any way the one it is desired to bring about. It is a fairly tall order when it is put like that, and goes some way to justify Mr. G. M. Trevelyan's plaintive remark, "It is very difficult to write good English prose". But an intelligent man with a little care and training can achieve it very fairly on the whole, and a man of genius can work miracles.

I have suggested the means by which the satisfactory presentation of the image is to be achieved. Calling up the courage necessary to make the observation in the present year of grace and cleverness, I may repeat that here, as at every other stage in the process, it is again a matter of selection and arrangement among given elements. This method has already been applied among the descending series of sub-images contained by implication in I^2, so as to discover just what is to be the actual content of O^2 that, as it stands in words, shall convey what is required to be conveyed. Now, to fit words to these sub-images is to break the latter up once more into elements each of which is capable of being represented by a word or group of words, and of selecting among the writer's memory-images of words and the possible arrangements of words those which are associated, with the greatest possible closeness, with these elements—in the most literal sense, those which *fit* them best. Among the factors to be considered here is first, of course, the choice of the words themselves, whose principles have already been discussed. But as we have seen already, this is not all. The *order* of these words is highly significant, as it is the instrument by which the relation between ideas is mainly to be perceived: and in particular it is on the order more than on anything else that depends our perception of their relative importance as factors in a given act of perception.

This order is in the first place determined by their grammatical relation—i.e., in the main (though with a modification of use and wont) by the logical relation of the ideas they convey. In a comparatively uninflected language like English or French, this order is in fact the main—sometimes the only—way of expressing these relations. I can write, "Balbus aedificavit murum", ' Murum aedificavit Balbus", "Balbus built a-wall". But I cannot write, "A-wall built Balbus". The order of words, in English at all events, is the main means of indicating their grammatical relation—that is, the logical relation of their respective content. This relation obtains primarily within the sentence, which is a self-contained unit, the expression in words of a single perceptual act. It may be a very simple act, as for instance, "The cat is black", where you have only three ideas—of a specific cat, of a colour, and of a very simple relation between them. It may again be an act of extreme complexity, as in some of the page-long but completely lucid sentences of Ruskin, or the curious groping advance of Henry James over the object of his vivid but myopic internal vision. But it is essentially a single act of apprehension of one complex object of a human experience.

The sentence, however, does not stand alone. It conveys the effect of one perceptual act: but the whole I^2 can only be perceived by means of a great number of such acts. So the sentences are grouped, and in modern writing most writers have adopted the handy typographical device of the paragraph. A paragraph is really a way of marking a pause—a rather decided pause—in the flow of perception. Perception moves in a series of pulses: it is not a steady stream of activity. And speech reflects this fact. The just-perceptible pauses between words are like the infinitesimal pause between the heart's systole and diastole, where it sleeps for a fraction of time between every two beats. I have known a phonetician deny any such pause: but its proof lies in the fact that we are conscious of reading two hyphened words a little differently from the same two words without a link between them. "Very bright pale blue eyes" neither means nor sounds quite the same as "very bright pale-blue eyes". Our writing has learnt to reflect this phenomenon by leaving little spaces between the words, a device which is comparatively modern. In the same way also, at the end of the completed act of perception there is a longer pause,

THE WRITING 181

the pause at the end of the sentence.* And at the completion of a system of closely related acts comes one still more marked, that we have learned to indicate by grouping our sentences in paragraphs, divisions of writing intermediate in the scale of subordination between the single act of perception conveyed in the sentence and the main limb or aspect of the subject which is the chapter.

But this grammatical, typographical, or temporal relation of words, and the logical relation of ideas to which it is parallel, are not the only kinds that require to be taken into account. They express the relations of contingency, causality, spatial, temporal, or associative contiguity, and so forth: but the arrangement of words which parallels the relative emphasis laid on the different elements in a given image ("He is a generous man, but he drinks like a fish": "he drinks like a fish, but he is a generous man") is a matter not only of grammatical relation but of rhythmical—that is to say, of the patterns made up by the words' accent and quantity. Prosodists are still at each other's throats over the precise connotation of these terms, and as my own studies in prosody have been confined to the analysis and appraisal, with occasionally the attempt, of actual practice, I will not venture on the "debateable land", but merely remind the reader of a phenomenon with which every English-speaker is familiar —that there are in English, as in some other languages, two kinds of syllables, which may be variously described as strong and weak, heavy and light, accented and unaccented, or (less logically in practice) long or short. The distinction between these two kinds is obvious even to small children, who in fact greatly delight in the patterns

* Though the story is against myself, I must quote here one of the finest Spoonerisms I have encountered. I was trying to explain the phenomena of punctuation to a class of students, and informed them solemnly, "You would naturally expect to find clawses at the ends of your pawses".

which it makes. The causes of the distinction are so far from obvious that very great scholars are at loggerheads over them: so I, as merely a little one, *passe outre*, to the surer ground that the whole of English speech consists of various arrangements of these types of syllables and of pauses, which form a sort of pattern of sound on time—a pattern conditioned by the facts that (*a*) in verse we hardly ever get more than three syllables and never more than four,* in prose seldom more than four and never more than five, without a slight pause: (*b*) in practically every group of two or over there will be at least one "heavy" syllable: and (*c*) that in most cases in English the pause comes just after a heavy syllable.†

This fact is of the greatest importance in writing. What it amounts to in practice is that our words as we use them will have different sorts of emphasis—that is to say, of sensory importance. If the maximum sensory importance can be assigned to the word of the greatest ideational importance, affective or cognitive, then naturally S^2 is helped to perceive the relative importance of the idea contained in it. Accordingly, in the writing of a sentence, it is the writer's business so to arrange his words, within the limits of their simultaneous grammatical arrangement, as to get most weight upon the most important. In every

---

* Some people would say "never more than three". But the tetrasyllabic feet exist, though perhaps as something of an innovation. You cannot scan the last lines in Mr. Masefield's *Sea-fever* otherwise than as Ionics *a minore*: and they certainly do scan, most beautifully. I myself once wrote a short poem, not good as poetry but very effective as metre, whose anapestic-iambic basis was heavily equivalenced with fourth pæons. (I did not realise the fact until I scanned it, by the way.) I fancy one could find tetrasyllabic feet in Mr. de la Mare and Mr. Milne.

† I say "in most cases". The general run of English is iambic, which is why continuous trochees sound uncanny and continuous dactyls are a physical impossibility. Cf. the effect of Shakespeare's and of Middleton's witch-verses in *Macbeth*. The latter had not a very sensitive ear, and in copying the octosyllabic couplet he wrote the more natural iambs, and killed the magic.

group of words, there is one word, or two at the most, which form, so to speak, the core of it, the central element in the perceptual act it involves. The writer who is able to use his tools will so build up the patterns of his rhythm that this key-word projects, one might say, above the rest of its neighbours. Take the last sentence. Suppose it ran: "The writer who can use his tools": the emphasis is naturally on "use". But I want to emphasise the idea in "can": so I change it to "The writer who is able to use his tools", where the natural emphasis shifts to the "able". In the phrase that follows, "will so build up the pattern of the rhythm that this key-word projects above its neighbours", "will so build up the pattern of the rhythm" gets its emphasis on "pattern" and "rhythm" automatically. But the remaining phrase, as it stands, has not enough emphasis on "projects". So "one might say" —a parenthetic and unimportant phrase of light quick syllables—is placed after it, as a shadow is placed to throw up a brighter colour. The effect of this phrase in low relief is further reinforced by the fact that it makes necessary a slight pause after "projects", which helps the important word to stand out farther. A pause next a word—particularly, in English, a pause after a word— always has this effect of emphasising it, giving it time to sink home. That is why the best place for emphatic words is at the end of a sentence or of some member of it. In speech the voice, in writing a punctuation-mark, may *insert* such a pause, without more ado. Take the phrase, "to enable him justly to form an opinion". The natural run of the words puts most of the weight on to "form an opinion". Now, pause before and after "justly" in speaking the phrase, or put a comma before and after it in writing: "enable him, justly, to form an opinion" swings the whole emphasis back on to "justly". The major use of punctuation, italics, capitals, etc., is to serve in this way as a set of expression marks which suggest the intonations of the spoken language. ("Have you seen the brass bottle?"—"Have you seen *The Brass Bottle*?") The phrase "he has come" can be spoken so as to convey four different meanings: and in writing we indicate these different intonations by ending it with the marks — . ! or ? The difficulties in "learning to punctuate" would be considerably lessened if people were taught to think clearly and to hear clearly. If they thought clearly they would feel the natural divisions or phases of the developing idea, and instinctively indicate these by a slight pause. If they heard, they would have no difficulty in distinguishing the value of those pauses we are accustomed to indicate by , ; : and . and the affective—cognitive quality of the intonations conveyed by ( ) " " ! ? — and the . . . which is now regarded as the hall-mark of the Really Intellectual Novelist.

It may be remarked also that the rhythm-quality of the sentence may have something to do in determining choice of words. English, being descended from half the languages under heaven, is very rich in words which, isolated, are more or less equivalent. I have spoken already of the need, in choosing words, to discriminate between the differences of associational overtone in two or more words of the same denotation. An important special case of this difference is where these overtones are not conceptual or affective, but sensory. Either word A or word B may do well enough as far as "meaning" goes. But A sounds better than B, is more attractive to the reader's ear, and so holds him better to the business of attending to O^2: or perhaps it has a vowel-sound more in harmony with the emotional colour of the sentence and its general content of sensory imagery—take for instance, the vowels in

So all day long the noise of battle rolled

and those in

> —Old knights, and over them the sea-wind sang,
> Shrill, chill, with flakes of foam.

Change these to

> So all the day the sound of fighting pealed

and

> —Over them cried the wind out of the sea,
> Sharp-sounding, cold, with foam-flakes borne in it.

There is no great difference of sense, and they both scan. But they are very considerably less effective.

One of the most important of these sensory overtones is the shape of the word in relation to the shape of the sentence. *Ceteris paribus*, the exchange of a disyllable for a monosyllable, or the other way round, may make all the difference. One can even make an artificial disyllable of the monosyllable by introducing some slight unaccented word, too implicit to be in any way conspicuous, and thus get the proper balance of the sentence, with the weights in the right place, like a good sword. It is even possible to shorten a sentence considerably by *adding* a word or two to it here and there.

This weighting serves for something besides emphasis. When I regard one object after another, my stream of perceptions will flow in an easy movement, without sharp breaks. If it is desired to make me feel as I should if I were contemplating these objects when in fact what I see is only a symbol of them, it is obviously advisable that my perception of the symbol should have the same flow and move at the same pace: and it is mainly the balance of rhythm that effects this, as the balance of a sword assists the thrust. If sentence goes easily into sentence, and so forth, the mind goes on unchecked, of its own momentum: and every dancer knows—or knew before jazz—that the effortless ease with which one moved through a dance came neither from one's own strength nor one's partner's, but from the impulsive momentum of their united weight, in perfectly counter-balanced rhythmical action. The power of compelling the mind to move in this way is one of the most valuable elements in a writer's technical equipment: it is partly, no doubt, a matter of the selection and arrangement of his sub-images, so that they compose into an inescapable whole: but in the main it depends on the actual writing. Why does one detective-story keep you out of bed and another send you to sleep before you get there? Both may have equally ingenious plots and a decent level of literacy and verisimilitude: but the former one has momentum as well: it swings. Nor is the quality confined to fiction: I know few men who have more of it than Burke.

The question of pace is of course bound up with this. There is slow writing and fast writing: and the slow writing has no need to be sticky, as is proved by the splendid adagi of the Prayer-Book. It is a question of avoiding or inserting heavy consonants, particularly gutturals and dentals, and of the relative proportion of long vowels in both the accented and unaccented syllables. "Like as the waves make towards the pebbled shore" is slower than, "And holds the eel of science by the tail", though they are both iambic decasyllables.

The use of rhythm to give relative emphasis slips easily into another, very valuable, where it indicates not so much the relative importance of the components in a perceptual complex as that of the affective factors in the percept—in other words, when it works directly to indicate the quality (and especially the intensity) of the emotions that form part of the experiend. In its more obvious manifestations this becomes *metre*—a regular and symmetrical pattern of sounds which accompanies S^2's perception of the content of the words with a sort of undercurrent of pulsation. The effect of this percussive accompaniment is twofold. On the one hand, like the regular beat of a drum or tick of a clock, it has a directly hypnotic effect, which fixes the mind on the recurrent stimulus and on the ideas associated with it, and thus cuts off the perception of those external to it, which of course intensifies those that are perceived. The effect of the cymbals and tom-tom in savage ritual is precisely analogous, and is of course repeated in jazz music, which is prized for this effect, as a species of dope: the fixed expression of a contemporary dancing crowd, the lifelessness of the faces, is often remarked on. There is the same thing again in the regular monotonous chanting of incantation: the S^2—or it may be S^1 as well—is sung into (*incantare*) a condition of insensibility to all stimuli but those directly associated with the chant itself, so that the effect of this has as little as possible to inhibit it. The value of this process, of course, depends on the nature of these associations. They may be those associated with the pattering *Hail Marys* of the rosary and with plain-chant and the swing of the censer as the Host is consecrated: or with the lilt of the pipes going into battle. Or again, they may be the conception of pleasure associated with the average nightclub, or the conception of the duty to deity associated with a West African ju-ju "custom". Or again, they may be simply the ideas that Milton or Mr. A. A. Milne is conveying in his very skilful verse. But whatever they are, the pulse that underlies them is a powerful adjuvant to the sensitising of the mind to receive their full quality, and to the inhibition of counteracting perceptions.

Nor is this, of course, the only effect of metre, for one

of the inevitable associations of strong rhythm is that of a certain emotional intensity. The reason, of course, is that the physiological processes of life—respiration and circulation very obviously, sleep, digestion, and the mechanism of reproduction less steadily but with a good deal of regularity in normal people—all move with a definite rhythm of their own. Now, the activity of any instinctive impulse is inseparably associated with an activity of what we call "emotion"—which indeed is merely the cognition of that impulse: and any such activity involves an intensification of *élan vital*—that is to say, a greater force in the process of living generally, which increases the force of those sub-processes that are its machinery and gives us a stronger sense of all their rhythms, which it may speed up as well as intensify; as is shown in the beating heart and quickened breath of a man who is undergoing strong emotion, in whom, therefore, instinctive impulse is strongly aroused. Now, all chains of associative process can work not only forwards but "in reverse": if I come to associate X with the smell of wet Harris tweed, then the scent of wet Harris tweed will remind me of X. So if strong emotion is associated with enhanced perception (conscious or subconscious) of natural physiological rhythms, then strong rhythm of any kind is likely to suggest to us strong emotion: and if the vehicle presenting any ideational content includes strong rhythms, we shall be specially sensitised not only to its content generally, but also to the emotional issues of that content. Hence the effect of Gothic vaulting, for instance:* and the association in all languages of metrical (i.e., regularly and noticeably rhythmical) speech with ideas highly charged with emotion—that is, with poetry. There is a good logical case for metre's being a mere accident of poetry:

* A friend of mine declares, at least half seriously, that "she can't feel devout in a church with a flat roof".

THE WRITING 189

but psychologically it is very like an inseparable accident. And strong rhythm, even though not metrical (e.g., Synge's prose, or Carlyle's) is not an accident at all, but a property.

From these observations it naturally follows that if S^1 is desirous of conveying in words an experience which is highly charged with emotion, he will find that to arrange the said words so that they are accompanied by a regular pattern or beat of accentuation, is a very valuable means to this. But the means must be used rightly, or it will defeat its end. In the first place, if his emotion is factitious, then the metre may be dangerously revealing. By sensitising S^2 to perceive emotion, it may make him, by that fact, a better judge of it, and therefore less ready to accept its semblance, more alert to distinguish between false and true, to the disadvantage, of course, of S^1's pretence. It is by an extension of this principle that comic verse gains half its effectiveness. When some very trivial or absurd idea is presented with all the accessories of one vitally important (as for instance when someone delivers pompous platitudes with the air of one revealing a new gospel) then, whether deliberately or without intention, the result is apt to be somewhat entertaining to people who have a keen sense of proportion. So when, in a sort of Black Mass of Apollo, a frivolous trifle of an idea is given the ceremonious accessories of intricate verse, it is more absurd for the contrast of the collocation, just as the schoolboy who is unmoved when Jones Minor appears with his tie hanging out would squirm with joy if the Head Master did it.

But even supposing the emotional quality is genuine, the rhythm must still fulfil certain conditions in order that it may be as effective as possible in enhancing S^2's perception of its content. First of all, though regularity is of its essence, it must not be too regular, or its hypnotic effect upon S^2 will be so complete and powerful that instead of being just sufficiently hypnotised to lose perceptions external to its content, he reaches a deeper stage, and ceases to be aware even of that—in fact, he goes to sleep.

The complete and uniform regularity of a clock's ticking is therefore likely to be inadvisable. To produce the maximum effect upon S^2, there must be a certain interference with this regularity—not enough to destroy our perception of it, but enough to prevent our being lulled beyond awareness. One of the great devices for this, and one early discovered, is the building up of the units in the rhythm-pattern into larger and more complex units, which themselves are arranged in a pattern of their own, superposed upon the others: the feet are grouped in lines and the lines in stanzas, which may themselves, as in some of the intricate forms of twelfth- and thirteenth-century courtly verse, be grouped again as parts of a formal whole, not "resolved", as a musician would say, until its end. The units of such a pattern are marked by a more perceptible pause than that between the sub-units composing themselves (i.e., there is a more marked pause after a line than after a foot, after a stanza than after a line), and these pauses are often further emphasised by some likeness of the sounds preceding, or more rarely following, them—by alliteration, as in early Teutonic verse, by assonance on the final vowel, as in early French, or by the complete similarity of the last emphatic sound and those following it that we call rhyme, and that Milton (who like most Puritans was a poor psychologist) dismissed as "the jingling sound of like endings". The essential function of rhymes is to mark the larger units of the rhythmical pattern and their place in the unit including them again, a purpose for which Milton himself uses it

THE WRITING 191

magnificently. In written verse there is also another device, that of writing each group of feet as a line by itself and marking it with an initial capital. Nobody who has read the Authorised Version of Isaiah in the traditional little numbered scraps of mechanically uniform length crammed in double columns, and then in Dr. Moulton's superb "display" of it to show the rhythmical structure of its form, can doubt the great use of this mode of arrangement, even though it may be as purely mechanical as the difference between a soft-iron sculptor's chisel and a fine steel one with a perfect edge.* The attempt to be original cheap by ignoring this device and reverting to the primitive mode of running the lines together continuously may make for prettier typography (no passionate printer but sets verse with a sigh), but it is rather as if a sculptor thought he was original because he made his statues of mashed potato.

A more subtle device, reinforcing this powerfully, is to vary the pattern a little within itself, without permitting its main lines to be destroyed. The variations keep us from being hypnotised to insensibility, but at the same time the pattern is regular enough to make us expect its repetition, to be alert for the fulfilling of the expectation, and to feel a certain pleasurable satisfaction when its fulfilment indicates that we have judged correctly in so expecting—a pleasure analogous to that which we normally take in the accurate performance of any action, such as a good stroke at golf. Take

* Dr. Moulton's *Modern Reader's Bible* (Macmillan, 10s. 6d.) treats the whole A.V. in this fashion, chaptering the narrative and argumentative parts so as to bring out the logical structure of the thought, which the ordinary text does its best to disguise, and printing the prophetic and other poetic books "displayed" (in the printer's sense) to show their form. It is done with a really exquisite ear for rhythm, and in spite of a remarkably ugly format is the Bible of all others for any man who wants either the content of the Scriptures or the form of the most gorgeous prose in English.

> I put my hat upon my head
>   And walked into the Strand,
> And there I met another man
>   Whose hat was in his hand,

and

> I settled my hat on the top of my head
>   And walked down into the Strand,
> And there I met with another man
>   Whose hat was in his hand.*

The second version feels more alive to us, because our perceptual processes have been kept more alive in receiving it. So the rich variety in unity that is one of the major glories of English verse, than which there is none more glorious in the world, does its part in creating the "life more abundantly" that is the end of writing as of all art.

Incidentally, this principle works in prose. There is not the same regularity of framework here: but the ear can be led none the less to expect a certain cadence, and the expectation can be fulfilled, deferred, or resolved into a greater satisfaction than that foreseen, or even at times disappointed with a shock like a discord.

These patterns of rhythm have a further value: they are a source of pleasure in themselves, as the arabesques on a Moorish tile, the tracery of a Flamboyant window, or the pattern of a Persian carpet are sources of pleasure. When I was a child of certainly not more than seven, I used to repeat to myself several stanzas of Milton's *Nativity Hymn*—those on the passing of the Old Gods. I had not the faintest idea who "Peor and Baalim" or "mooned Ashtaroth" might be, and only a very hazy one what it was all about, but it gave me the same kind of delight that I had in the colour of velvet—I can remember, in fact, associating the two. And I was by no means a

---

* From Dr. Saintsbury's monumental (and delightful) *History of English Prosody*.

THE WRITING

literary child: I must have been fourteen or even older when I presented my governess with a nine-word essay, and informed the pardonably indignant lady that I had no more to say ... which was perfectly true.

The associative value of the pleasure is obvious. If the image I^2 is directly associated with a pleasant experience, S^2 will be more inclined to attend to his perception of it, and so to receive that perception more vividly. Precisely the same principle works in advertising: if the idea of X's suet or Y's sparking-plug can be associated in your mind with that of a charming young woman or an engaging pup, then you have a certain subconscious association of pleasantness with the suet or the sparking-plug, which may determine you to choose them when you meet them among others with which you have no associations at all or which merely spoil for you a favourite view.

More subtly than this, the pattern of the rhythm may *as such* suggest emotional qualities which reinforce those it is desired should be aroused by the actual ideas contained in it. We all know the very definite emotional quality of the visual rhythms of Gothic architecture, the sense of aggressiveness, languid incompetence, smugness, ill-breeding, or gracious dignity that may be felt in certain kinds of furniture, and I have seen a pattern of abstract lines (in a modern German theatrical decoration) that was fairly greasy with obscenity. Now, just as these visually perceived non-representational forms have a strong affective quality as such, so the same thing is true of those aurally perceived. And the writer who knows his job will put his writing in the form which he can charge most fully with the emotional associations that fit its content.

This is not only a matter of pure rhythm. I have spoken already of the process of association linked with the quality of the sound as such: and the compound pattern

—the harmony—of the sound and rhythm (i.e., of the quality of the sound and its disposition in time) may also be used to imitate some natural (or other) sound associated with the image to be presented, as in the enchanting water-music of Spenser, the chatter of little birds in Nash's spring-song, the toll of Sidney's dirge, or the cry of the lute in Wyatt's *Forget not Yet* and in the lovely song in the Aberdeen *Cantus*, before Geneva silenced Scots courtly verse:

> In a garden so green, of a May morning
> Heard I my lady pleen of paramours.
> Quoth she, "My love so sweet, come you not yet, not yet?
> Hecht you not me to meet, among the flowers?"
>   Eloré, eloré, eloré, eloré,
>   I love my lovely love, eloré, lo!*

We may even have such complex *tours de force* as Mr. Kipling's echo of the Dead March at the end of *Follow me 'Ome*:

> Take 'im away, 'e's gone w'ere the best men go.
> Take 'im away, with the gun-w'eels turnin' slow.
> Take 'im away, there's more from the place 'e come.
> Take 'im away, with the limber and the drum.
>   For it's "Three rounds blank", and follow me,
>   And it's "Thirteen rank", and follow me,
>   O passing the love o' women,
>   Follow me, follow me 'ome,

or the similar one of the Last Post that ends *Cholera Camp*, to say nothing of the drum-and-fife quickstep in *Troopin'*.

There is even verse where the pure abstract pattern of the sound is the main thing. Some refrains, like the *eloré* one above, are like this in whole or in part—"Mironton, ton, ton, mirontain-e" or "With a fal la la la la"—though most of the ballad ones have a content-value as well, like

* I am quoting from memory. Hence the modern spelling.

THE WRITING 195

the arabesque of leaves round an illumination. "The broom blooms bonny and sae it is fair. . . . And we'll never gang doun tae the broom ony mair", of *Sheath and Knife*, is an example, or

> There were three sisters in a bower,
> *Edinburgh, Edinburgh,*
> There were three sisters in a bower,
> *Stirling for aye,*
> There were three sisters in a bower,
> There came a knight to be their wooer,
> *Bonny Saint Johnstoun stands upon Tay,*

and so with the moderns in the flaming background of Rossetti's *Troy Town* or the fantastic heraldry of *Two Red Roses across the Moon*. Sometimes the arabesque border is studded with illustrative miniatures, as in the wild refrains of *Sister Helen*.

These, of course, only use this abstract or semi-abstract kind of pattern as decoration round a main image that itself is sharp and clear and well defined, as a medieval statue stands in a carved niche. But we may have *objets d'art littéraire* that exist for this decoration, as a carved pendant does, or a pattern of pure line on the face of a wall. Swinburne, of course, is the great example here: the content of idea in his verse is rather an accompaniment to the metre than vice versa, and one can take just the same sort of pleasure in it that one does from looking at a Persian rug or the interlacing jets of an old French fountain. Logically, it should indeed be possible to make patterns of words without any ideational content at all. Psychologically, however, it is impossible to do this satisfactorily unless S^2 is ignorant of the language used. If anyone read to me a meaningless but melodious series of Arabic words, I should enjoy it as I enjoy

> Knights of Logres and of Lyonnesse.
> Lancelot and Pelleas and Pellinore—

or, for that matter, the mouth-filling sixain that begins

> Barbara, Celarent, Darii, Ferioque prioris—

which is simply a mnemonic for the moods of the syllogism. As a child, in fact, I used to like the look of French on the page, and dislike German, without knowing a word of either. But I am unable to enjoy, say, Miss Gertrude Stein, and would be, though she sang like the harps of Heaven, so long as she used a language that I know. The reason is not, I submit with all modesty, because of my intellectual limitations, but because I cannot limit my intellect enough: to anyone who, by nature or training or both, is sensitive to the qualities of words, one of their inevitable and ineluctable associations is that with the idea of possessing meaning. To tear this completely away is quite impossible: to attempt to ignore it is to produce a fresh association, extremely strong—the very positive sense of an absence of meaning, of the process of consciousness impeded and insane, with its insanity, too, in the absolute, not set in relation to a norm of sanity. The effect of Swinburne, however, is quite different. The meaning, as a rule, is negligible, but it is there, and knowing it is there one can ignore it, take it for granted as one takes the surface of the decorated wall. Sometimes, of course, the meaning is too prominent to permit that, as in the things where after all Swinburne was greatest, like *The Garden of Proserpine*, which may be nonsense as eschatology but is great poetry for all of that, as the perfect image of a real mood, emotionally if not intellectually valid. Then his idea-content, though still rather the ribs in the leaf than the wine in the cup, as it is in the Cellini chalice of Milton's *Nativity*, works as a sort of intellectual accompaniment or undersong to the emotions of that marvellous metre.

Normally, however, it is the idea-content that matters,

THE WRITING 197

the knowledge of human cognitions and conations and of their quality as experience: and the form of words by which this is conveyed has only for a secondary function its enhancement of the perception of this by the effect of an abstract non-ideational pattern. That is merely like the accompaniment to a song, or at best the air to which the words are set.

And, just as the air may be harmonised between parts, so this rhythm-pattern need not be only a melody. I have spoken of two distinct sets of rhythmical principles which govern the arrangement of words in use. One gives the relations, including the relative emphasis, of different ideational elements. The other forms an abstract pattern reinforcing the emotional quality desired. Both these coexist in any one piece of writing. In prose, the former dominates by a good deal. In verse, as we have seen, the latter may. But in verse again they may rather be coequal, coinciding with and strengthening each other, and there is another usage that can be magnificently effective, though it takes a great technician to bring it off. This is where the sense-rhythm and the sound-rhythm are both perfectly clear and perfectly fitted to their subject, but instead of coinciding they cut across each other, as a wind may blow across the run of the tide. (There are magnificent examples of this in Shakespeare's later verse, and in *Paradise Lost*.) The effect is a strong tumult of perceptions, in which, none the less, they retain their very complete and perfect clarity, an ineluctable truth to their relation, and this gives a sense of enormous energy, controlled and directed by a will that can hold it. But there is not much writing like this at any time. It is a privilege of the very great.

The ideal of writing as such would then seem to be that kind of it which is the most transparent, which reveals most perfectly and with least admixture the image of that whose embodiment it is. There is nothing very novel in this view. It is so obvious, in fact, that it runs a serious danger of being forgotten, for writers are apt to be Very Clever People, or at all events, Clever People are apt to be writers. (It is the easiest art to imitate convincingly.) And it is the mark of the Clever Person, all through history, to panic at obvious things, whether true or not. There is, however, another reason why this particular platitude is unpopular. Perfectly transparent writing, writing through which every shade and line of the image contained in it may be seen so clearly that they are inescapable, is an ideal about as possible of fulfilment as the ideal of perfect moral goodness, and difficult aims are unlikely to be popular in an age where the only virtue we preach is tolerance, interpreted as a passionate objection to any demand for the practice of the rest.

Nevertheless, there are always people with courage enough to attempt impossibles, and even now and then to bring them off, and though transparency in writing is unfashionable, there are writers who make a valiant bid for it. Transparency means a good deal more than simplicity. Simple writing, of course, may be an excellent thing: but to give a simple expression to something whose essence is to be highly complex, may be to veil that essence considerably. Very little of Donne's writing is simple: yet none the less, when he is at his best, it has the transparency of deep sea water. We must look into it, and look close: but if we look long enough and close enough, we can pierce to a perfect image of what it holds.

The ideal of "simple writing" has this of truth. It should always be as simple as possible, which is not to say that in any given case it need be what we call simple absolutely. It must fit the image, however that may be. That the image itself should be simple in the sense that its sub-images are so chosen and co-ordinated that when they are all perceived the whole is graspable on one act of perception, and that each of them serves to enrich the content of the whole—such a simplicity is always desirable, if singularly difficult to attain. There is no clear writing unless there has been clear thinking to precede it. But the image, once formed, must be embodied fully.

In practice, this means that the words must be—another shocking platitude—first rightly chosen and then rightly arranged. Their core of primary meaning must have the percept "true in the middle of it", as a singer should sing in the middle of the note. As many as possible of its ideational overtones, and of its sensory too, must harmonise with this central percept and enrich it: as few as possible must be discordant; and these, if existing at all, must be rendered mute. And the words so chosen must have such a grammatical relation, must make such a pattern of sense-order, as to show as completely as possible the relations (including that of relative importance) between the sub-percepts building each major image, and between the images composing these. Again, the order of the words in rhythm must be one where the sound of them, simply as such, reinforces the quality it is desired to give the experience of their content, and sensitises the auditor to receive this. Finally, if the words are recorded visually, their spatial arrangement—the paragraphing and so on, and such devices as the punctuation—should supplement all these by making it as easy as possible to perceive them, and avoiding the introduction of counter-suggestions.* All of which means, of course, that no word exists in literature for itself. Words have no rights except as a vehicle, though as that they are the

---

* I have just read a MS. whose every sentence is treated as a paragraph. The effect is to give an exasperating joltiness to a story that is meant to be dreamily romantic.

richest, fullest, and most sensitive—incomplete as they are—that man has yet devised for conveying experience. Each of the other arts can do some one thing better than the greatest literature: but none of them can do all, or a tithe, of the things of which literature is capable. And no other save drama can follow the living process of the mind in its shifts and turns, not even music, which has, alone of the rest, the dimension of time, but is far more limited in its range of content; while drama itself is limited strictly in time, and further in dealing with the inarticulate. Lord Burleigh in literature can be overdone, and has been considerably so in recent fiction: but he has a due and possible place there, all the same, while in drama he can only be a joke. Literature also has one more advantage. The protean quality of its material form gives it immortalities denied its neighbours. I shall never see the paintings of Apelles, or listen to the airs of Casella's lute: to see the *Man in Armour* or the *Venus of Melos* I must go to the Glasgow Gallery or the Louvre: but I can hear Dante think by stretching my hand for a book I bought in Bisset's for one and sixpence, of which there are thousands of copies in the world, any of which would carry the thought as truly. A brief dance of the air—words are no more: and yet they may overendure a pyramid.

> Not marble, nor the gilded monuments
> Of princes, shall outlast (a) powerful rhyme

So much, then, for the nature of the medium. The question arises, how does S^1 make use of it, how, at this latest stage of his creation, does he force the system of sounds we call a language so to enclose his individual thought that it is no longer a vision within himself but can drive like seed "over the universe"?

The psychological outline of the process is already

THE WRITING 201

familiar. In his endeavour to project I^2 upon the consciousness of S^2, S^1 has already found it necessary to seek among the implications—including the associations—of its components, for those which most reveal its essential significance. Now, if he is practised in the use of words—and just as a painter is in the habit of making little sketches of anything that interests him, so a writer is accustomed within his mind to fit words to anything that happens to interest him at the moment, though he may not take the trouble to write them down—if he is so practised, it is probable, or rather it is certain, that some of these reinforcing associations are already with phonic images, that is to say, with words as such and with the rhythmic or other patterns of articulate speech. These last may possibly precede the words a little: it is not an uncommon experience in writing of anything strongly charged with emotion for the image of the *shape* of the sound, so to speak, to arise before that of the words composing it, just as one may hear the tones of an approaching voice before distinguishing the words it speaks. The business of writing as such, psychogenetically considered, is simply a process of analysing down each image in the structure I^2, or rather in any given part of the structure, to a series of components whose images can be conveyed in single words or very small groups of them (a verb and adverb, a noun and one or more attributive adjectives, any two of these with a conjunction or preposition) and of seeking among the associations of these fragmentary images for the words which are most intimately associated with their precise significance in that ideational context. These words are then built together in such a way that their relation and effect in modifying each other parallel as closely as possible those of the images whose symbolic equivalents they have become.

Now, in order to do this, S^1 requires certain qualifications. We have seen already that he must have the power of analysing very delicately the images with which he is dealing, so as not only to perceive their component parts, but also to discriminate among these and select those charged at present with most significance: and that he needs also an equally delicate sense of the interrelations of such images, and a liveliness of apperceptive power regarding them that is only possible to a well-stored and well-organised mind. But before he can get the product of these gifts satisfactorily laid out on a few sheets of paper, he needs in addition to these, or rather as a specialisation of the last, that among the apperception—systems so brought into play should be a very large and well-organised body of verbal images. To put it more concretely, he must have a memory well stored with words, so that the image formed of any idea calls up the image of the words which would contain it, and these words arrive in consciousness with a full apperceptive charge of all their possible associations.

Quite what is implied in such an apperceptive sensibility to verbal and other phonic images is a little difficult to formulate, for words are a medium unlike any other. One can see that a sculptor must have an extreme sensitiveness to visual-motor sensory stimuli, a musician to auditory-motor, and so on. And since the O^2 which the writer is producing is materially a pattern of sounds in time, as much as music is, it is obvious that he must respond to auditory-motor stimuli as sensitively as the musician. The stimuli, though, are not quite of the same kind. He needs the same sense of rhythm and of tone-quality, but while on the one hand there are no consonants in music, on the other he makes very slight use of pitch (in the European languages at all events)* and so

* I understand that in Chinese at any rate the significance of a word may depend on the pitch of its utterance.

his ear must be rather differently attuned. But there is more to it than that. If anyone read me a melodious piece of Arabic or Persian, it would strike on my consciousness just as a tune does, for I know neither language. But if they read me an equally melodious piece of English, then though I should receive the same sort of auditory-motor percepts, I should also receive another sort as well, in the shape of probably visual and certainly conceptual images, not merely associated with the auditory (as the *Pastoral Symphony* might make me think of the country), but actually conveyed within them—these, too, being not discrete but built up in elaborate systems of relationships, proper to themselves, and not imposed upon them by my imagination. The *Pastoral Symphony* may make you think of Hertfordshire and me of Deeside or the Barvas crofts: but a landscape in Spenser, though it may *remind* us both of different country, conveys a specific image of a particular place, which is neither your Hertfordshire nor my Deeside or Hebrides, but Spenser's County Cork, which is known to neither of us: and we perceive it as such. And Beethoven can convey to us what he *feels* of Napoleon, but Tolstoy could say also what he *thought* of him. The writer thus requires not only an auditory-motor sensitiveness, but a power of forming and relating concepts from both sensory and conceptual material: he must respond to ideas as such, and to their relations, especially to those of deductive and inductive interactions between the particular and the general concept. As among artists in general, this quality of conceptual ratiocination is needed most by the writer and least by the musician. With regard to visual sensitiveness as such, a man can be a writer with very little of it, but he will hardly be able to do creative work of any force, for if his S^2 is a normal-sighted person he will fail to appeal to a large part of his usual range of perceptions, and the image presented will have the incompleteness of a play in the dark. Finally, I think it may be said that just as a Solitary Wasp has a more than ordinary sensory sensibility to the presence of a certain kind of grub which is necessary to her reproductive activity, so a sculptor will have this sensibility to the quality of different sorts of plastic material, a musician to sounds as such, and a writer to the sensory qualities of words as such and of their significance in association with ideas. This sensibility may be greatly developed by training, but in itself it would appear to be an innate characteristic of the individual. It is certainly true that there are people who derive considerable pleasure from words simply as such—some place-names, for example. The title of Mr. Hergesheimer's *Balisand*, for instance, gives me great pleasure, and that from no association with the book itself, which struck me as being for the most part simply a clot of dead words, surprising from the author of *Java Head*. The place-names of West France have attracted me for as long as I can remember: and the reason must be their pure shape and quality as words, for the pleasure dates long before I had been in France, and my nearest inherited connection with that country-side goes back to the middle of the fourteenth century. So medieval words took the Pre-Raphaelites, who now and then went rather drunk on them, and laid themselves open to "the amorous colocynth"—which certainly is a lovely word in itself! Who said "the most beautiful phrase in English is 'halldoor' "? And everyone knows what Milton could achieve out of a mere geographical catalogue, or the names of a dozen or so Asiatic deities.

Let us see what happens to a writer who lacks the elements of the sensory-intellectual complex just described. Suppose he is insufficiently sensitive to the relation between the word, purely as such and in its symbolic value, and the idea—that he has a slovenly sense of exact

THE WRITING 205

connotation, and "uses words loosely" as we say, content to employ those whose significance is *approximately* equivalent to the idea. In that case, even although the percept under the words is clear enough (which it cannot be if it is more than sensory, for conceptual thinking is necessarily verbal, and even sensory, if elaborate, needs words to register the differences), then the percept will not be clearly conveyed to S^2: the words will pucker over it, as it were, as an ill-fitting suit deforms the shape of the body. They will introduce irrelevant associations: they will fail to introduce those which might have served to strengthen the primary image: and they may even distort the bare outline of that, by conveying not X, the idea intended, but Y, which is not by any means the same thing, as when a student described to me Macbeth's entry into "Duncan's sleeping *compartment*", with a pleasing suggestion of the Night Scotsman, or another made Chaucer Controller of *Costumes* in the Port of London, an office not assigned to him by history. A mind insensitive to the relation of word and idea tends to be guided in proceeding from one to the other by a mere association of habitual contiguity without regard to individual shades of significance: hence its automatic reaction to any idea is the word, or more usually the stock-pattern group of words, habitually attached to each of its vague and undifferentiated experiences of the idea. Hence come journalese and all habitual forms of jargon, which serve in fact as a substitute for thought: a man who has been confronted with some object claps a ready-made generic label on it, and feels exonerated from the need of any further reaction.* Again, a man with no sense of visual

---

* Everybody who writes, especially if he has to write for money, should read a certain story of O. Henry's, *Calloway's Code*, in the volume called *Whirligigs*. It combines considerable entertainment with an Awful Warning.

stimuli is badly handicapped in creative writing: for creative writing is essentially the projection of expetience as actually experienced by someone or other—that is, of the actions and passions of human beings: and therefore the conveyance to S^2 of an image of such experience will be greatly helped if that image can appeal to the whole range of percepts by which he would witness it in actual fact. Now, no man can create an image in visual terms unless his mind is charged with images in themselves visual: which is impossible unless he is sensitive to such images. This sensibility may be imaginative rather than sensory, however. (In Milton's case, for instance, there is a remarkable sensibility to visual images: but even before his blindness he appears to receive them in the first place less from actual sensory experience than from the description of them in literature: he is a townsman's poet. Shakespeare, on the other hand, makes you feel that he had actually *seen* what he described.) This point in the writer's qualifications has more to do with earlier stages in the affair: but written words are visual signs in themselves, and the written language has many delicate overtones of association which are not so perceptible in the spoken one. It is more obvious that if his feeling for auditory-motor perception is weak, he may choose his words with an accurate sense of their ideational content, but his writing will none the less be dead and mechanical, for it will lack the overtones given by the auditory-motor pattern which should accompany it. It will stimulate the completely conscious levels of S^2's mental processes, but will go no deeper, and consequently be at the mercy of his subconscious impulses, which may tend to inhibit the fully conscious impulse to focus his attention on it. S^2 will not "warm to the subject", as we say, unless he has already a very strong bent to it. The writer therefore who has been able to find an image for his experience and to

THE WRITING 207

prepare that image for projection in words needs for the accomplishment of this final stage all these discriminations that have been mentioned—of the verbal associations of ideas and of the visual and especially the auditory-motor associations of words and of the possible arrangements of words: and finally, with these, the will to make use of them as far as possible, and a sharp discontent with anything less than the completest equivalence he can achieve between the image and the words conveying it.

When in practice he puts this mechanism into action, it is seldom he finds this equivalence immediately. If he dwells too long and intensely on any element in I^2 at large, he runs the risk of seeing it out of focus, or even of losing touch with its fellow-components. Perhaps his wisest course, certainly that followed in actual practice by many writers, is thus to create first a verbal structure roughly corresponding to I^2 as a whole—in other words, "to get the thing down anyhow", in a rough draft of his complete O^2. He will probably do this on paper, of course, so that he can recall it to his memory. This draft pins down I^2 for his own perception, so that neither the image as a whole nor its components ii^2 or their ii^3 and so forth, can slip away from him. The draft, in short, can convey I^2 to *one* mind—that is to say, to the mind of S^1 himself. It does this because I^2 is already there: which is why so much opaque writing or dead journalese is perfectly satisfactory to its authors.* It conveys a meaning to them, and "the ψcal anal of the ϕa of Σg reasoning discovers some int facts de the rel.^{n} of πs" conveys a meaning to me. But the rubbed-down and loose-fitting journalese of

---

* The famous Jutland Despatch is known to us all: and I have lately received a note in answer to a dinner invitation that left me most completely in the dark as to whether its writer was dining with me or not.

the one and the student shorthand of the other (which translated is "the psychological analysis of the phenomena of syllogistic reasoning discovers some interesting facts concerning the relation of propositions" in a code I devised as an undergraduate for lecture-notes) do not do very much to convey a definite image to S^2. So with the rough draft. S^1 himself can see through it his image embodied at last. "After long toil and tempest's sad assay" he can look across the room and realise that his meaning is stored now not "in some close corner of his brain" but in a completely tangible pile of manuscript, which would exist if death caught him next moment. But he would do well not to misinterpret his strong and quite natural sense of satisfaction. His prince is still in prison, for all of that: the image is only seen through a glass darkly. *He* sees it because, having pondered it long enough to get it down, he has already seen it pretty vigorously. But for other people to see it, who have not had his past experience of O^1 to direct their perceptions, he must somehow force the glass to transparency; that is, he must go over his draft again, seeing it no longer from within, but from S^2's point of view, from the outside, as, precisely, the object of a new experience, which he hopes will coincide with that remembered from O^1. Where the glass is opaque, he must work until it is transparent, testing the words and their arrangement by pondering them in conjunction with the image underlying, until he apperceives a fresh and more satisfying association between the image and some other words.*
The more he does this, up to a given point, the more vivid the image of both words and meaning: but after that point, the words themselves and as such become so prominent that the meaning fades, and he finds himself staring blindly at marked paper. If he is wise, he will put

* See Appendix B.

THE WRITING

the thing away, and not think about it until he finds he has regained fresh vision.

Perhaps the final stage of the affair will be to rewrite the book clear through as a whole, and as rapidly as possible, so that the swing of it bears him along, and he is always conscious of it *as* a whole, and can test each part in vivid relation to that. When he has done this, O^2 is created: and in practice this material body he has made for the image in his mind will already be clothed and protected in O^3, the written words that have recorded it. His book is written, and has passed out of himself. It no longer lives of his life, like an unborn child, but has being and existence of its own, though only potentially yet, for it is not read. His experience now can be relived by someone else: but first its embodiment must reach someone who can relive it, can transpierce that body again and grasp its soul. And in hope of this he sends his work into the world, taking the chance, first, that the experience itself is worth conveying, or is vivid and individual enough to need it: second, that all his labour has in fact conveyed it: and third, knowing quite certainly that like any other "spel" it must be to some a stumbling-block and to others foolishness, he stakes on the hope there are some who will find it neither . . . and that they will not be foolish so to find it. He may doubt of all these things: he may even doubt of them, like Browning's *Pictor Ignotus*, till they choke and inhibit the impulse he might have had. If he is genuinely an artist, then he will doubt, for the world and time are large and his art is only part of himself after all, and how can he know he is not deceiving himself, as he has seen so many men go blind? But his moments of violent certainty carry him on: he takes his chance, and sometimes of worse than this, for knowing that no good cause was ever lost except through its own supporters, he may doubt again that he is harming what he would give his soul for, and blinding the very eyes he would enlighten. He must face these doubts: and if they are more than doubts, have the courage to destroy what he has made: and if they stay doubts (the best he is likely to get), have the courage then simply to turn it loose, and leave it to sink or swim in the world about him, with such advantages as he can give it of a decent format and a reputable imprint. Which having done, he turns his back on it, and faces forward to another work.

CHAPTER XI

THE READER

"I must leave my labour to the man that shall come after me, and who knoweth whether he shall be a wise man or a fool?"
Ecclesiastes

O^2, WE take it, the book which embodies the experience gained by its writer from some earlier object, O^1, has come into existence as itself a possible object of experience. But that this object should be experienced, which is the aim of all S^1's elaborate chain of activity, is not possible without the collaboration of a second subject, S^2, the reader, who is necessary to the completion of the whole process. Accordingly, we must study his part in affairs.

Theoretically, it is a fairly simple matter. Practically, it is in fact rather far from that, as anyone may know who has ever seen a Variorum Shakespeare. But, as S^1, with the hopefulness that is needful to the artist, writes almost always primarily for the perfect reader, it may be as well to sketch first what he hopes will happen, and consider the actualities later on.

O^2—or rather, as we have seen, O^3—comes into the hands of S^2 as a lump of dead matter: to wit, an assemblage of certain sheets of paper, on whose surface marks have been made with a black fluid. Yet this fragment of matter may conceivably have a spiritual force, which in turn may have as potent a drive on matter as anything inside an H.E. shell. Rousseau and other men made marks on paper: there ensued the guillotine on the Place Royale, and a sequence of stricken fields until Waterloo: besides some other things. And yet men can sit down in the midst of libraries, and set forth schemes of materialist philosophy, using a means that itself gives them the lie, and is a great deal more surprising than most enchantments. S^2 can conjure Helen from the shades without the aid of Mephistophilis's glass: he needs only to look down at the marks on his paper . . . and understand what he has seen within them, which may perhaps be a more exacting task than any dramatic piece of necromancy.

He looks at the marks, and by a power of habitual association they call up to his mind certain words—certain sounds, that is, that form a pattern. And these words and the pattern in which they have been arranged at once suggest to him certain ideas, which, as he proceeds through one page after another, he finds have been built up in a design: and this design, whatever it may be, reflects a definite phase of human experience.

Perhaps these ideas may be conceptual—of things that no man can ever perceive with his senses, like a billion as such or duration or causality as such. He is given one of these ideas after another, in a particular order, and each of them presented from a particular angle, in a particular relation with its neighbours. As he goes through the whole series he finds them grouping and re-grouping, no more as a series but as a structure. At length they form for him a single concept, most probably a very complex one, that is the "meaning" of the book as a whole—the concept of a relation between many concepts, as in Croce's *Æsthetic* or Dr. Einstein's book on "Relativity"; or of the relation between various functions and qualities of concrete objects, as in James's *Principles of Psychology* or J. A. Thomson's *Zoology*. And this concept, once it has penetrated his mind, takes its place there, is related to other concepts, already or subsequently present—becomes, in short, a fact of S^2's experience, to which he reacts as he does to any other fact presented to him, by intellectual analysis and comparison, by conscious and subconscious apperception, and by certain instinctive impulses which rise to his consciousness as certain emotions: any or all of which reactions may have an effect upon his subsequent conduct.

Or again, the ideas are not of abstract concepts, but of images in terms of sensory percepts, of certain individual personages, doing and being and suffering certain things, in specific time and place and for given reasons—people as real, perhaps, as his wife across the hearthrug, except that they do not exist objectively, any more than causality does, or the billion, or duration. He forms a percept of these people and their experience by grouping together a number of sub-percepts, which have been presented to him as standing in a given relation to each other. These percepts have a specific affective quality: they arouse emotion of a certain kind. As he goes through the book they group together, until at the close he finds himself aware of a certain phase of life seen as a whole—perhaps, too, seen more clearly and intimately than he is in the habit of seeing anything in "real life" outside his immediate personal experience, and certainly seen in such a way that they rouse a perfectly definite reaction. This total experience is admitted by his critical intellect to be a valid reaction to the data-percepts as he has now perceived them: he accepts it as part of the content of his mind, a datum for reasoning in his future contact with other experience, direct or indirect, of anything analogous to its content, a memory which can be apperceived to other percepts and aid in their interpretation and in the formation of concepts based upon them. In short, it gives data for the interpretation of life, and consequently for the intelligent reaction to life in his personal conduct.

This is the process as S^1 hopes for it, and in fact it may actually take place, entirely, in certain of SS^2: O^2 may be able to convey the experiend, and may meet with somebody who is capable of experiencing it fully when he perceives (as he might not "in real life" have perceived) the objects that are capable of causing it. S^2, however, may derive a good deal from O^2 without being completely capable of this. He may grasp, for instance, the nature of the experience, and feel its quality truly, but less intensely. I do not suppose for a moment I ever feel the emotion that Shakespeare experienced over *King Lear*: but when I see Lear's story through Shakespeare's mind, I perceive the *kind* of experience it gave him, and guess, with some awe, at a depth and intensity my capacity is too small to comprehend. I can feel his smaller emotions more completely, *when I am made to see their objects as he saw them*, though I might not so feel if I saw them for myself. I love Doll Tearsheet, and laugh at her: if I met her in the flesh, it is probable enough I might do neither, or even fail to notice her at all. But if I met her in the flesh after meeting her in Shakespeare, I might see more of what he saw in her, when he met her, or her components, in Paris Garden: and whatever universe of possible action governed my immediate apperceptions concerning the lady, these would be greatly richer in their content, and my action on them correspondingly effective.

Again, S^2 may fail in intellectual comprehension, yet still be profoundly moved by the emotion which is part of I^2. I once sat through a performance of *Romeo and Juliet* next an old lady of the charwoman class: it was a touring company, with no stars, and they gave us the whole play very competently. I hardly think it is snobbish to assume that my neighbour had a less full intellectual comprehension of the play as such than, say, Dr. Bradley would have had. But there was no doubt she echoed its emotions. An Aberdonian shows feeling, in actual fact, as little as an Englishman does in theory: but the tears ran down her face as we came to the end, and she turned to me and said very fervently, "Ech, it's a graund play yon!" I imagine the author, if his ghost were present, would be better satisfied with her reactions than with those of certain professors of literature.

Conversely, there may be a complete intellectual comprehension: but no emotional reaction at all, or merely, perhaps, a feeling of discomfort. S^2 understands that S^1 has seen certain things, and has felt about them in a certain way. He can understand all that is told him about these things, including that they cause certain emotions. But he does not feel these emotions. This reaction is less satisfactory to the author, and not only to the author of creative work. Darwin, for instance, would have been very disappointed if readers of *The Origin of Species* understood what he was saying to them, but remained completely untouched by the interest in it he had hoped to arouse in them. But even if S^1's reaction is thus seriously incomplete, his perception of O^2 can at least enlarge his outlook with regard to the possible content of human experience. He has not shared the experience of S^1, but he has realised the existence of at any rate the percept at its root, and perhaps of objects corresponding to that percept. From S^1's point of view, *c'est déjà quelquechose*.

One or other of these possible reactions is what S^1 has hoped for in his reader: the first, if possible. And if his work is of any value at all, then some of them, or quite possibly all of them, will happen in certain cases, at all events. He may not know that they have, but he hopes, at least: and with luck he may even receive that most precious praise, the only one that counts from people unknown, of finding that someone has *understood* his work, has got from it just what he meant to convey. The "word" he has created has been heard, and now there is someone else who knows as he knows.

There are other possibilities, of course. A book goes through many dangers in the writing: and even supposing it has evaded these, it is faced in the reading with nearly as many others. We will assume that O^2, whatever it is, is a competent piece of work as it stands finished. Its subject and the setting-forth of its subject are completely capable of conveying its theme, and themselves are set forth in turn in language that is a transparent case for them. Now the first risks that this work will have to run are those of the malperception of the words. S^2, in the first place, may not know the meaning of certain among them, or what is more dangerous still, he may know it vaguely, or perhaps even not know that words can have clear meaning. He may, in short, only half-know his mother-tongue. This is, in fact, a terribly common condition, and one it is difficult to avoid, perhaps, in a nation compulsorily half-educated. I append some instances, all of them actual cases, taken at first hand from the work of training-college students, all of whom had received a secondary education, and all of whom were intending to become teachers. I should add in justice that the later years of their school life were during the war, when schools were understaffed and in many ways considerably handicapped . . . but they had all had their primary education under normal conditions: and in England, a primary education is all that is received by 94 per cent. of the population. I asked a newly entered class, as an exercise, to write sentences containing certain given words. Many of them, of course, did this quite correctly: but some of the rest gave me, among other specimens of the sort, "The orator sought to eliminate the chief factors in his speech". "She was so condign." "If we eliminate the causes of the war, we find that Germany was to blame." "When the danger was over, the company transpired freely." Other specimens, mostly from London University students, include, "Shelley writes of far-fetched themes, dealing more with morality than with real life". "Scott was unconscientiously preparing himself for the future exercise of his genious" (sic). "Through these works runs a strong local current of scenery." "The Elizabethan stage was without dresses." "An outflow of stories poured into the country." "The pivot turns round a central character." This blindness is not confined to unfamiliar words. In England, at any rate, I had to explain to every new class of students that *and* and *but* were not quite interchangeable. The general impression seemed to be that such small words could not matter very much. Here are two actual examples of conjunctions as used: I give my word of honour that the two quotations are reproduced verbatim. The first is from a London student's essay, on a subject chosen by himself from a list of half a dozen.* "The study of Roman literature, which was chiefly political, had a great influence upon the political affairs of the time. For it was at this time that famous painters like Raphael began to be admired." The other is from a letter in the *Daily Telegraph*, protesting against Miss Scott's design for the Stratford Theatre: "If, as your correspondent remarks, the plan is an example of English architecture, then let women keep their place as women, and let men do these jobs, as they have always done."

Now, people who use words in this way in writing are not very likely to receive clear images from those that they encounter in their reading. The same sort of thing may happen to a man reading another language than his own, or an unfamiliar form of his own language—an

* Not set by me.

average Englishman loses, for instance, the finer flavour of both Burns and the best parts of Scott, and unless he has been fortunate in school, may be in the same predicament with Chaucer, even with Spenser. But there is only too much evidence that the difficulty is far too common with regard to plain King's English. A surprising number of university students, asked to "answer not more than six questions" will answer seven, or will offer answers to both A and B, which are plainly labelled as alternatives. There are forms, of course, that justify some vagueness: the clerical troubles of the Inland Revenue must be considerable, but they ask for them.

The result of this blurred perception of word-values will be, of course, that the words read by S^2 will convey only a rough approximation to the ideas and images that S^1 has intended. And the total image perceived by means of O^2 will be as unlike that intended by S^1 as (I hope) certain amateur snapshots are unlike me. Certain important sub-images will not appear at all: others will be distorted, or half present: and the relations between them will ipso facto be falsified.

In a case less extreme than this, S^2 may be aware of the direct ideational meaning of the individual words within a given context, yet may fail to perceive their important overtones. For an obvious instance, it takes a good classical scholar—a first-rate Latinist, at all events—to get the full, complete, and perfect quality of almost any sentence of *Paradise Lost*. I have myself a fair sense of English word-values: but when I read Milton I am aware that I am only receiving the equivalent of the transposition of an orchestral piece for the piano, or at best for a quartette. I have the outline of the content clearly enough: I have sufficient philosophical background to cope with the ideas, which in any case are neither very abstruse nor personal to Milton: and I have ear enough to appreciate the auditory values. But I have not the classical background to pick up more than about one in three of the implied allusions that enrich the texture. I can guess how much enriched that texture would be if I knew my Vergil as well as Milton did: but that is about as far as I can get. The chains of apperception Milton intended to forge hang into space so far as I am concerned. I know they are there, but I cannot follow them. And a reader with still less classical equipment might not realise that they are there at all.

Now, S^2's acquaintance with S^1's particular range of implied allusion may be as scanty as mine with this of Milton's. This is not always the result of a lack in general education. The scholarly critic is often as unsafe here as the Man in the Street, though the defect may lie in different directions. To take a very obvious example, suppose S^1 is using words with reference to an implied philosophical or theological background, and S^2, professional critic though he is, has not (as in contemporary England he probably will not have) the smallest acquaintance with any branch of philosophy. He will lose the words' third dimension almost completely. Or again, suppose S^1 makes use of some analogy drawn from a delicate observation of country life, and S^2 is a townsman, to whom trees are trees, with no more to it than that. Again there is a leakage in the meaning. Shakespeare, for instance, is given to using technical terms (though never very abstruse ones to his own audience) in a more or less metaphorical fashion that derives half its force from his extremely delicate sense of both the direct and the analogical values, as with the double sense of *sessions* and *summon* in the sonnet that begins

> When to the sessions of sweet silent thought
> I summon up remembrance of things past.

It is more subtle than a common metaphor . . . and but for the *sessions* that gives a key at the beginning (it is much the most obvious of the allusions) one would miss the full force of several later phrases, like, "And weep afresh time's long-since-cancelled woe".* All Shakespeare's writing has this many-dimensional quality —increasingly so in his later work, as he drops the more obvious forms of it, using less of the actual pun or adduced comparison, and more of these swift allusions in solution, that give (in an age as sensitive to word-values as the early seventeenth century undoubtedly was) a sort of iridescence of sub-meaning to the definite primary content of the word, so giving to this content the depth and richness that perception at large would have to a mind like Shakespeare's—a richness agony to some lesser minds, who grow angry with envy at the sight of it. This sort of resentment, indeed, is not uncommon. S^2 may be aware, just as a parvenu is aware among gentlemen, that there are overtones of some kind or another that he is unable completely to pick up. And if he has a touchy temperament, he resents his half-conscious sense of inferiority, and transfers his resentment to O^2 that causes it, rationalising it in curious ways.†

Again, the words may have altered in meaning with lapse of time. This is the greatest weakness of the medium, for S^2 may not have sufficient historical knowledge even to know that this change may have occurred, let alone to comprehend the original sense, or even to realise it from the context. There is a noble collect in the Prayer

---

* There is the same echo in "cancel and tear to pieces this great bond", where there is a similar double sense of significance in *bond* itself—the direct sense of a legal obligation and an echo of that of being trapped and fettered.

† A vindictive hatred of art is stronger and more widespread (at any rate in Protestant countries) than educated people are accustomed to realise, and sometimes reaches an extraordinary and rather ghastly pitch of rancour.

Book that begins, "Prevent us, O Lord, with thy most gracious favour, and further us with thy continual help". If to S^2 "prevent" means only to inhibit, and in addition he has no Latin and is not capable of putting the two halves of the sentence together, he will not guess that the word which puzzles him may have a second, less familiar, meaning. Very frequently, of course, he will not trouble to think that a word in the Prayer Book means anything at all—an indifference apparently shared by many clergy, to judge by their treatment of the greatest prose in the language.

Closely connected with this lack of word-perception, there is another possible channel of leakage. S^2 may be deficient in the power of comprehending relative emphasis. Say to him, "Mrs. X has a snub nose, but she is charming", and he will read it, "Mrs. X is charming, but she has a snub nose" . . . or even simply, "Mrs. X has a snub nose". He has, in the former case, grasped the meaning of most of the words, but he has not grasped the meaning of their arrangement, that reinforces the "very little one" in the middle. Consequently, though he may be aware of the components of the image, he will not grasp their mutual interrelations, and so will have a distorted sense of their sum: he may perceive ii^2 and yet have a false perception, or none, of I^2. This kind of failure, in fact, is heartrendingly common. The number of people who can write an accurate précis of any narrative or argument is almost negligible, as I know from sad experience as an examiner. Ask the average English undergraduate to summarise the content of a chapter of Burke (who is, one would think, a fairly lucid reasoner) and the odds are at least five to one that he will give you, very carefully, all the incidental illustrations, and leave out, just as carefully, what they illustrate. As for the average newspaper-reporter, I leave the calculation of the odds to anyone who has done much public speaking, or who reads, perhaps, a couple of daily papers—an amusing if disconcerting exercise. What happens, apparently, is that S^2 picks out from the images presented those that interest him as such and in themselves, and proceeds to let his mind drift in apperceptions of his own, starting, to be sure, from the images presented, but determined not by the relation in which they are presented, but by the dominant interest in his own mind: and as S^2 is not capable of analysing ideas, he fails to distinguish his own from those of S^1—a failure very familiar, for instance, in gossip.

S^2, again, may grasp the direct implications of the words, including those of the logical relation between their contents. But he may fail entirely to comprehend the secondary but important significance of the pattern of their arrangement considered as such. In the most obvious example of this, he has no sense of the significance of metre: indeed, it is not so very long ago that children in school were deliberately *trained*, in reading verse aloud, to ignore the metre. This, for some reason, was thought to be "natural" by people who apparently had never seen a dog wag its tail or heard a baby drumming with a spoon. Most children, in fact, have a keen and delighting sense of rhythmical values: they tend to read verse in a chant, as poets do. And to train this natural sense into atrophy is as educative as training a man to be colour-blind. In fact, to read the greatest verse of Shakespeare for the purely intellectual content as such and alone is like preferring to take one's Titian from a photograph. A great deal of what Titian or Shakespeare meant remains, of course: but much (and often the main thing) is ignored.

With regard to verse, at all events, this mistake is perhaps less common than it was. But few people realise that prose has shape also, and that this shape may be quite definite, and counts. One notices this often when reviewers quote. Even when the quotation is there, precisely, to show the writer's "excellent prose style", it may have its back broken, its cadence mangled by mispunctuation, and perhaps a word or two altered here and there, till the writer can hardly know it for what he wrote, and the reader of the review is justified in wondering why it was praised.

This defective sense of rhythm means inevitably a defective perception of relative emphases, and also at least a very uncertain sense of the emotional significance of what is read. And when, as frequently happens in creative writing, a grasp of the quality of certain highly specific emotional reactions is the whole aim of the creation of O^2, to ignore in this way its emotional significance is like buying a Rolls-Royce to keep the coals in—a complex object, laboriously created, and very valuable for a special purpose, is, to put it mildly, somewhat underemployed.

There may be also a defective perception of the sound-values other than rhythmical. A gross example of this is the (comparatively recent) carelessness of the Southern Englishman over the enunciation of his r's, owing first to the adenoids endemic in an urban population and then to the prestige of the metropolis causing this adenoid-affected speech to be imitated by neighbouring communities. It is a somewhat quaint phenomenon that although a man is socially damned for omitting a mere initial aspirate, a very unimportant sound phonetically, he can murder his r's as much as ever he likes, and people will still continue to ask him to dinner. And yet a man who is tone-deaf to r is nearly as handicapped in dealing with much great English literature as a man who is colour-blind to red would be when he went round the

National Gallery. Some of the most exquisite sound-patterns in Milton, Shakespeare, and Spenser derive half their value from the skilful use of this sound among the rest, especially in conjunction with the liquids, to which it adds the needful virility. The r-sound, of course, is not the only sufferer. The marvellous range and play of English vowels is dulled into a colourless monophone by the adenoised Cocknification of the language that is now affecting even the upper classes: it is sad—and rather serious—to reflect that an Oxford education should completely unfit a man for reading aloud the finest prose in English. To ignore the true value of the sounds of literature is to ignore some part of the given O^2: and since each such part is ex hypothesi significant, to ignore some portion of the total meaning.

The manner in which S^2 is handicapped by an inadequate sense of oo^2—the actual words or groups and arrangements of words that go together to make up O^2—is closely connected with, in fact overlaps, the results of a faulty perception of ii^2. It will of course bring this about in any case. But there may at the same time be other causes. S^2 may have a clear comprehension of the words, severally, that embody any specific i^2, and yet fail to grasp that fully, or even at all. This is surprisingly common—much more so, in fact, than anyone would easily realise who has not been through the whole "press" of a single book that has happened to be extensively reviewed. I shall illustrate unblushingly from my own press-cuttings, not because I have suffered worse than other people, but because, if Smith says Jones has declared that S is P and I say Jones said nothing of the sort, Smith may be right and I may be mistaken; but if Smith says the heroine of my new novel is a dark Czechoslovak of twenty, and I say she is a fair Canadian of thirty-five, I may claim in this case to speak with more authority. I am not talking here of critical opinion. It is natural that people should differ in that: I have observed, without very much surprise, that *The Times Literary Supplement* describes as "a fine exhibition of strength in design and execution" a book of which the *Sheffield Telegraph* remarks that "the authoress has tried to ally the methods of Elinor Glyn with the sentiments of Annie S. Swan".* But one does expect that a professional reader should know what a book has actually said, however he may disagree with the statement, or dislike the writer's method of presenting it. Yet even as I am writing this very sentence there arrives a New York summary of my last novel. The hero of the book is the son of a small Scots laird, who has farmed his father's little estate ever since he grew up—a fact that has a good deal of bearing on the story. But he appears in the summary as *Captain* Keith. I have tried to trace the psychological origin of this rather surprising commission, but remain at a loss. In summarising the plot of another book, a reviewer makes it turn on a *mariage blanc*, which in fact does not exist in it at all. And the review in which this summary occurs is not in the *Little Pedlington Gazette*, but in what is generally considered—by myself among other people—as the doyen of our literary weeklies: the writer thought the book sufficiently important to give it a long notice in large type, and was obviously not prejudiced against it, for the critical part of the notice was most friendly, and showed he had read with a good deal of enjoyment. Again, there is another novel of mine which ends with a marriage enforced by circumstances and their own past actions on two people who know it must mean disaster. Fault might no doubt be justifiably be found with this, as an unnecessarily painful conclusion: indeed, my own conscience was

* Quotations verbatim.

rather troubled over it, for that reason. But one would hardly expect that the book should be condemned because of an inappropriate "happy ending". Yet more than one reviewer has so condemned it. Again, it was a very important weekly, to whose opinions I give considerable weight, which quoted in inverted commas part of a sentence I had actually written, applied it to a subject to which it did not belong and of which my (fully stated) opinions were exactly opposite, and damned me heartily for saying the exact reverse of what I had said. Here, perhaps, one might have suspected a certain impatience: but in the other cases there was obviously no sort of desire, even subconscious, to misrepresent the book. Yet after this it is perhaps not so startling to find a Boston reviewer describe a novel as "happenings which *begin* when two men in the Scottish Highlands face each other at fifteen paces on the field of honour", when in fact the book has no connection with the Highlands, and the only duel mentioned in the whole of it is fought somewhere after the end of its last chapter! * I could add a good many other examples to these, and so, I have not the least doubt, could anyone else who cherishes a collection of press-cuttings. I have merely taken those that first came to hand as quotable without much explanation. I am not attacking reviewers as a class, and I do not suggest that any of these gentlemen had any intention of misrepresenting, or even that all reviewers misrepresent: I have just found a cutting from the *Glasgow Herald* which summarises the contents of a critical book of nearly five hundred closely printed pages a great deal better

---

* This is hardly, perhaps, a really fair example. The poor man had obviously been led astray by that abomination known as the blurb—in other words, the publisher's ecstasies that sprawl over the front of the paper jacket. That of the American edition was not very lucid, and the reviewer had—well, economised effort a little. We are all mortal: and he was sportsman enough to give no opinion.

than its author could have done, and gets the summary and some thoughtful criticism into the space of about five hundred words. The point of the citations is that it is possible to find these crude and obvious misapprehensions in the perception of professional readers, dealing with a very short novel with a very simple story, printed in large clear type and so straightforwardly presented that someone always remarks that a thing as simple as this really can't be Art. What then can we assume may sometimes happen to a casual amateur let loose on St. Paul's Epistles or on the later novels of George Meredith?

The result of this defective perception upon the total percept of I^2 will depend, of course, on how many of ii^2—and also on which of them—are thus falsified. Probably nobody reads a book for pleasure and takes in every single detail of the sub-images. But one man may overlook nothing of importance, another may miss the whole point of the plot, or the clause on which turns the conclusion of the argument: and while in the one case I^2 is not materially distorted, in the other it simply has not been seen at all—S^2 has substituted for it a kind of I^3, built up in part of some of I^2's components, but containing also others apperceived to these, which have no place at all in the real I^2. For instance, it is a very common phenomenon, in all fields of perception, that when a man has seen A, which in his experience is normally accompanied by B, he is apt to believe sincerely that what he has seen is not A but (A + B). The gentleman who introduced a *mariage blanc* into the plot of *The Half Loaf*, and thereby somewhat surprised the said book's author, probably did so because, as a reviewer, he had read a good many books in which the opening situation was somewhat similar, and had been followed by the one he attaches to it. (That, in fact, was a very popular plot some years ago.) So with the "happy ending" which distressed reviewers of the other book. A happy ending, in a novel, usually means a wedding: therefore an ending "indubitably matrimonial" must be a happy one, which they were right in declaring to be wrong . . . only it does not happen to be there! The debate in the Commons on the Revised Prayer Book showed some excellent instances of this fallacy.

Akin to this, perhaps, is what sometimes happens when S^2's experience of life has been rather narrow. One or other of a set of ii^2 may disagree with this experience, and he fails to notice that the unfamiliar image is presented as occurring in a setting which differs from that of his daily life, and consequently condemns it out of hand. A New York reviewer, for instance, is rather pained because the hero of a certain novel takes off his hat to his wife when he says good-bye to her—the hero being a Scots gentleman of normal decent manners. A friend of the author's objected to the same novel that it puts the reader off by a glaring improbability on the first page: the improbability turned out to be the mention of a forest wall as of "weathered granite" . . . "which of course is much too expensive for walls in woods". The wall in question was in Aberdeenshire, where in fact its stones "are alive to this day to testify": the lady objecting had never been north of Bedford. There was a Boston critic of a first novel who patted it gently on the head as a very pretty and promising piece of work, then shook his own and gravely informed the author that she had better not write about Scotland until she had been there. She happened to be a Scotswoman born and bred . . . but it may be added as excuse for him that the scene was a district still free from the tourist. Conversely, if ii^2 fit his preconceived ideas, he may swallow considerable improbabilities without turning a hair, and accept as true to life a pseudo-realistic I² which is far remote from it: the American lady who stuck at the raised hat might have made no objection to an English country gentleman dining at home in a white tie and tails, as I recently saw one do in a Hollywood film.

The malperception of some among ii² is probably the commonest source of a hitch in perceptive process at this level. But the omission to note the specific relations obtaining between the images may also distort the perception of I². For instance, a large part of the point of *Othello* depends on the fact that although the hero is brought to behave as a man temperamentally jealous, he is really very far from being such a man. Iago, indeed, who knew him pretty thoroughly, actually says as he considers the data of the plot he is beginning to form,

> The Moor is of a free and open nature
> That thinks men honest that but seem to be so.

Yet even people who ought to know much better, speak of him as a study in jealous rage, because they have failed to grasp the development (i.e., the mutual relation) of the processes by which Othello is made to act as Leontes might, and without which he would be the last man so to act. Yet if he were in fact another Leontes, the whole play would be merely a blank verse *Maria Marten*. And there is really quite a difference.

This failure to note relations between ii² sometimes takes the form of a failure to infer from ii² actually presented other important ones intended to be inferred, but left to the imagination of S². S¹, in effect has said to him, "Here is 2 . . . and here again is 3", and expected him to think, "Oh, that makes 5", and regard this 5 as part of the data for the next development of the perceptual process. But he has merely answered, as it were, "Yes, 2 . . . and 3. . . . Very well, what next?" And when the "next" assumes "5" he is puzzled and cross, and wonders what the author is driving at. He has read too passively, and not given the writer the collaboration asked from him. Or perhaps he did not know that $2 + 3$ made 5, and thus was unable to make the deduction required. Again the I^2 appears to him imperfectly.

At a profounder level of perception there are other dangers, that are harder still for S^1 to guard against, and perhaps, since they are matters less of carelessness than of temperament, more difficult too for S^2 to avoid, if he happens to be prone to them by nature. Suppose that S^2 has a perfectly clear intellectual perception of ii^2 and of the various interrelations through which they form the total image I^2. He knows exactly the stages by which Macbeth came to murder Duncan and can give you in order, numbered and labelled, the subsequent events that led to his death. He could give you an able and perfectly lucid précis of Lady Macbeth's arguments and of those which her husband produces to counter them, and write learned notes upon the cat i' the adage, the various contents of the witches' cauldron, and whether it was a *shoal* or *school* of time. And he will not have the ghost of a notion what the play means. It will not even occur to him, in fact, to wonder whether it does mean anything but that William Shakespeare, having to earn a living, described with quite remarkable incorrectness a passage or two from early Scottish history, more accurately rendered by Hume Brown. Or if he does decide there is a meaning, then Lady Macbeth is the President of the L.C.C., trying to induce the Chairman of the Board of Works to burke the plans for the new drainage system which in fact did not go through about five years before the play was written. This is not an actual specimen, to be sure: but a Miss Winstanley has described *Hamlet* as a sort of political cartoon upon these lines, giving Shakespeare's views about the Scottish succession.* S², in fact, may grasp the subject clearly, and remain completely oblivious of the theme, as a man might make a perfect drawing of a sewing-machine, and be able to name every part of it, without having any notion of what it was for.†

Now critics who look at art from this point of view may be as intelligent as Euclid himself. But my charwoman in the gods at Aberdeen had a deeper sense, by a lot, of æsthetic values. As Aristotle might have led them to see, art is essentially discipline for emotion—that is, a discipline for instinctive impulse. And the greatest art is apt to deal with the most powerful and most fundamental impulses. But its interpretation—whether in general as the science of æsthetic or in specific aspects as criticism—is terribly apt to fall into the hands of men whose instinctive impulses are shallow and feeble. (This may be masked by their feebleness of will, as it often is among very "arty" people.) As a result, the portrayal of the quality of very profound and equally powerful emotion is described and analysed as if a man should describe a picture as an area of so many square feet

---

* Miss Winstanley is a teacher of English Literature.

† A very common modification of this divorcing of the theme and subject takes the form of regarding the events described in the book as if they were real life, and discussing them as such. For instance, at the opposite end from Miss Winstanley, someone once wrote to prove that Hamlet was a woman in disguise, in love with Horatio: and we may have learned essays on the professors he sat under at Wittenberg, on whether Brabantio kept a butler or not, on whether Bottom was a trade-unionist, or on the flowers that bloom in the spring around Elsinore. Which is rather a compliment to the author, certainly, since it shows his book is carrying conviction. But (though even Dr. Bradley has not escaped it) to treat Hamlet as a product of Wittenberg instead of remembering that Wittenberg is (for the play at least) inferred from Hamlet, and he from something more than Saxo Grammaticus, is to ignore completely the nature of art. *Hamlet* is not a record of certain facts in Danish history: but the record of a state of mind of Shakespeare's, which he is trying to induce us to share by presenting us with stimuli to produce it.

of oil-painted canvas containing so many square inches of flesh colour, so many of blue, so many of green, and so forth, all accurately catalogued by shape, area, and colour: and omit to mention that it happened to be a portrait of Monna Lisa.

In some cases, at least, this may be due to bad initial training: the reader simply does not know what to look for, as a man who has no experience of horses will not know what he is seeing when he buys one. We have to *learn* to read, and we only begin the process after we have learned to identify words in print. A baby or a savage, seeing a picture, does actually perceive it as a mosaic of flat colour: the power to see it as representing something comes later. And although this later development would come naturally to anyone growing up among civilised people, a false conception of literature (or of any other art) may be inculcated by education. It is no exaggeration, as the Commissioners on the Teaching of English would sadly agree, to say that people are frequently trained to believe that the right and proper way to read a book is to worry at one little snippet after another, without relating them: or to draw up a summary of its subject-matter. Which is rather like saying that if you ran me through a mincer, or extracted my skeleton and set it up, the result would be me, and having contemplated it for a while, you would enjoy the full pleasure of my acquaintance. If the victim of this form of education has been born with any feeling for art at all, he is seized with nausea at the bare idea of a book, and ceases to read as soon as he is able . . . which at all events is better for his soul than if he had gone on to read in this way. If he has not, he continues as he has been taught, and becomes in time a certain kind of scholar, and probably edits a school edition of Shakespeare or a series of potted versions of famous novels, to be published in twenty-six fortnightly parts, for the purpose of teaching the masses to love literature.

Education is not always the trouble, however. The root of the matter may go deeper than that, to the most fundamental dichotomy of human nature—one as deep as sex (though in fact it cuts across that) and productive of rather more trouble, if anything. A fails, in the last resort, to assimilate the inner core of B's work, not because he is stupid or badly trained or reads carelessly, but because A and B are two different kinds of men. There are many kinds of people in the world, but at bottom all of them fall in just two classes, which it is very difficult to define. Perhaps the handiest label, for practical purposes, is to call them the Shakespeare men and the Milton men—a description which has at any rate the merit of suggesting nothing discreditable to either. The reader will probably recall a famous verse about

> Every little boy and gal
> That's born into the world alive,

but the Milton-Shakespeare formula is clearer cut, for although probably every "little Liberal" is of the Milton type of mind, not every "Conservative" is of the Shakespeare. Mr. Baldwin, for instance, is, and Mr. John Buchan: while Dean Inge and Lord Birkenhead are certainly Miltonic.

Now, between men of these two classes, however much they may like and admire each other, there lies what a student once called "an unbreachable gulf". You may find it drawn for all time in the mutual attitude of Shakespeare's Antony and Octavius Cæsar. The distinction between them appears to be that the one can only love what he can look down on and so tries to force life into the mould of himself: he cannot, and resents what he may not so force, ignoring it when he can, and when that is not possible, seeking to destroy it, with the eager resentful hate that is born of fear. The other has an essential humility.* He takes the impact of life as it comes upon him: and if he is strong, will not be dazed by it, or lose the power to choose among its values: he accepts its antinomies as they arrive, and if he is intelligent seeks their law, without trying to impose one from within himself. The one sees life steadily, but never whole: the other whole, whether steadily or not.

There are good men and bad of both kinds, wise men and fools. Each class has produced great men in all walks of life, and it would seem, as we look back on history, that now the one class is dominant, and now the other. The division, too, may cut across social classes, but on the whole the typical gentleman and the typical free peasant are of one type (which is why these two can understand each other) and the typical bourgeois, of all levels, of the other, from Soames Forsyte, let us say, to Elmer Gantry. A friend suggests that what I am trying to describe is merely the clash of Catholic and Protestant: but this division is in practice no clearer than the political one I have rejected. One is the more likely to prefer—if he understand it—the one faith, the other the other: but that is all there is to it in practice. The sincerely devout Presbyterian Montrose falls into the same class as Sir Thomas More: James VII and II, who gave up three kingdoms for the Church of Rome, is as much a "Milton" man as, say, John Knox.

However we label them, the types exist, and recognise each other by what would almost seem a sort of instinct. As much as they may like and admire each other, there

---

* It is only a proud man, of course, who can achieve humility in the true sense of the word, as only a humble man can be really proud.

is always a certain fundamental disharmony. To the Milton man the Shakespeare man is a sprawling tangle of inconsistencies: and he disapproves, from his soul, of inconsistencies. Yet the Shakespeare man, thanks to his balance between opposites, has a richness and easy rounded vitality which tend to arouse the intense and bitter hatred that comes from a sense of inferiority to what, on one's own most cherished principles, one should be comfortably free to despise. On the other hand, the Shakespeare man has less difficulty in understanding the Milton man: but he is very well aware that at bottom the latter will never quite be able to grasp the things that matter most vitally to himself, and feels in face of him that terrible helplessness that comes of knowing that what one is trying to say cannot be understood by the person hearing it: so, like a man who speaks before deaf judges, he in turn is afraid, and men hate what they fear.

This fundamental antagonism shows in matters of art as well as everywhere else. It is why even great artists may fail to understand each other, why a superb scholar like Dr. Bradley, one of the finest minds that ever wrote about the plays of Shakespeare, is ill at ease with *Antony and Cleopatra*. When a smallish man of the one kind comes on the work of a great man of the other, the reaction is bound to include a certain hostility. If the smaller man is of the Milton type, he will tend, too, to ignore what he disapproves of, if his principles say he ought to like the author: or if there be not any such compulsion, to see these elements exclusively. The history of Shakespeare criticism would illustrate these statements very fully. The effects on fundamental comprehension, when S^1 and S^2 belong to the two classes, are too obvious to need further pointing out.

So far, we have considered S^2, as one might say from

S^1's point of view. He has existed for us merely as S^1's collaborator, the recipient, more or less sensitive, but passive, to whose conscious perception O^2 has been offered. But in fact to consider him only thus is inadequate, for S^2 is an autonomous personality. He not only perceives, but actively reacts to what he perceives: and these reactions depend on the subject reacting no less than on the object to which he reacts.* The preceding section, indeed, has already suggested this, for the "fallacies" in reading which it describes depend on causes within S^2 himself. Nevertheless, I have taken them, for convenience, as merely the flaws possible in a medium whose end is just to receive a perfect impression. It is necessary now to go a little farther, and consider S^2 no longer in terms of S^1 but in those of himself.

It is as well to face boldly the fact that we are discussing what S^2 *ought* to do, supposing him a normal human adult of reasonably developed intelligence, confronted with a book—that is, requested to receive certain percepts which call for reactions of a certain type. What he has first to do is obviously to make sure what these percepts are, both individually and in the mass. He must know, that is, just what the book contains, receive a true impression of I^2, and infer, if possible, what this particular image is intended to convey to him. And this perception, if the image in question is complex or unfamiliar, requires his collaboration in the process. It calls, that is, for an exercise of the will. He must attend to it, and in terms of itself, and not be tempted, we might say, to listen

* There is an interesting parallel to this in a well-known phenomenon of hypnosis. The "subject" may be apparently completely under the "control"—that is, with the consciousness closed to any perceptions but those presented to him by the hypnotist. But if the latter suggests, for instance, that his subject should knock down his mother, then deep-rooted convictions will reassert themselves against the control. So a man "loses himself in a book" only so long as it does not counter some deep-rooted and important disposition.

in English when he is spoken to in French or Latin. This itself may call for a good deal of conscious effort, especially when, for historical or temperamental or other reasons, the writer's mental background and range of apperceptions is very markedly different from his own. He must take the images or concepts presented to him as they are grouped in their actual presentation: that is, he must accept the form as well as the content of O^2, a lesson that seems remarkably difficult to learn with regard to literature at least, and more especially with regard to the literature intended as the "score" of drama, for we cut about and dislocate our Shakespeare as we would never dream of doing with Bach or Rembrandt, Rodin or Christopher Wren. If he fails to do this he runs the risk of failing to make those inferences from juxtaposition of ideas that are as much a vital part of the work as anything that is actually presented in it. He must, then, attempt to see all the components of O^2 in relation to each other and to the whole, if they are worth considering at all; and see the whole as growing from the parts—that is, as something more than their mere sum.

But it is not enough to do only this. A man does not exist only to read a book, let that book be the greatest ever written. He is not only the reader of *The Divine Comedy*: he is a man, as Dante was a man. And the nearer he is to Dante's size of a man, the more will his universe hold besides Dante's book, and the more intimately will he relate to each other the parts of that universe, with the book among them. He needs that relation, in fact, to comprehend it, for all through his reading he has already been asked to make certain apperceptions of images in the book to others not directly presented in it. If Shakespeare says, "Cancel and tear to pieces this great bond", he is asking us to relate Macbeth's state of mind to what we already know of the compulsion of a legal obligation. If we do not do that, we do not understand what is said to us. If he alludes again to "the mightiest Cæsar", he expects us to recall, as we pass the words, what we know about a great historical figure, and through that, our own impression of great men . . . and so forth. There must be this readiness on our part to a certain activity in relating what he tells us to what we know. It is not enough merely to accept the images he actually presents. We must also evoke other images, to fulfil them.

Now, suppose S^1 has a fuller and richer range of experience, in that particular universe of it, than S^2, or even suppose that in this they are fairly equal, but that their experience is not coterminous, as in fact will necessarily be the case, since no two of us have identically the same. Obviously, the more fully S^2 makes relevant apperceptions to S^1's images, the more will his own perception be enriched. The new images will transcend and vitalise those possessed already: he sees too that inference springs truly from datum, but goes farther and deeper than he had means to carry it. Or, if so much as this is not the case, he finds a clearer expression—that is, a clearer definition—of some image or concept that is already part of his mental furniture. But suppose again that S^2 is superior here? Suppose Shakespeare is reading Miss Ethel Dell? Again he will apperceive the images presented to others already present in his mind: and instead of the two blending to enrich each other he will find that the new images refuse to be related to the others, and further that in point of fullness and of truth to perceived objective reality they stand comparison very ill with those already present in his mind. They render inadequately what he knows or infers, already or from the data given him.

This process of testing goes on through all layers of

the business, from the primary perception of the words as in relation to ideas, a relation vague and cloudy upon the one hand, or intimate and organic upon the other, down to the apprehension of the central theme from the completely experienced work of art—a theme which may be, at the one extreme, the reaction of a feeble little mind to some half-comprehended aspect of human experience, on which it has only a thin and narrow outlook, at the other the all but intolerably intense reaction of a vast personality to some huge synthesis of ultimates.

Between these phases of the perceptive process comes the corresponding testing of the component images and of the sub-images that build up these, for their truth to objective fact and subjective experience and to the interrelation of the two. He judges the known by conformity with his own recollection, and the unknown by its congruity with the known, or when that standard is impossible, he will take the author on trust when he speaks of unknowns if his presentation of the known is accurate. Conversely (to quote an instance noted lately), if an eminent authority on Comparative Religion shows that he thinks "the Immaculate Conception" is a phrase for the same thing as "the Virgin-Birth"—a point on which any Roman Catholic charwoman, not to say sixpenny manual of devotion, could have enlightened him in a couple of minutes—what he says, or infers, about Patagonian creeds will be accepted with a certain reserve.

I do not wish to be taken as implying that the reader must savour and test in this detailed fashion every book that happens to come into his hands. If he is going to describe it to someone else, he should, as a simple matter of decency, form a reasonably accurate notion of what it contains. But if he is only reading for his own sake, the case is different: for life is short, and the annual output of books is staggering. These standards apply to the books that he finds worth reading, on the preliminary evidence—either the opinion of a competent judge, his own inference from what he knows of the author, or a brief preliminary inspection of the book. It is possible to tell a live book from a dead one (which is the most important distinction of all, though many reviewers never think of making it) by reading a couple of pages taken at random. A writer who shows certain qualities here will ipso facto be incapable of certain others: it is not necessary to hear me through the whole part of Brunnhilde before deciding I was not intended to be a successful operatic singer. In fact, an expert and hardened publisher's reader can tell a dud almost by smelling it, though if his firm are what is technically known as tripe-merchants, he may have to read farther to guess if the thing is fairly likely to sell . . . a question far more difficult to determine, for badness is no more guarantee here than merit.

To read alertly consists then in a delicate balance between passive recipience and active reasoning, the latter including not merely an explication of what is implicit in the perceived ideas but a testing of those by their apperception to ideas not thus implicit, but already present in the reader's mind. Among these latter will be certain concepts that give, as it were, a norm for human reactions. For instance, if S^2 has present in his mind a clear idea of coherence of thought as a desirable quality of human mental process, he will "test for this", as a chemist would say, what he reads. If he has a definite concept of what is involved in honesty to facts, or a concept (which does not mean a formula) of beauty, he will test for that, and so on, in proportion to the number and clarity of the standards already formed by his evaluation of past perceptions—by the organisation, that is, of the recollections derived from past experience in the light of certain derived normative concepts, or "ideals" as we generally call them.

In short, S^2 is not only the recipient: he is also, whether consciously or not, the judge, the critic. And his critical judgment of O^2 will have value precisely in proportion to the clarity and volume of these ideals—that is, to the range of percepts he can clearly recall and the fullness of their organisation into systems which have definite significance as such.

It is to be observed that just as there are sources of error in the process of perceiving the actual content, so there may be such sources in that of evaluating it as perceived. Some of these, of course, arise directly from some prior malperception of I^2: a man can hardly judge what he does not know. I may quote here a letter from Sir George Arthur to the editor of a famous daily paper: "Your dramatic critic in his clever if condemnatory review of M. Bernard's *L'Âme en peine*, makes one slight error which rather upsets the balance of his other remarks. He alludes to Robert as a former 'passionate admirer' of Marceline, who retains 'a deep affection for his old sweetheart'. On the other hand, the author describes—and the audience, with the exception of your critic, seemed to accept—Robert as the unhappy heroine's brother." There are also some other errors, peculiar to this stage, in the form of prejudices that bias the judgment, as for instance an à priori view of what is or is not probable, ranging from a syrupy optimism to the point of view of Miss Eden's Mrs. Douglas: "Nothing is too bad to be true, Mr. Douglas, and nothing is true that is not bad."* A certain intellectual laziness, again, may cause him to trounce an author for having the temerity to put forth work which does not correspond to the label

* *The Semi-attached Couple* (1830).

commonly applied to him: or for the same reason, if S^2 find within O^2 assumptions, forms, or images that are unfamiliar, he may dislike the effort required for their assimilation: there is a charming little song in Tennyson's early work—

> A spirit haunts the year's last hours
> Dwelling amid these echoing bowers:
>   To himself he talks;
> For at eventide, listening earnestly,
> At his work you may hear him sob and sigh
>   In the walks;
>   Earthward he boweth the heavy stalks
> Of the mouldering flowers:
>   Heavily hangs the broad sunflower
>   Over its grave in the earth so chilly;
>   Heavily hangs the hollyhock,
>   Heavily hangs the tiger-lily—

of which a *Blackwood* critic, in 1849, remarked, "What metre, Greek or Roman, Russian or Chinese, it was intended to imitate we have no care to enquire. The man was writing English and had no justifiable pretence for torturing our ears with verse like this." Conversely, the critic may take *omne ignotum pro magnifico*, especially if it has some easily grasped relation to what he knows, exaggerating or reversing it. Both this reaction and that previously mentioned are very familiar in the history of criticism.* Perhaps the most common source of error, however, is an uncritical acceptance of fashion—of fashion as an autonomous standard, at least, to be followed

---

* Every professional critic of any art should have read Professor Saintsbury's *History of Criticism*. He might find it useful also to read a few periodicals of the time when responsible reviewers hailed Marie Corelli as a genius, and nothing less than the *Saturday Review* used to come out on the day of publication with a column-long laudation of Sir Hall Caine's latest. It is a fairly sobering experience. And everyone knows (though most of us have forgotten) what eminent critics said about John Keats.

THE READER 243

or revolted against as such, for the sake, whether consciously or not, of the critic's personal prestige. A book dealing with certain subjects, using certain images or certain technical devices, is highly praised by the group of people whose judgment, or whose prestige, S^2 admires: and so he feels there is kudos to be had in praising any book which deals with these subjects, or uses these images or these devices. At one time a liberal dose of "sensibility" went down very well with the average highbrow audience, and anything that went weeping à la Werther was reasonably certain of applause: at another the mode was all for violet sins set forth in appropriate hand-painted adjectives: or everybody (in between these two) was trying to "be Early English before it was too late" and highly approving anyone who did likewise, whether he did it convincingly or not: and it is not so many years ago that any book was sure of a success if it took one of its characters into certain places that all of us visit daily but don't talk about—at any rate, not if we are civilised people. As obverse to this, there is the negative fashion, that certain images or certain assumptions simply "aren't done" by anyone worth considering: a novel, for instance, whose heroine was unchaste would have had as little chance of mercy from the average critic of the 1860's as one whose heroine was voluntarily otherwise would have had from certain neo-Georgians between the War and say 1925. The one standard condemns *Anna Karenina* and the other nearly every play of Shakespeare's: and both condemnations have been duly made, on this ground. Which recalls a favourite remark of Euclid's.

The best safeguard, perhaps, is a little knowledge of history, coupled with honesty and a sense of humour. These qualities will probably save the critic, if he is careful and goes cannily, from at least two opposite extremes of danger—that of being merely "a vane blown with all winds" and that of developing into a critical diehard, particularly that direst kind of Conservative, the man who has always prided himself on being Modern, and trumpets, *Athanasius contra mundum*, to a world that has long since taken his doctrine for granted, or dismissed it to where old theories go when they die.

The critical judgment, whatever its quality, goes (at least in regard to creative literature) through either or both of two concurrent channels. A full critique of any work of art would certainly take both of these into account, but in practice one or other may be neglected, and fashion is apt to approve of this neglect, and concentrate almost exclusively on the one, assuming that no really cultured person would ever bother his head about the other. Which "the other" may be depends upon the date.

On the one hand the critic of O^2 will consider chiefly the content—the phase of experience that it presents. He reads *Esmond* as an account of certain events in the reign of Queen Anne. The events are more or less likely to have happened: they invite, as events, certain emotional reactions or ethical judgments. S^2 will judge them first with regard to probability, given certain data, and proceed, thence, to consider them as a perceived aspect of human conduct. Now, it is perfectly right that he should so judge: the author has intended him to do that, to apperceive this conduct, considered as such, to the standards by which he judges conduct in general. But besides this, the book itself is an object of experience: and to savour it fully he must combine with this former judgment another, must seize and evaluate the experience received from it, as such—a thing that many men find rather difficult.

This amounts to saying that judgments of literature involve standards which are logical, ethical, and æsthetic. To put it like that will certainly sound startling to anyone who has been bred in the late tradition, determined so much by reaction from the Victorians. But none the less, in a full criticism of any literature, this ethical element will be present somewhere, even if it merely takes the form of stating, as Lamb did of the Restoration comedy, that moral standards here need not apply. Literature is essentially a presentation of human experience which includes within it the dimension of time: and this commits it to presenting human conduct, as seen and experienced by a specific intelligence. And the man whose experience of conduct as such is apperceived to no conceptual standards is what we call a moral imbecile. The result of any given such apperception may of course be an act of judgment affirming that the standard apperceived does not apply in this particular case, that—as seemed very startling to the 'nineties—Alec d'Urberville's mistress was (as Hardy defiantly called her) "a pure woman": or even as with the Lamb I have just referred to, that in this specific case no standard is relevant. But in the normal developed mind at least, some standard is invariably present, and will be a datum in its experience of conduct (and consequently in either the presentation of that conduct or in its reaction to such presentation) as much as the æsthetic standard with which, indeed, as the Greeks saw long ago, it is closely associated genetically. Both the conception of ethical "rightness" and that of beauty, together with that of truth (the logical standard), can all in fact be subsumed under the notion of something consummate, needing no alteration: so that truth might be described as perfect perception of being, goodness as perfect action, and beauty as perfect revelation of being in action.*

* The three qualities thus formulated correspond in a rather interesting fashion to the three Personæ of the Trinity, the Spirit, the Creator, and the Logos. In fact, the respective relations are also parallel.

In assessing the value of any given object, we lay stress on one or other of these aspects, according to our purpose at the moment: but it is false logic wholly to separate them.

S^2 then, we take it, has experienced O^2, and is aware of his own experience of it, as having certain specific qualities. Now, suppose this experience to be of such intensity that it demands perpetuation—demands, that is, to be re-embodied and conveyed to a fresh series of subjects: and suppose that the natural means for this conveyance is writing. Then the whole cycle will begin afresh. S^1's O^2 becomes for S^2 the O^1 of a process similar to that which S^1 has previously gone through, and he contrives a fresh O^2 of his own to embody the experience derived from it. The series of OO^2 which is *Lyrical Ballads* becomes to Coleridge an O^1 whose ensuing O^2 is the *Biographia Literaria* . . . which in turn may again be written about by X, whose critique of it is criticised by Y in *The Times Literary Supplement*: and in severe cases Y may even have Z in the correspondence columns "upon his back to bite him", or at least to derive a nutriment for his muse which goes back at five removes to the original OO^1 that started the poets. So Pelion piles on Ossa in the Bodleian. It is rather alarming when one comes to think of it.

This new O^2, the critique upon the original, may fall into either of two classes. The writer may describe the former O^2, now the O^1 of his present activity, as it stands—that is, endeavour to reproduce in his reader the impression it produces upon himself: or he may describe the impression upon himself in relation to certain previously formed concepts—that is, he may judge as well as describe. There is a third possibility, of course, in practice. X, writing a column notice of Y's *Studies in*

Certain Aspects of Z, may ignore Y almost completely, and write about "certain aspects of Z" himself—not necessarily even those which Y has considered: a certain great Sunday paper produces an instance of this nearly every week. But even then, X probably thinks he is writing of Y's book, and in fact does show the effect it has had on him . . . which may be to his discredit or to Y's: it all depends on the particular case.

The process of S^2's production of the new object will take the course of that which produced its stimulus: its quality depends on the same factors. It may be weaker, more derivative, for criticism of a kind is possible to less penetrating and prehensile minds than first-hand creation, since the experience that serves it as stimulus is already *arranged*, so to speak, and dissected out from the mass of life at large. In actual fact, this is true of the bulk of current criticism at any time since the founding of literary periodicals, the more as so much of it is produced not from any real interior stimulus, but from some such external compulsion as grocer's bills. If (even with the grocer's bill in the background) the reviewer is genuinely interested in the book he is "doing", then his work will have life in proportion to the vitality of that interest: but even then he is not likely to have time or space to give more than a rough image of his impressions—part of which, too, may easily go west if a good murder comes in during "making up". In the circumstances, indeed, it is surprising that the general average level of reviewing is—I will not say as brilliant, but as honest, as it undoubtedly is, in this country at least. We all know, of course—both authors and those who wrestle with "library lists"—the perennial and trying type of reviewer who is trying to convey not an impression of the book but one of his very clever and notable self: he will always be with us, for in the nature of things reviewing must often be done by the very young, or by the dispirited who grow resentful, and try to assert themselves at someone's expense. But there really seems to be less than there used to be of the latter at all events—very much less than fifty years ago: while the former is less apt to show itself in denigration than in praising the second-rate but fashionable: and it is probably better to call Stephen Phillips the greatest poet since Shakespeare than to muddy the reputation of Charlotte Brontë . . . or is it? The point would be worth a little debate.

It is better, of course, to avoid both errors alike: the reviewer, though little esteemed by his editor, is charged with a very important social function. He copes with the roaring spate of ink at its sources, and directs his flock to the channels he thinks most profitable. If he has a sensitive and well-stored mind and some power of conveying the impressions made on it, he may do really valuable service to authors and the reading public alike by acting as a kind of liaison officer. But no man should be asked to do this for long, at any rate for the present flood of novels: the enormous mass of competent near-literature is bound to dull his palate sooner or later: and the better he is, the more cruelly will the mass of the bad torment him.

A man may attain to be a critic who may never fashion any creative work: but it must not be forgotten, nevertheless, that criticism itself may be great creation, as witness Aristotle. (Dante wrote criticism, for the matter of that, and admirable criticism it is: if it has not worn as well as his poetry, it is only because in the natural course of things ideas "date" far sooner than emotions.) We have a pernicious habit, in this last century especially, of thinking of "art" as separate from life: but an object of art is an object like another, an experience of it an experience like another. Assuming the same qualities in S^1, his experience of a sunset and of a sonnet may demand perpetuation with equal intensity.

Now, this embodiment may take the form of a critique, as when Coleridge writes about the *Lyrical Ballads*, or Bradley about Shakespearian tragedy, or Aristotle about the tragedy of the Greeks. But it may not. The experience derived from the object of art, or from a complex sequence of such objects, may also become a theme whose conveying subject is not a direct image of themselves or of the actual impressions derived from themselves, though it may include images from their content. *Paradise Lost* is derived fully as much from Milton's experience of five great literatures as from his experience of seventeenth-century England. *Il Penseroso* and its twin derive perhaps in even larger proportion from art than from what we are pleased to describe as "nature", forgetting that art is itself a part of nature, being a human activity as much as eating, and the Iliad as much a phenomenon of human action as the Battle of Bannockburn. Indeed, a great part of nineteenth-century literature, as of Renaissance, as of Latin again, derives from an experience of art.

There is no essential danger about this: but there is one accidental to it always, and a very dangerous danger it may be—that a man may pass from this experience of art to an experience solely by means of art, and so divorce art from the rest of nature, to its inevitable impoverishment. He reacts to art as it were in a vacuum, with no contact upon the rest of reality: which, so far at least as living is concerned, is too much like hoisting himself with his own bootstraps. Art is a most potent means of discerning not—art—that is to say, all of the rest of life: but it is through the latter, and chiefly through the latter, that a man can really attain to see into art.

CHAPTER XII

THE EFFECT OF THE PROCESS

"The poet, described in ideal perfection, brings the whole soul of man into activity."

S. T. COLERIDGE, *Biographia Literaria*

OUR consideration of the process of literature began by taking it, and art in general, as primarily a function of human living. But like all such functions, it has a cyclic progress, and takes effect in turn on human life. We have looked already at the specific reaction of a man in immediate contact with an art, that is to say of the reader quâ reader as such, and have noticed one of his possible further reactions—that this contact may induce him to write in turn. But the effect of art is larger than that: it cannot be studied only in terms of itself, and therefore we must look at it for a moment in its effect on human life at large. To put our present problem in concrete terms, what is it that a man gets out of books?

The immediate answer, of course, is "That depends". It will depend, in the first place, on the man, and in the second on the particular book: the man is the more important of the two, for Shakespeare got marvellous things out of mere journalism, and certain men, out of Shakespeare . . . I need not continue! A man, too, gets different things from different books, or even from the same book in different moods.

He will find in books, on the one hand, an escape out of life, which may grow into a substitute for life: and on the other, they may provide him with a discipline in life. These divisions are not mutually exclusive. The use for escape may grow into the substitute, but on the other hand, as I hope to show, it may link itself

THE EFFECT OF THE PROCESS 251

to the use as a discipline, by aiding a man to reach a condition of being in which his perceptions have a chance to clarify.

The greater number of readers, probably, look to art to provide a substitute for life. In our present type of semi-civilisation, a large number of people are maladjusted to their environment, without being able to get away from it or to alter it: or at least without any effective realisation of a means by which they can achieve either of these. The natural human being finds his fulfilment in three things: in effective impact on his environment (i.e., work and fighting), in human relationships, and in his relation to something supra-human. To miss any of these will adversely affect the others: and in the average industrial community the first for certain and the two latter probably are bound to be wrong for a large number of individuals. The mechanised repetition of unthinking labour is not work, in any real sense of the word: it does not demand the activity of the personality that an old-fashioned wheelwright or weaver or shepherd could enjoy, but rather a repression or at best a setting aside of a large and important part of the personality, which dangles unoccupied and gets into trouble, as a man's teeth go wrong if he lives on pap. The human relationships of a number of such people are naturally impeded, for none of them can be in a healthy state. And the outlook on things trans-human is apt to be impeded equally when people of this sort are left to move in a world of taps and levers, where effects are seen divorced from adequate cause, and men create causes without seeing their effects. The consequence, in people who are naturally normal, is a furious discomfort and a desire to escape. And as every psychiatrist knows only too well, one very frequent consequence of this is the creation of a subjective world to which the subject retreats from the world about him. If he has a powerfully creative temperament, this fantasy-world may be embodied in creative literature of a high quality, depicting a world that is nearer his ideal: *The Earthly Paradise* is largely a case in point, although it is not so exclusively a "substitute-fantasy" as Morris himself and some of his critics have thought it.* All art, in fact, would come in a certain sense under the head of "substitute-fantasy", for in all of it the artist is creating a phase of life more perfectly adapted to a specific purpose than any of the actual life about him. This purpose is the complete revelation, to himself and others, of a certain thing: and this thing may simply be the fulfilment of his desires, which in this way he may "both enjoy and miss". The non-creative man cannot do this so effectually. He may, and often does, build up a web of protective fantasy, within which he lives a dream-life that may become much more real than the objective world, so that he acts on its assumptions in the latter, and we say he is hysterical or insane. The difference between the hysteric describing adventures he has not had and Morris coasting the shores of old romance, both as a substitute for modern London, is partly a matter of the intellect, and even more, perhaps a matter of will. Morris, like Disko Troop, could "keep things sep'rate", and also could discipline his personality into building up from his fantasy an organised structure that involved no mere vague play of instinctive impulse, but a rational analysis, and a firm volitional direction of the self—that is, that employed the whole of his personality to reach a definite and external end, in a specific relation to objective reality.

The man who is neither a creative artist to make an object corresponding to his *desideria* nor an hysteric to

---

* This desire to escape into another milieu may determine elements in writing with a very positive primary content, as when a novelist chooses to stage in another century a theme and subject that could have been set in his own.

THE EFFECT OF THE PROCESS

be deceived by these into considering them fulfilled objectively, is, left to himself, in a condition rather unsatisfying. His dreams are so much better than reality: but he cannot live in them sufficiently for them to provide an effective escape from it. They are vague and static, and lack vividness. Accordingly, he needs, and seeks, a stimulus. He may find it—at some stage he probably does find it—by falling in love, when the rush of nervous energy caused by the stimulation of a powerful instinct provides him with the vitality he needs for more vivid and more effective fantasy: when reality breaks in and contradicts him, he falls out of love, and has a fresh chance to dramatise himself in a picturesque and interesting rôle, of the disillusioned hero with a tragic past . . . e da capo. He may find the needful stimulus in beer, or in some more obnoxious substitute, or perhaps in some other handy hypnotic agent, the broadcast lecture or the Savoy Band, that dulls his perception of normal external reality, and so leaves more strength to the inner fantasy-life. Or he may find a better means to his purpose in the cinema, which owes its enormous success to a double reason. In the first place, it is a perfect means of inducing this hypnosis: it is cheaper than beer, more respectable than the pub, there is no risk of trouble with the police: and the darkness, the physical relaxation, the incessant music, the continual flicker on the fixed bright screen, combine to make it powerfully hypnotic without any more noticeable bad effects than a headache that can be attributed to the office. Beyond all these extremely real advantages (he could not label them, but he loves their effect) it does more: it directs his dreams, enriches them with new material, or rather with fresh combinations of the old, and by representing them objectively, helps their vividness, his sense of their "real" existence, and gives him, as it were, a kind of hope.

Now, this is precisely what very many people—the majority, in fact, of the reading public—desire of art, and particularly of literature. Thanks to the "progress" of last century, they have little access to the plastic and graphic arts, that once, in some form, were as common as fire and water: and these, being static, have less of this dream-directive power in any case. Music, which is now more easily available, has the hypnotic and sensuous power to make dreams effective, but it does not enrich their actual content as such. Hence the popular arts are drama, the film, and literature, which can do this, and therefore provide the most effective dope. Drama has colour and the vividest objective reality, but in practice it is expensive, and means a good deal of physical discomfort. When you are earning £4 a week or less, 2s. 4d. is a considerable sum. And for 2s. 4d. or even 4s. 6d., you have (in London at least) to stand, perhaps for hours, on a cold pavement, and to sit for three hours more on a very hard and backless wooden seat with no room for your legs and far too much contact with your neighbour's boots, to say nothing of only seeing about half the stage, in a crazy perspective at that, and hearing imperfectly. For anyone with an income under £300 and anything to do out of office hours to be a regular playgoer means an heroic devotion to the arts, or else an appalling emptiness of life. I am not sure that the former quality would make anyone stand three hours in an east wind to see the average musical comedy.*

The film, of course, is perfect for the purpose: but still it requires a definite place and time, and a little money. One cannot turn it on in an A.B.C. or in the Tube at a rush-hour—places from which escape is very desirable,

---

* People stand fifteen at times, of course. But I think there is a touch of "collector's frenzy" here: they collect first nights as other people do stamps, or as a friend of mine collects routes to the Continent.

THE EFFECT OF THE PROCESS 255

and sometimes the only way of dodging insanity. But a book is portable, and costs little or nothing.* It has not the hypnotic adjuvants of the film, and demands a little more mental effort: but it does pretty well on the whole when one can't get better. It provides ready-made the variations on one's pet fantasy that one's own enfeebled vitality cannot stir. The variations, of course, must not be too considerable, or it does not supply what is wanted: but the fact that they are there keeps consciousness alive, retains the vividness of the fantasy. The curious deadness of average bookstall fiction is really an asset from this point of view. The dull sense of language and the vague and inaccurate images are in this connection very positive merits. If the image is precise, that means it exists as something outside S^2: and he wants it to exist inside him. The vague image can be "adapted to fit"—and perhaps, too, is more in consonance with the other vague images that form the previous content of his mind, and so takes its place more readily among them. And precision of thought, or even of perception, demands an unaccustomed effort of will. So also with the reach-me-down characters. If these had personality they would exist in themselves, and S^2 would not be able to identify himself with them. If they have none, he can shoulder them out of the way, adopt their adventures and their attributes, or shove these on to the people whom he knows. To the doll-like heroine with the golden curls he gives the vacant enormous eyes and fixed heart-shaped mouth of his pet film-actress, and uses the synthesis as a *persona* for what he would like to find in Miss Jones of the Ling-gerie. The villain who gets

---

* Authors, as everybody knows, don't have to pay rent or buy boots or ink and paper. It was the *Daily Herald*, organ of the demand for fair maintenance, that ended a most appreciative review by saying, "This is a book to ask for at your Free Library" . . . and it only cost the price of two gallery seats and a quarter of toffee, with no necessity to stand in queue!

it in the neck in Chapter XXX is exactly what he feels about that beast Smith: he can't tell Smith off, or he would get the sack, but he does enjoy it when the hundred-per-cent he-man lands him one on the jaw in the Great Open Spaces, under the eyes of the fascinating Miss Jones, who has become a lovely Russian princess with millions in diamonds and Athabasca Preferred. And he, of course, is the hundred-per-cent gentleman, with fifteen inches added to his chest: and when that beast Smith has had him on the carpet for being ten minutes over his proper lunch-hour (the racing-special was awfully late that morning) it is very soothing to his injured feelings to throw Black Steve's gang neatly through the window . . . et cetera.

We all do it, of course, or have done it at some time or other. The precise type of fiction we choose depends on which of our various unemployed instincts happens to be most active habitually. Miss Jones of the Ling-gerie spends her spare time in the arms of a white-robed Sheikh. She is not quite sure what a sheikh is, certainly, but at all events he is picturesque and impassioned and probably misunderstood . . . in short, Childe Harold without Byron's wit, and consequently much better for the purpose: and if one lives in London it is pleasant to dream of a land where there are no bus-fights and it never rains. Her married sister, semi-detached in Balham, with a kitchen-sink in the background and a completely unexciting husband, is bored and would like to be an expensive vamp, all pearls and fatal attraction and tiger-skins, with a background of boiled shirts and sinuous barons, and no reference to Bow Street or Lock Hospitals. So she patronises Michael Arlen and Elinor Glyn, and generally the cares of a menage keep her feet on the ground sufficiently to prevent her from growing into another Edith Thompson: which is fortunate for her Bywaters

THE EFFECT OF THE PROCESS

at least, though the lady probably enjoyed her trial, until the limelight was turned off at last, and she found herself faced with a very objective rope.* Young Jones, again, likes to think of himself as a mysterious gentleman with a tragic countenance and a soul empurpled with disillusioned vice. In objective fact he does nothing more picturesque than to get mildly if somewhat unpleasingly drunk at intervals and pick up an inexpensive girl in the street: but to his looking-glass, and to anyone who will listen, he is all the things Baudelaire thought of himself, or at least as many of them as he can imagine or find images for in the fiction he affects.

Now, the ultimate effect of this sort of thing depends. In the first place, the nature of the fantasy-images will have a certain bearing on results. Little Tibbits of the Gents' Hosiery, who is the heroic he-man aforesaid, will have more difficulty in realising his ideal objectively than young Jones will in resembling, to himself, his notion of a purply gorgeous sinner. And it was easier for Mrs. Thompson to play at being a Robert Hichens heroine than it would have been for her to behave—with any degree of consistency at least—like a heroine of Mrs. Henry Wood. On the other hand, little Tibbits's he-man ideal may induce him to take a "Poly" course in boxing, which is good both for him and for subsequent little Tibbitses: and on the 4th of August, 1914, it may send him into the recruiting-office, and lead him by ways that were not in his books to a gallant death somewhere by Vimy Ridge, saving a civilisation . . . for what it is worth.

* I do not see any reason for not hanging a woman if she happens to deserve it: but I very much doubt if Edith Thompson did, or if she would ever have come to her trial if her lover had not taken her seriously and acted on her hysterical fantasies. Without him she would probably have done less damage than a good many similar and quite respectable neurotics whose fantasies take the form of dangerous gossip. A doctor (or a priest) with a caustic tongue would have met her needs far better than the hangman.

And Miss Jones, if she does not do that (and after all, she was useful in the Waacs and did some very plucky things on munitions), may contribute to the said civilisation by acquiring sweet speech and a certain fastidiousness. The danger comes when the ideals give a shoddy delight in nine-carat-gilded vice, or, from another angle, when as with poor Edith Thompson, the boundaries of real and ideal grow vague, and the fantasy is not merely an occasional holiday, but the normal life within which one moves and acts. That may lead anywhere from senseless habitual boasting or lying gossip, to Broadmoor.

This substitute-fantasy must always hold a considerable risk. If it encourages instinctive impulses of value, the risk, as I have suggested, will be less. But Don Quixote had high and chivalrous ideals, and yet got himself (and Sancho) into trouble. The only thing that will keep S^2 really safe is, as with other "short ways out of London", to know when to stop, to be able to bring a certain intellectual criticism to bear on his fantasy and its relation to life, and to pull himself up when he has had what he can carry.

Given that these conditions are fulfilled, the dangerous drug can become a wholesome medicine. It should be used as medicine rather than food, or at any rate as one uses wine or tobacco. It is deadly to live with a substitute for life—that way lies rot of both the mind and will: but it is sometimes needful, if not imperative, to escape out of one's life for a little while. The kind of book that without distorting or loosening a man's normal perception of his surroundings can lift him out of them—including out of his own nervous stresses—and give his recuperative forces free play for a while would not be needed in a perfect society: but it is as valuable to the average present-day citizen as tobacco was to a soldier at the Front . . . and a shortage of that would have probably lost the war.

THE EFFECT OF THE PROCESS

There is a special corner on Parnassus (low down, no doubt, but very comfortable) for writers of really good "thrillers"—the sort of story that without making much demand on one's intelligence does not offend or nullify it at least, but can transfer perception and emotion from oneself and one's surroundings for two hours, and give one's nervous-system a chance to "sleep". This may seem to put a brutally low estimate on a deal of competent and careful writing; it takes far more art to write a good detective-story than a second-rate piece of elaborate introspection. But to take pure story-telling on these lines is not, I submit, to underrate its value. One of the most sensible things Ruskin ever said (and startling as the statement may be, he said quite a number with a remarkable amount of wisdom in them) was to the effect that there are good books of a day as well as good books of all time :* and those that I am thinking of are a valuable class among the former, though I cannot be quite sure that he would have thought so. For the sake of a very deep and real gratitude, I will tell here two personal experiences that will explain exactly what I mean. Some years ago I found myself "up against it". I had had, for a longish time, certain personal troubles, that were causing a good deal of nervous strain, and as a matter of fact was in very bad health. Then my job came to an end, unexpectedly. I had no money, no sort of influence, and no professional training of any kind, except a completely useless Arts degree. It was, no doubt, a commonplace situation, but it comes with some freshness to the individual. I was too dazed with fatigue and shock at the time to have any very active hold upon religion: mine has always, I fear, been a matter in the main of intellectual conviction, and one needs emotion in emergencies. So I went home to my lodgings rather "far through", and if I had chewed

* *Sesame and Lilies.*

on the situation all night, would probably have landed in either a nursing-home or a pool of the river. As it happened, I had by me a novel of Mr. H. C. Bailey's. Now, I should not call Mr. Bailey a great novelist: but he is a very competent and vigorous craftsman, who can tell a good story well and keep it moving, with no violence to the facts of human nature, and who gets an echo of the Elizabethans into the cut-and-thrust of his lively dialogue. I have forgotten most of the book's content, but I know it showed decent and likeable people undergoing misfortunes that were convincing enough, and getting out of them partly by luck, but still more by their own courage and resolution . . . the matter, after all, of all true epics. I took the book up and read it straight through: it took me clean away from my own affairs, and I woke next morning braced in body and mind and ready to put up a decent fight for it. And in the end, I won—for that campaign. *The Cherry Orchard*, no doubt, is finer art: but the effect of Tchekoff on me at any time is rather like that of incipient influenza, and if I had read him in those circumstances he might have sent me under altogether. It is a fact that an unfortunate ex-officer, down on his luck much as I was at that time, saw a certain clever play and went home and shot himself. It was not the dramatist's fault, of course: he wrote what he could, and he wrote it very competently, and the play would be the last concause of a series. But if the unfortunate Major —— had, instead, read Mr. Bailey (who artistically is no less competent a writer than the author of the play in question) he might have lived and made good.

My other tale is precisely similar, but even at the risk of a dull repetition I will recount it for the sake of thanks. I was in a nursing-home, with an operation coming on next morning. I had damaged my cheekbone, causing an abscess to form in a cavity of it, and although by that time

THE EFFECT OF THE PROCESS

the pain was a good deal relieved, I had had no sleep for a week without morphia: and between a good deal of previous pain and the strain of anxiety common to most people at the end of '16, I was pretty tired, with a negligible amount of fight in me. I had an idea, too, that the operation might possibly mean disfigurement for life—a prospect one does not enjoy in one's early twenties: and to sum up in the vernacular, I was in a blind blue funk, and very much afraid I was going to show it. Then a friend arrived, and lent me John Buchan's *Greenmantle*, which has more than a reminiscence of the ballads in it. It pulled me together and shamed me out of my funk, and when they got me on to the table next morning, I could chaff the Theatre Sister quite cheerfully.

No doubt, of course, this was a sort of Dutch courage: but at any rate it was better than none at all, and just then I had very little of my own, and could not lay hold of material to reforge it. Even when the book does not turn up with quite such providential appropriateness, the recollection of "pluck facing luck" may be a useful thing to carry about: and adventure-fiction of all sorts is just that, whether it is Jack London or the Odyssey. About the oldest piece of English literature (it is probably of the sixth century or thereabouts) is the song of a minstrel who is down on his luck: he has lost his job, in fact, and feels up against it. So he tells over to himself the gallant stories that were his stock-in-trade, stories of Eormanric, Wayland, and Beadohild, and heroes who had won through by resolution; and at the end of each story comes the heartening refrain,

þæs ofereode, þisses swa mæg.

—"That was got over, so may this be." Deor knew one good use for his own literature. And a minor application of that may come in lesser crises of fatigue. No doubt to take Jane Austen instead of a cocktail is to read her for less than the motives she deserves; but even at that she is better for nerves and palate than miscellaneous nips of sweetened gin ... and a man is no worse critic (or worse Christian) for keeping his nerves and digestion in good order, as that most admirable and charming lady would very certainly have said herself.

Also, at best, this lesser use of literature shades into the truest function of all art, the discipline of a man's reactions to life. The reaction to his inner and outer universe of a fully conscious being with volitional autonomy—i.e., with the power to choose between possible reactions, to respond to X, the more distant recollected stimulus, rather than to Y, which is vividly present—is a sufficiently complex matter, and in practice shows very various results. One man will risk all that he values most to adjust a trifling physical discomfort: another will bear the extreme of physical and moral torture rather than utter a specific monosyllable or make a trifling gesture with his hand. The immediate reaction in any special case depends on the balance present between two elements—one the strength of the instinctive impulses involved, including their relative strength as compared with each other, the other a twofold perception of these impulses, and of their various stimuli, both within and without the subject's own personality: where this balance is delicate and habitual it may become almost automatic in action, so that we find the subject respond to the unprecedented in the manner of the young typist in the recent Westminster floods, who fell asleep in normal homely surroundings, and waking to find her bed floating in darkness, showed in a nightmare of fantastic perils an unhesitating courage and a cool resource that it would be impertinent to praise.

The factor that ultimately determines what this balance

shall be, in any given reaction, is the phenomenon we know as will, which consists, primarily, in a more or less vivid perception of a certain idea of the self as desirable to be realised, plus a more or less strong instinctive impulse to realise this self—an impulse which is a specialised form, of course, of the general primary urge to continue in being which is common to all organic entities. Which is as much as to say that what a man is in any given circumstances and what he will become in relation to life depends on the strength of vital impulse in him and on the clarity and range of his perceptions of ideas and of the data for their just formation. He must, in fine, *be* strongly and *know* clearly if he is to be an adequate human being.

The former determines the energy with which this ideal self will be desired. On the latter depend its nature and its vividness—that is, the power of its image in the subject's mind to evoke the fullest response of instinctive impulse.

Now, the amount of *élan vital*—of general impulse—in any specific individual is partly a matter of his innate equipment, as determined by heredity and pre-natal circumstance: one man is born with more "vitality", as we say, than another. But his later nurture may do much to develop the full extent of his possibility of this, or on the other hand to choke and weaken it: and as he becomes an autonomous personality he himself may either weaken or develop it, by his own conduct, which either exercises or misuses the powers of mind and body that are its instruments. But to develop them demands the perception of an idea—that of the desirable condition for these powers: and in fact the nurture he receives from other people depends on their idea of this condition and the means to it. Further, the use he will make of vital impulses will depend on ideas formed of their result. So that what a man becomes in relation to circumstances (and within the world of our experience at least no being can be conceived as existing absolutely) depends ultimately on the perception, by himself and the other people who "educate" him, of subjective and objective entities and qualities and of their various interrelations. To put it briefly, what a man is and becomes depends in the long run upon perception—mainly, though not entirely, his own perception.

In any given situation, the percept that will be immediately effective in determining a choice between reactions is that of the ideal* conception of the self in reaction to that particular situation. Captain Oates goes out and dies to relieve his comrades, or Christopher Robin, aged three, tries not to spill his bread-and-milk at supper, when either of them might more easily have done otherwise, because they have each an ideal self in terms of which their reaction is decided, possibly not without a certain struggle. When the "situation" in question is the generic one of being alive as a human being in this world, the relative ideal has its largest connotation, as the concept of the most desirable sum of the subject's reactions to the sum of human circumstances as cognised by him. Obviously, then, this concept or image (for it may be either, and most often, probably, is a complex of both) must be built up of various concepts and percepts, which will include ideas, both perceptual and conceptual, of qualities of both the self and the not-self about it; and important among these will naturally be those of relative values. This value-element is very necessary, for unless the ideal self arouses desire—unless, that is, it stimulates conation, "attempt"

---

* "Ideal" is used here in its colloquial sense, to mean "the concept of that possible self which is considered most desirable". This does not refer only to moral qualities, but to the whole self as such, though naturally the idea of its realisation will become very closely bound up with concepts which are clearly ethical.

THE EFFECT OF THE PROCESS

in some specified direction—it will have no effect in guiding the actions and consequently the development.

Now, in practice, if the concept of the ideal self is based on percepts which do not harmonise with objective reality, then its realisation, which is essentially that of a relation between the self and such reality, will not be possible, while the attempt to bring it about will land the subject in various misrelations that may range from mere absurdity to disaster. Again, unless there is a just concept of values—that is, a perception of first things as first—the subject will spend his available energy on attaining an ideal which is opposed to his completest possible development, or to that of the race of which he is a unit; and we may have a man with a splendid natural gift of *élan vital* using it to float fraudulent companies, to form a large collection of glass rolling-pins, or to hit a ball in certain given ways. Elmer Gantry (to quote no instance from real life) is a fine and not unusual instance of this, and so, in fact, are all really successful rogues.

Now, the attainment of conceptual truth is a matter of knowledge, including that knowledge of the valid processes of thought that enables a man to make just inferences, and which, when systematised, we know as logic. Knowledge comes, in the first place, through the direct experience of the individual, and consists, in the true sense, not of an agglomeration of percepts, but of their fusion in an organised unity, together with what can be inferred from them. But the direct sensory experience of the individual as such is inadequate: a man only lives to threescore and ten or thereabouts, which is not very long when one thinks what there is to know.

To implement his own knowledge, and also to give him the means of organising it (without which it remains completely useless), he must correlate it to the recorded knowledge of the race in which he is a unit. This knowledge refers to all aspects of conscious life and some of unconscious, and in its process of development has been organised in great bodies of related concepts and percepts, whose organisation makes inference possible within them, makes it possible to relate to them new percepts of individuals, and further to make new inferences from these that lead to the creation of new concepts, which may be added to the common stock.

For practical convenience we divide this organised knowledge in three great groups. The first of these is that organised knowledge of the "material" world we know as science, and the second is that organised knowledge of the "spiritual" world we know as philosophy.* With these, there is a third—man's organised knowledge of the relation between those things which he perceives and infers and the subject (individual or collective) who perceives or infers them: that is to say, art.

Now, all these three systems are of vital moment. But that of most immediate *practical* importance is art. I say "most immediate", not "greatest". There is no "greatest", as a matter of fact. There can be no true study of a man's interactions with environment (including his past and future selves) unless there is a definite conception of that environment: that is, there is no art without a science and a philosophy. But knowledge of that environment, however copious and accurate, is useless to man as a living and functioning being, unless he can relate it to himself: and as his own personal knowledge of this

---

* The distinction between these two is in fact pragmatic, as matter is now seen to be conceivable in terms of pure energy, which are the only terms in which we can conceive of spirit. A more logical distinction would probably be, therefore, to call science man's organised knowledge of what is actually perceptible by his senses (including what he infers as so perceptible, as in astronomy and palæontology), while philosophy is essentially his organised knowledge of what he can infer from what is so perceptible without being able sensorily to perceive it.

THE EFFECT OF THE PROCESS 267

relation is limited, he needs to supplement and implement it with the body of racial knowledge, of recorded experience as such, that we know as art.

Such knowledge takes effect in two directions upon the development of the individual. This development, as we have just observed, depends on two factors, clarity of perception (including perception of values) and vital energy. And art provides a discipline for both.

To perceive, fully, an object of art is to observe a certain phase of human experience through the perception of another mind. When this other mind has greater perceptual powers than that of the immediate subject (when S^1 has a greater power than S^2, that is), the latter's own perception is enhanced with regard to the object that is being perceived. If I look on quiet village life for myself, I may be bored. If I look on it through Jane Austen's mind, I shall not: and if I look on it through my own after seeing it through hers, I am less likely to be bored than I was, for now I shall have a somewhat enlarged conception of the experience that may be latent in observing it. If, on the other hand, the other mind has less perceptual power than that which looks through it—if Shakespeare, say, is reading Mr. Michael Arlen—he will be made to realise, if he reads critically, how the world appears to a narrower range of vision. This naturally palls a good deal sooner, but a little of it may be useful and entertaining, if it is not allowed to lead to snobbery: and of course he may usefully reperceive the presented content, as Shakespeare did with Cinthio or Greene.

This perception of recorded experience has a twofold value. It *extends* the content of the subject's perception by placing before him percepts he could not have obtained from his own contact with objective reality: I have never murdered a king or sailed the Spanish Main with Sir Walter Raleigh, but I have read *Macbeth* and Hakluyt's

Voyages. Further, it *intensifies* the subject's percepts of his own contact with objective reality: Browning's painter cries

> Have you noticed there
> Yond cullion's hanging face? A bit of chalk,
> And trust me, but you should, though!*

Art trains a man to a new understanding of his own direct percepts, by showing him the fullness and richness of content in the corresponding ones of other people.

It is worth noting that these two enhancements act in regard to percepts of values as well as to those of any other category. Hence they train towards the formation of an ideal for the self which shall be clear, related to reality, and conducive to the development in the subject of those qualities on which he sets a value. Now, mankind is in a process of evolution. Millions of years ago, inorganic entity evolved from a certain nebula into a world. Then, somewhat inexplicably, organic life appeared, and continued the process, rather more rapidly. Then organic life became conscious of itself, and again continued the process, this time not passively, but as so to speak in partnership with the other forces manipulating the materials. This implies that the Cosmos ran a serious risk. Evolution could no longer go on automatically in one direction. The material had begun to take a hand in the process: the potter's clay moved of its own accord. If man used this new potentiality to collaborate with the force that was developing him to high levels, well and good. But there was now the possibility that he might refuse so to collaborate, in which case he would be worse off than his seniors, the unselfconscious brutes, who could not get out of harmony with these forces. In the theologian's phrase, there would be a Fall. There was, with its inevitable

* *Fra Lippo Lippi*.

consequences: but there was still the possibility, both for the race and for the individual, of developing a power of harmonious and *active* collaboration with the developing force. And in order to do this, the individual and the race need a conception—at least proximately true—of the end of such development. The most valuable ideal self, whether racial or individual, will thus be that which provides the highest conception of such development in terms related to possible means of attaining it. And art is the great key to the racial experience in developing such an ideal, and to the data for its refashioning for the individual. It is obvious, of course, that the art which reveals most clearly the ideal of highest evolutionary value in terms of the most intimate contact with existing realities (including possibility) will be that most effectual from this point of view: and that art which induces the formation of an ideal which is evolutionarily retrogressive, or which is divorced from contact with the actual conditions of fulfilment, will be proportionately less valuable. St. Paul's famous advice to the Philippians* is founded on a perception of this fact: and a sound piece of practical advice it was.

This use of art to discipline perception is not its sole service to the evolutionary process. It shares this, indeed, with science and philosophy, though it is of more practical value than they in regard to one of the most important series of percepts—those of a man's own relations to what is perceived. But with regard to the discipline and training of these reactions themselves, it stands alone. Science can tell us of the things that cause them: philosophy can provide a standard for measurement: but art, besides helping these two, can do a third thing.

It portrays for us a man's reactions to circumstances. There are certain sciences which do this as well: in art,

* Phil. iv. 8.

however, they are shown no longer as general concepts, but as they appear in individual cases—that is, in the terms in which they must be experienced. I may conceive with my intellect of Love, or Anger, or Valid Reasoning: and my conception may be the same as yours. But except as abstract ideas, I do not experience them. In my actual reactions to life, on which I have to base my development (or, if you prefer, to work out my salvation) I love, I am angry, I reason, more or less validly: so also do you, and being another person, somewhat differently. Your loving and my loving, your anger and my anger, are sufficiently alike for us to be able to call them by the same names: but in our experience and in that of any two people in the world, they will never be quite completely identical. Now, art admits to a range of individual experience of human reactions, perceptual and conative. This latter point is vitally important. Art gives us knowledge of the way in which *élan vital* actually works, in individual cases and in the specific channels we call the instinctive impulses. The presentation of these includes data for a perception of the relative values of such exercise of it, that train us to perceive the relative values of our own conations, an important point in guiding our choice between two possible alternative reactions, and so in determining our course of conduct.

But beyond this result, there is yet another, for art can directly exercise those same specific activities of *élan vital*, can stir in us the various instinctive impulses which, permitted to develop into action, are our impact, so to speak, upon what we perceive. It trains a man, as he perceives the matter, in feeling: that is, it habituates him to make certain instinctive reactions to given objects. Art is always a presentation of certain percepts *in a manner to stimulate certain specific instinctive impulses*, which reach the consciousness as certain emotions. The artist's central

THE EFFECT OF THE PROCESS 271

and deliberate purpose is precisely to make his audience feel in a certain way about certain things: and if his technique is adequate, and the relation of reaction to percept sufficiently implicit in human nature, he will make them so react. To borrow a familiar instance from Aristotle, he shows them certain events in the life of a man, and rouses their pity and terror for such events in human life generally: and so trains them to this reaction later on, whenever they encounter such events.

It follows that when this exercise of the impulses is stimulated on lines which are consonant with evolutionary development, this latter will be furthered, and conversely. To train men to see first things as first is excellent: but it will be of very little service if they are not also trained to *endeavour towards* first things first, to respond to them with the most powerful and most positive conations. This is where art is of the extremest value in achieving "the measure of the stature of the fullness of a man". Science and philosophy may train him in the knowledge of Means and End: but art not only helps him in the effort to see both these as they are for his own self: by developing also his instinctive impulses, it develops the Energy without which the Means are useless to the End. By awakening the latent life in him to positive and definite reaction, it arouses desire for "life more abundantly". And he cannot gain that life unless he desire it. Nor can Man unless men have been taught to do so.

APPENDIX A

SINCE the development I have traced of *Othello* from a more or less vague idea in the mind to a work of art is only conjectural—though the conjecture is based on a close study of facts—it may possibly be of service if as well I trace the development of the content of a novel unimportant in itself, but of which I can speak from actual first-hand knowledge, my own *Quiet Lady*. This has a very simple plot, with simple and clear-cut issues, so it may serve very conveniently as a sort of laboratory guinea-pig.

The beginning of it, so far as I can remember, was a novel of someone else's, which took the Nietzschian standpoint, dear to the feeble, that it is a mark of strength to grab what one happens to want, irrespective of any other considerations—the object of desire in this case being a man who was somebody else's lover. The "strong" lady in the tale had some sort of hold on him, and used it as a lever to marry him, for which the author apparently admired her. I made the obvious reflection that it would have shown more strength on her part, in the circumstances, to give him up; and for a time left it at that. Apparently the idea stuck in my mind: I found myself thinking, vaguely, of a novel where this should happen, the title of it being *We that are Strong*. The subject, like most subjects of fiction, was old, but it took my imagination because at the time I happened to catch a glimpse in real life of a situation which though not the same as this, had certain emotional parallels at least. The two worked in my mind, and the situation grew more concrete, changing from an abstract problem in ethics to an actual situation between individuals. It was not much of a plot: but I began to see the situation with a particular "atmosphere", as it were. The effect I wanted was one analogous to that of a certain piece of music I vaguely remembered, which has a fragile and haunting melancholy. Also I happened to see *The Immortal Hour*, in Sir Barry Jackson's production. At one moment in the piece, the lighting severs two figures from the rest, holding them on a different plane from the others behind them, as if they were enclosed in their own world. The moment had a profound emotional effect, that took me greatly.

I am not sure of the chronological sequence of these ingredients: I rather think I had seen *The Immortal Hour*, in fact, before reading the novel, and I know that I read the novel before I wrote that one of my own which precedes *The Quiet Lady*. At all events, as the course of time went on I saw my skeleton plot as a *design*, with the emotional colour of the tune, and with one figure standing clear and still in a frame of brightly coloured moving action. By this time, I had to have a shot at it, or choke. The sheer technical difficulty of what I wanted to do was what fired me more than anything, I believe. I had just been writing fiction long enough to be profoundly thrilled by pure technique. I began to hunt for my persons, setting, and action.

I had the bare outline of the latter, of course: and the general emotional tone of what I had seen gave me the personality, and appearance, of my central figure: she must be rather small, fair, but not brightly coloured, self-contained, but with deep emotions and a strong sense of the values of conduct—"a sense of honour". The other woman must be a marked contrast. She must be a "sympathetic" character, or the sacrifice became mere quixotism. But the contrast must be there, for the sake of design. I began to see her as a big woman, fair, brightly golden, open and straightforward. As for the man between, he must be of value enough to make the sacrifice real—which meant with some stability of character: he must be honest enough to stick to his bargain (I had made the lady's "hold" on him a formal betrothal) but with strong enough emotions to make it difficult, and obtuse enough emotionally to have made it: further points, his obstinacy, hot temper, and so on, are partly racial traits derived from his background, and called into the surface of the design to motivate his part in the book's action.

I saw all three vaguely in the mid-nineteenth century —mainly because it seemed an escape from my own, but more logically because it was a period when the idea of impersonal values in conduct was fairly familiar, however they might be confused or traversed in action. And because it was country I knew very well and loved, I saw them in the country by Aberdeen. Then I suddenly realized that in sketching in background in an earlier book I had touched in a story that would serve. This is the passage as it stands in *Without Conditions*:

> He was clearly and legally Crawford of Skrine, as his father might have been before him if he had lived, as his capricious old grandfather assuredly had been, and as he himself had very nearly not, his lairdship saved only by the luck of a late will, for old Alexander, fifteenth of Skrine, had never forgiven his son's defiant marriage to a Macleod of the Outer Isles, the daughter of a poor gentleman, with no inheritance beyond the fair tall beauty of her race.

The "father", John Crawford, would do for the man I wanted: I had already drawn his son, and to give the latter's father a natural family likeness would produce very much the kind of figure required. The description of Mrs. Crawford in old age suggested that in her youth she might have been much what I wanted for my second woman: her Highland background would set her remote from my heroine, and give variety. Add the heroine and her renunciation to the episode I had sketched in *Without Conditions*, and I had action enough to get along with.

My second woman I christened Flora—a common name in the Highlands, and one that had the kind of colour I wanted. My heroine took rather a lot of naming: I find that a half-page of the draft MS. is full of names I had been trying over. Eventually I recalled one in Oldmachar Kirkyard, Burnette Silver, that had charmed me as a student. (I had to drop the "e", to my regret, to prevent English and American readers from putting the accent on the wrong syllable.) If Flora was Highland, and a countrywoman, Burnett should be East Coast, and town: and the Georgian houses in the Chanonry of Old Aberdeen, where the real Burnette is buried, were just right, while for Flora there was a very suitable setting in a place I knew rather well in my native island, the *Lonay* of the book.

By this, I had my setting, the principal people, and the outline of the action; the time was fixed by the fact that my hero's son was born in 1819. That gave me about 1816 as a date, which fitted well enough, and gave me a chance of making my hero an ex-soldier of Wellington's, which helped to provide him with a solidifying past. I had drawn his home, and hinted at his father, in *Without Conditions*, so they were to my hand.

I need not go into much more detail, I think. Given these data, incidental action, to relate the people and the events, the events and their sequelæ, could be inferred from them, or from what I knew of the places. The fire at Coll, which helps to give action to John Crawford's stay there, and causes Mad Neil's outbreak, whose effects on Flora lead to her quarrel with John which brings about his formal betrothal to Burnett Silver, is a very close description of an actual experience of my own, at that same place: only the dramatis personæ are changed. Mad

Neil, by the way, was first thought of as female, a reminiscence of an old crazed beggar-wife who used to come about my grandmother's kitchen when I was very small: she attempted to murder John, who was rescued by Flora, and I shifted the rôles because John required all the creditable actions I could give him to prevent the reader who took Burnett's side from being too annoyed with him for sympathy. The psychological processes of Neil's outbreak after the fire are a commonplace to any student of abnormal psychology, although of course I did not give my facts as I should if I had been lecturing upon them!

The technical tricks have some little interest. I gather from reviews that I did succeed in making Burnett the dominant figure in the book. This took a lot of trick-work to bring off, as until the very last chapter she *does* nothing, for most of the book she disappears from sight (Chs. III-X inclusive and Chs. XVI-XVIII inclusive, out of XXI), while Flora, her rival, is an active character with a considerable number of adventures, which show her a vigorous person, and in a creditable light. Flora has never heard of Burnett till Ch. XIII, and John forgets her for Chs. III-XII, so that I could not use anyone's recollection. All I could do was to begin and end the book with her, and begin it by showing the ironic contrast between her attitude to John and his to her, so that the reader might remember her when she reappeared. I used Flora, too, as a contrast, not only of personality but of "painting". Flora is seen almost always by daylight—in bright sunlight, in fact, at first and for some time: Burnett never is, and at first, at the end, and at her first reappearance between, in half-lights. Flora is strongly associated with out-of-doors, even when she is actually seen in the house: Burnett only once gets as far as an open window. Flora is associated, by her dress and by references to sea, sky, and the paint not uncommonly used for doors in the Lews, with bright blue: Burnett, by her dress, her needlework, and the moonlight in which she appears and makes her exit, with dim pale green . . . and so forth. Most of these tricks of "painting" were cribbed from Chaucer.

The other ingredients of the book were chosen to produce the effects I wanted, and had similarly to be deduced, with that end in view, from the data of the action, in such a way that they also forwarded that. But I do not think I need go into further detail.

APPENDIX B

As an actual specimen of the development of a short piece of writing, I will give the opening paragraph of a recent novel and its various stages in the writer's MS. I may add that the writer in question is a slow starter, so that the process of development here is rather more elaborate than usual, and that she was further handicapped inasmuch as she was describing an actual place very well known to her.

The passage as printed reads:

> The moon sailed glorious, drowning the gleam of stars in a clear sky. It was near midnight, and the sober folk of Aberdeen were long since bedded: in the strip of the Auld Town that reaches northward, a little inland from the coastwise dunes, there was only the sea wind about the High Street, the scent of the ebb, and the low murmur of the surf by Donmouth. The blind grey houses slept in the translucent pallor, huddled together with their backs to open fields. Only where the larger dwellings of the Chanonry stood square and separate in shadowy gardens, the flow of the moonshine gleamed on a woman's face in a dark window, where she leant out high above the uncoloured fragrance of the flowers.

The first draft is as follows: the words italicised have been crossed out at once: those in parentheses have been crossed out in a subsequent revision.

> Save (on a cloudy night) under cloud, there is no darkness in the high summer of north-eastern Scotland: and to-night the full moon (drowned) (quenched) drowned the pale gleam of stars in a clear sky. It was near midnight now, and the douce burghers of Aberdeen were long since bedded: in the strip of the Auld Town that reaches out northward, a little inland from the coastwise dunes (to Bishop Elphinstone's crown and the *dumpy* stark twin spires of *the remnant of* what remains erect of the Cathedral) there was only the south-east wind to go about the High Street and carry the scent of the ebb-tide (to the empty quadrangle under Bishop Elphinstone's crown)

(past King's College crown) and *the* with the scent the murmur of the surf by Donmouth. The (stark) blind grey houses (slept blindly) (crouched) slept (under) in the translucent pallor, huddled together with their backs to (whispering) (the cold) open fields of *standi* (whispering) moving corn, *wide to the rim of trees where Don crooks crozierwise abo* Only where the larger houses *the white of the moon lay on a woman's face* (in their shadowy gardens) framed in an open window high from the flowers (whose colour the moon transmuted to a web of fragrances invisible *as fragi music* and haunting as the fragile music).

The last sentence, "Only . . . gardens" has then been struck out, and "Only where the larger houses of the Chanonry stood square and (isolated) separate in *their* shadowy gardens the flow of the *moonlight* moonshine lighted a woman's face (within a) (high in) in a dark window, where she leant out high (over) above the uncoloured fragrance of the flowers" has been substituted. The paragraph is then copied out again, and reads:

(Save under cloud, there is no darkness in the high summer of north-eastern Scotland, and to-night the (illegible word) *full moon* broad moon) The moon drowned the gleam of stars in a clear sky. It was near midnight, and the douce burghers of Aberdeen were long since bedded: in the strip of the Auld Town that reaches out northward, a little inland from the coastwise dunes, there was only the (south-east) (onshore) onshore wind to go about the High Street, and carry the scent of the ebb-tide (past the College crown) and with the scent the murmur of the surf by Donmouth. The blind grey houses slept in the translucent pallor, huddled together with their backs to open fields (of moving corn). Only where the larger dwellings of the Chanonry stood square and separate in shadowy gardens, the flow of the moonshine lighted a woman's face in a dark window, where she leant out high above the uncoloured fragrance *of the flowe* of the flowers.

The version in the fair-copy MS. reads as in the printed text, except that "about" is given as "to go about":

APPENDIX B

"to go" has been struck out in either the typescript or the proofs.

The author desires to add that she would not care to give this passage as a specimen of her prose: it is chosen here, first because it is not dependent on anything preceding it, and secondly, because it has an unusual amount of fumbling visible in the draft.

INDEX

Aaron's Rod, 121
Absalom and Achitophel, 19
Abstraction, 86
Action, 105, 118, 134
Æsthetic, 212
Æsthetics, 9
Alighieri, Dante, 10, 17, 84, 90, 248
Amour courtois, 31
Andrea del Sarto, 129
Animals and man, 17
Anna Karenina, 243
Answer to Davenant, An, 107
Antony and Cleopatra, 121, 233, 235
Apology of Heroick Poetry, An, 126
Apolonius and Silla, 45
Apperception, 68, 131
Apprehension of theme, 84 seq.
Aristotle, 231, 248
Arp, Herr, 19, 20
Arrangement, see Form
Art, def., 22, see Artist, Collaboration, Continuance, Conveyance, Discipline, Élan vital, Ethics, Humanity, Life, Matter Media, Motive, Philosophy, Science, Sex, Spirit
Art-impulse, 29 seq., 73
Artist, 35 seq., 67 seq., 73, 77, 202
Ascesis, 89
Association, 68, 158, 174
Atmosphere, 105, 118, 274
Austen, Jane, 74

Background, 106, see also Atmosphere

Background of English Literature, The, 103
Bailey, Mr. H. C., 260
Balzac, H. de, 60
Barnes, Bishop, 61
Bates, Miss, 81
Baudelaire, C. de, 141
Beauty, 245
Beethoven, 205
Belle Dame sans Merci, La, 156
Belles-lettres, 103
Bergson, Prof. H., 32
Biographia Literaria, 84, 250
Biography, 103
Blackwood's Magazine, 242
Book, 42, 78, 169, 211
Bradley, Dr. A. C., 231, 235, 249
Brillat-Savarin, 31
Brontë, C., 99, 138, 153, 158
Brontë, E., 99, 106
Browne, Sir T., 59
Browning, R., 207, 268
Buchan, Dr. J., 261
Bulldog Drummond, 25

Calloway's Code, 205
Cantus, The Aberdeen, 194
Catherine of Siena, St., 89
Causality, 129, 161
Certain Notes of Instruction, 107, 124
Characters, 53, 106, 118, 129, 132 seq., 275
Cholera Camp, 194
Cinema, 62, 253
Classification of the arts, 21, 39
Cocknification, 224

Cœurs purs, Les, 105, 146
Coleridge, S. T., 84, 136, 249, 250
Collaboration, art as, 42, 211
Complaint of Deor, The, 261
Conceptual thinking, 125, 203
Constant Nymph, The, 97
Construction, 55, 143 seq., 160 seq., 163
Continuance, art and, 26, 32
Conveyance, 20, 78 seq., 95, 101, 142
Conveyance, art as, 19, 42
Corelli, M., 156
Coriolanus, 51, 150
Courage, 89
Cranford, 106, 122
Creation, 65
Criticism, 103, 235 seq.
Croce, Dr. B., 212

Dane, Miss C., 100
Danse sur le feu et l'eau, La, 78
Darwin, C. R., 215
Dauber, 142
Day-dreams, 112, 252 seq.
Dayton, 61
Design, 160, see also Form
Development of subject, 56 seq.
Diagram of art-process, 27
Discipline, art as, 262 seq.
Dobson, Austin, 91
Donne, J., 19, 89, 90, 198
Drama, 43, 50, 129, 254
Dreams, 101, 112, 151, 154
Dryden, J., 19, 126
Duncan Gray, 25

Earthly Paradise, The, 252
Ecclesiastes, 24

Effect of literature, 251 seq.
Egoist, The, 25, 129
Élan vital, 32, 33, 71, 78, 87, 94, 100, 112, 117, 263 seq.
Emotion, 38, 39, 64, 70 seq., 86, 103, 113, 161, 188 seq., 193, 222, see also Instinctive Impulse
Emphasis, 162, 181, 221
English Traveller, The, 57
Eothen, 103
Epipsychidion, 121
Eroica Symphony, The, 50
Escape, literature as, 258 seq.
Esmond, 104
Essay on the Literature, Arts, and Manners of the Athenians, 29
Essays of Elia, The, 103, 121
Ethical values, 244
Evolution and art, 30 seq., 268 seq.
Experience, 18, 24, 50, 69, 88, 104, 246, 265, see also Intensity
Experiend, 81
Expression, art as, 18 seq.

Fallacies of criticism, 241 seq.
Fallacies of reading, 216 seq.
Faure, M. Élie, 78
Fiction, 43, 104, 129
Figure of speech, 27, 175
First Men in the Moon, The, 149
Follow me 'Ome, 194
Fra Lippo Lippi, 268
Freud, Dr. S., 32, 33, 107
"Frieze" books, 98

Garden of Proserpine, The, 196
Gascoigne, George, 107, 124

INDEX

Gaskell, Mrs., 104, 106, 138
Gauguin, 141
"General", The, 146
Goody Blake and Harry Gill, 64
Grammatical order, 179
Greatness, 73
Grierson, Dr. H. J. C., 103, 173

Hamlet, 26, 34, 47, 89, 176, 231
Heart of Darkness, 106, 122
Hegel, 115
Henry, O., 205
Heresies of criticism, 60
Hernani, 60
Herrick, R., 91
Heywood, T., 51
History, 103
History of Criticism, A, 242
History of English Prosody, A, 192
Hobbes, T., 107
Holy Ghost, The, 153
Hormé, 33
Humanity, art and, 17 *seq.*, 251 *seq.*
Hypnosis, 151, 187, 236

I^1, I^2, 83
Illusion, 147
Imagination, 65, 69
Immortal Hour, The, 274
Inspiration, 153
Instinctive impulse, 29 *seq.*, 62, 70, 73, 87, 103, 111, 122, 136, 152, 155, *see also* Emotion
Intellect, 69, 70, 81, 85, 98, 103, 122, 128, 133, 134, 150, 157, 159, 161, 173, 203

Intensity of experience, 24, 38 *seq.*, 59, 78, 88, 188
Itylus, 158

James, H., 180
James, W., 212
Jane Eyre, 44, 99
Jargon, 205
John of the Cross, St., 89
Jonson, B., 35, 158
Journalese, 205
Julius Cæsar, 45, 150
Jung, Dr., 32

Kennedy, Miss M., 99
Kessel, Monsieur J., 105, 143
Kinds of literature, 103
King, H.M. the, 61
King Lear, 89, 214
Kipling, Mr. Rudyard, 194
Kubla Khan, 156

Ladies of Lyndon, The, 99
Lamb, C., 75, 245
Landor, W. S., 25
Language, 79, 173 *seq.*
Last Tournament, The, 176
Laziness, 91
Legend, 100
Leighton, Miss C., 97
Libido, 32, 33
Life and literature, 250 *seq.*, *see also* Humanity *and* Effect
Life-impulse and art, *see* Élan Vital
Life-force, *see* Élan Vital
Literature, passim, *see also* Art
London, Jack, 261
Lord Gregory, 19
Lost Kinnellan, 116, 119
Louis, St., 89

Love, 90
Lowe, Prof. Livingstone, 130

Macbeth, 26, 150, 230
McDougall, Prof. W., 36, 107, 151
Mackenzie, Miss J. M., 11
McNeile, Captain, 25
Mahon, Patrick, 34
Malvolio, 45
Man of Property, The, 121
Marinetti, Signor, 18
Marlowe, C., 25, 89
Marseillaise, La, 61
Matter and art, 21
Measure for Measure, 48
Media of art, 21, 38 seq., 204
Medium, 153
Memory, 63, 65, 107, 108, 113, 151
Meredith, G., 227
Metaphysic of Ethics, The, 103, 121
Metaphysics and art, 18, 33
Metre, 187, 222
Milton, J., 37, 173, 176, 192, 196, 206, 218, 224, 253
Modern Reader's Bible, The, 191
Momentum, 186
Mood, 113, 114
Morris, W., 252
Mortality and art, 18, 24 seq.
Morte Darthur, Le, 121
Motive of art, 22 seq., 29, 33 seq., 41
Moulton, Dr. R. G., 191
Mozart 125
Music, 203
Mystic Experience and Philosophy, 93

Nash, T., 194
Nietzsche, F. W., 273
Nunn, Prof., 33

O^1, O^2, 27
Ode on the Intimations of Immortality, 156
Ode on the Morning of Christ's Nativity, 192, 196
Odyssey, the, 26, 261
Onomatopœia, 194
Organic sensibility, 24, 37
Origin of Species, The, 215
Othello, 44, 124, 229
Outline of Abnormal Psychology An, 108, 151
Outline of Psychology, An, 37
Outline of Zoology, An, 212
Outside the Law, 93
Overtones, 174, 184

Paradise Lost, 25, 197, 218, 249
Patience, 25
Paul, St., 227, 269
Pelléas et Mélisande, 121
Penseroso, Il, 249
Philosophy and art, 266
Pickwick Papers, The, 27, 104, 118, 122, 124
Pictor Ignotus, 209
Plato, 10, 30, 76
Plot, 51, 105, 121, 129, 134, 148, 163, 273
Poetry, 103, 129, 188
Pollock, Sir F., 93
Pre-image, 96, 101
Prince of Wales, H.R.H. the, 61
Principles of Psychology, The, 212
Process of art, 9, 26, 83

INDEX

Psychanalysis, 106
Punctuation, 183

Quiet Lady, The, 273

Reader, 146, 147, 162, 211 *seq.*, 251 *seq.*
Reason, 70, *see also* Intellect
Reason of art, *see* Motive
Refrain, 184
Religio Medici, 59
Religion, 90
Rhyme, 190
Rhythm, 181 *seq.*
Road to Xanadu, The, 136
Romantic Revival, The, 145
Romaunce of the Rose, The, 31
Romeo and Juliet, 214
Ronsard, P. de, 18
Rosary, 139
Ruskin, J., 259

S¹, S², 27
Saintsbury, Dr. G., 192
Samothracian Victory, 50
Sayers, Miss D., 92
Science and art, 17, 18, 68, 266
Science and humanity, 17
Scientific writing, 103, 128
Selection, 64, 148, 179, *see also* Construction *and* Writing
Self, development of, 264 *seq.*
Sentence, 180
Sesame and Lilies, 250
Setting, 129, 134, 135, *see also* Atmosphere *and* Background
Sex and art, 30 *seq.*
Shakespeare, W., 34, 43 *seq.*, 75, 122, 145, 158, 197, 206, 219, 222, 224, 233, 250

Sheath and Knife, 195
Shelley, P. B., 29
Shepherd, Miss Nan, 96
Shirley, 99
Shylock, 138
Sidney, Sir P., 194
Simile, 176
Sir Patrick Spens, 25
Sister Helen, 195
Sound-quality, 184 *seq.*, 223
Spenser, E., 194, 203, 224
Spirit, art as function of, 21
Stein, Miss G., 19, 165, 196
Stevenson, R. L., 106, 121, 129
Still She Wished for Company 149
Stimulus of literature, 59 *seq.*, 61, 78, 117
Subconscious processes, 94 *seq.*, 106 *seq.*, 128, 135
Subject, 44, 51, 66, 74, 101 *seq.*, 124 *seq.*, 163
Subjects, suitable, 60
Sublimation, 34
Substitute for life, Literature as, 251 *seq.*
Swinburne, A. C., 195
Symbol, 27, 61 *seq.*, 79, 94, 117

Tales from Shakespeare, 75
Tamburlaine, 25
Technical terms, 81, 173
Temperament, 130, 141, 232
Tempest, The, 44
Templeton, Miss J. S., 11, 40
Tennyson, Lord, 176, 242
Teresa, St., 89
Tess of the D'Urbervilles, 245
Theme, 44, 50, 74, 84 *seq.*, 101, 127, 130
Theology and art, 36

Thompson, Edith, 256
Thomson, Prof. J. A., 212
Three Sitting Here, 165
Tintern Abbey, 68, 103
Toc H, 61
Treasure Island, 129
Trevelyan, Mr. G. M., 175, 178
Trinity, The Holy, 245
Troilus and Cressida, 44
Troopin', 194
Troy Town, 195
Troylus and Creseyde, 44
Truth, 245
Two Red Roses across the Moon, 195
Typographical arrangement, 180, 191

Unity of impression, 98

Valediction forbidding Mourning, A, 19

Value of experience, 24, 78, 88, *see also* Intensity *and* Stimulus
Villette, 138
Visual factors, 203
Vitality, 73, *see also* Élan Vital
Volition, 76, 89, 122, 140, 151
Vulgari Eloquentia, De, 17

Wallace, Mr. E., 142
Webster, J., 89
Whose Body? 92
Will, *see* Volition
Willcox, E. W., 156
Winstanley, Miss L., 231
Winter's Tale, A, 44, 55
Wisdom, 101
Wordsworth, W., 24, 64, 102, 156
Wuthering Heights, 99
Wyatt, Sir T., 194

For Product Safety Concerns and Information please contact our EU representative GPSR@taylorandfrancis.com
Taylor & Francis Verlag GmbH, Kaufingerstraße 24, 80331 München, Germany

www.ingramcontent.com/pod-product-compliance
Lightning Source LLC
Chambersburg PA
CBHW061435300426
44114CB00014B/1692